101 Answers to the
Most Asked Questions about the End Times

MARK HITCHCOCK

101

ANSWERS

TO THE MOST ASKED QUESTIONS ABOUT THE

END TIMES

Multnomah®Publishers *Sisters, Oregon*

101 ANSWERS TO THE MOST ASKED QUESTIONS ABOUT THE END TIMES
published by Multnomah Publishers, Inc.

© 2001 by Mark Hitchcock
International Standard Book Number: 1-57673-952-X

Cover image by Tony Stone Images

Scripture quotations are from:

New American Standard Bible® © 1960, 1977, 1995 by the Lockman Foundation.
Used by permission.

The Holy Bible, New International Version (NIV) © 1973, 1984 by International Bible Society,
used by permission of Zondervan Publishing House

Holy Bible, New Living Translation (NLT) © 1996. Used by permission of
Tyndale House Publishers, Inc. All rights reserved.

The Holy Bible, King James version (KJV)

Multnomah is a trademark of Multnomah Publishers, Inc.,
and is registered in the U.S. Patent and Trademark Office.
The colophon is a trademark of Multnomah Publishers, Inc.

Printed in the United States of America

For information:
MULTNOMAH PUBLISHERS, INC.•POST OFFICE BOX 1720•SISTERS, OREGON 97759

ISBN 0-7394-3031-9

TABLE OF CONTENTS

Introduction

Inquiring minds want to know what the future holds for this planet: What are the signs that the end is at hand? Is America mentioned in Bible prophecy? What is the Rapture? Who is the Antichrist? What is 666? When will Armageddon occur? Will there be peace in the Middle East? What do we know about life after death?

The questions are almost endless. Many of them are questions you have probably asked at one time or another or heard someone else ask. I have asked every one of these questions myself.

My own interest in prophecy really took off in my early twenties when I began to read the book of Daniel in the Old Testament. My heart was filled with questions and a bunch of confusion. That's when I decided that I needed to learn what the Bible teaches about the end times. Here I am, twenty years later, sharing with you the fruit of my odyssey to answer my own questions.

As I have traveled around speaking at prophecy conferences and spending time with the people at my home church, I have discovered that no matter where I go, people have the same questions about Bible prophecy and the end times. Over the years I have collected and compiled the most frequently asked questions about Bible prophecy and the end times. That's what this book is about.

Here are two more things that make me qualified to answer tough questions: First, for the last ten years I have been the pastor of Faith Bible Church in Edmond, Oklahoma, where people want to know the bottom line on things. Second, I have two sons (if you're a parent, you'll understand why this qualifies me to answer hard questions).

This book will focus on answering 101 of the specific, most asked questions that people like you and me have about the end times. Along the way I will hopefully answer *your* questions about the last days—questions about what will happen in the final drama of the ages.

To make the book more accessible and user-friendly, these questions are organized into eight sections:

1. General Questions about Prophecy and the End Times;
2. Questions about the Rapture;
3. Questions about the Antichrist and His Kingdom;

4. Questions about the Tribulation;
5. Questions about Armageddon;
6. Questions about the Second Coming;
7. Questions about the one-thousand-year reign of Christ (the Millennium);
8. Questions about the Afterlife;
9. At the end, there is one final question just for you.

Before you dive into this book, let me share five personal thoughts with you that I hope will make it a better read. First, I hope you understand that there are many opinions about the end times. In this book I'm endeavoring to lay out what I have come to believe, based on rigorous biblical research, about how the final drama of the ages will play out.

I am fully aware that good Christian brothers and sisters disagree with me on numerous points. That's fine. The only essential that we all must hold on this topic is that Jesus is the one and only Savior from sin who is coming back to earth to judge the living and the dead. However, when ·writing a book like this, an author has to make some decisions and interpretations. I'll do my best to show you how I reached my conclusions, but I hope you'll feel free to disagree and yet keep reading with an open mind.

Second, the questions in the book are not listed in the order of how frequently they're asked. The questions are grouped in clusters, with each section laying the groundwork for the next. However, each question can stand alone. So feel free to skip around. Just keep in mind that without some of the foundation in previous answers, you might miss a beat here or there.

Third, throughout this book I will be using masculine pronouns (he/him/his), but my intent is to include female readers as well unless the context clearly indicates that I am referring to a male.

Fourth, since there are many references to Scripture sprinkled throughout the book you will get the most out of it if you keep a Bible handy as you read and take a few extra minutes to look up some of the main references. After all, God's Word is our only source of truth for the future.

Fifth, as you read this book please know that I have already prayed and asked the Lord to use this book in your life, to answer your questions about the end times, to give you a greater interest in the study of Bible prophecy, and to draw you closer to our wonderful Savior who is the ultimate subject of all prophecy and the final answer to all our deepest questions.

"The testimony of Jesus is the spirit of prophecy."
REVELATION 19:10

GENERAL QUESTIONS ABOUT PROPHECY AND THE END TIMES

It's very difficult to prophesy, especially about the future.
CHINESE PROVERB

Only one generation in three has a chance to witness the end of a century. Rarer still, only one generation in thirty gets to see the end of a millennium. We have been privileged to experience the transition from the end of one millennium to the beginning of a new one. People seem more interested than ever in what the Bible has to say about the end times.

- 18 percent of Americans expect the end times to come within their lifetime.
- 53 percent of Americans believe that some world events this century fulfill biblical prophecy.[1]

What should we expect? What does the Bible tell us will happen in the end times? Is there a scriptural blueprint that shows us where the world is headed?

The purpose of this section is to provide an overview of what the Bible reveals about the last days. We'll accomplish this by answering general questions about prophecy and the end times.

But first, to whet your appetite, here's a little chart that summarizes the grand scope of things from here to eternity!

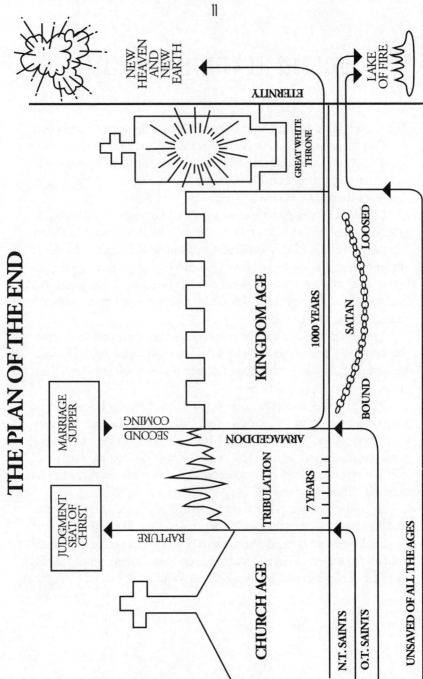

THE PLAN OF THE END

ONE

WHAT DOES THE WORD PROPHECY MEAN?

The English word *prophecy* comes from the New Testament Greek word *prophetes* (noun) or *propheteuo* (verb). Very simply put, this word means to speak for God, to be a mouthpiece for the Lord, to speak divine revelation. The prophets in both the Old and New Testaments were used by God to communicate His truth to men.

The most common image of a prophet is of a predictor and prognosticator. Biblical prophets foretold the future with 100 percent accuracy. They announced the Babylonian Exile, the coming Messiah, the coming of the Antichrist, and the end of the world, among many other events. This aspect of a prophet's ministry is often called *foretelling*. It has to do with coming events. The prophet was God's spokesman for previewing the future of Israel and the nations.

This predictive aspect of the prophet's mission is the primary focus of this book. *101 Answers to the Most Asked Questions about the End Times* is focused on the future, unfulfilled Bible prophecies of the last days or end times.

However, it is important to remember that the prophets also had a message for the people of their own day. This aspect of the prophet's ministry is sometimes called *forthtelling*. It has to do not so much with coming event as with current events. The prophet declared God's message to his own generation, always calling people to God's truth for them in that moment: "Thus saith the Lord!"

In both of these aspects of the prophetic office, the overall purpose was the same. Whether the prophet was forthtelling about current events or foretelling about coming events, the goal was to call people to trust the Lord and to submit to His will for their lives. Now, as then, prophecy calls us to live our lives in conformity with God's Word.

Two

How much of the Bible is prophecy?

A young pastor commented to a former seminary professor that he didn't preach on prophecy because "prophecy distracts people from the present." His professor replied, "Then there is certainly a lot of distraction in the Scriptures!"

Few people have any idea just how much of the Bible is prophetic in nature. The following statistics shed some light on the matter.

Total Verses in the Bible	31,124
Total Number of Predictions in the OT	1,239
Total Number of OT Verses that Contain Predictions	6,641 out of 23,210
Percent of the OT that is Prophecy	28.5 %
Total Number of Predictions in the NT	578
Total Number of NT Verses that Contain Predictions	1,711 out of 7,914
Percent of the NT that is Prophecy	21.5 %
Total Number of Separate Prophetic Topics in the Bible	737
Total Percent of the Bible that Is Prophecy	27 percent[2]

So if 27 percent of the Bible is prophecy, it seems it would be unwise to disregard it.

THREE

ARE THERE VALID PROPHECIES OR PREDICTIONS ABOUT THE FUTURE OTHER THAN THOSE FOUND IN THE BIBLE?

Throughout history there has been a constant parade of people who claim to know the future. From the oracles of ancient Greece to Nostradamus, from Edward Cayce to Jeanne Dixon, from the tabloids to the modern psychic hotlines, the stream of alleged prognosticators goes on and on.

While some of these crystal ball gazers may be able to hit upon something that does actually occur, it's not because they know the future. It has more to do with the law of averages: If you "predict" enough future events, one of them is bound to happen eventually. Like the old saying states, "Even a clock that doesn't work is right twice a day."

In order to accurately predict the future, one must either be omniscient (know everything), omnipresent (be present everywhere), and omnipotent (possess all power)—or have a direct connection with the One who does meet those requirements.

Read what God says about His unique ability to disclose the future.

"Present your case," the LORD says.
"Bring forward your strong arguments," the King of Jacob says.
Let them bring forth and declare to us what is going to take
    place;
As for the former events, declare what they were,
That we may consider them and know their outcome.
Or announce to us what is coming;
Declare the things that are going to come afterward,
That we may know that you are gods;
Indeed, do good or evil, that we may anxiously look about us
    and fear together.
Behold, you are of no account,
And your work amounts to nothing;
He who chooses you is an abomination.
(Isaiah 41:21–24)

If someone proclaims himself a prophet of God but his prophecies are not 100 percent accurate, the Bible says not to listen to him.

> "But the prophet who speaks a word presumptuously in My name which I have not commanded him to speak, or which he speaks in the name of other gods, that prophet shall die.
> "You may say in your heart, 'How will we know the word which the LORD has not spoken?' When a prophet speaks in the name of the LORD, if the thing does not come about or come true, that is the thing which the LORD has not spoken. The prophet has spoken it presumptuously; you shall not be afraid of him." (Deuteronomy 18:20–22)

Only the true God can predict the future, and He can do it with 100 percent accuracy 100 percent of the time. All others who claim to predict the future are imposters.

FOUR

ISN'T STUDYING BIBLE PROPHECY ALL JUST SPECULATION?

Bible prophecy has often suffered as much at the hands of its friends as in the hands of its foes. Date setting, "newspaper exegesis," attempts at identifying the Antichrist, and reckless speculation have turned many people off from Bible prophecy. Added to this is the frustration many people feel in wading through all the different views of the end times.

Therefore, many of God's children simply choose not to study Bible prophecy at all, thinking of it as an exercise in futility. I have personally heard many people say that when it comes to the last days, no one really knows for sure what is going to happen, so why waste time on it?

It is certainly true that a small group of overzealous speculators have tainted the legitimate study of Bible prophecy. And it is true that there are a number of views on last day events. But this should in no way dampen our fervor for studying the end times. Almost every area of theology has its quacks, and there are differing views on numerous subjects in the Bible. We should not allow this to scare us off from discovering God's truth on any subject He has revealed to us.

As we have seen, over a quarter of the Bible contains prophecy. It seems clear, then, that God intended us to study it. We should analyze Bible prophecy with humility, excitement, and expectation.

FIVE

WHAT ARE THE MAJOR VIEWS ON THE END TIMES?

One of the primary reasons the average Christian avoids studying Bible prophecy is that there are so many different views about it. A person might be brave enough to pick up a few books to brush up on his knowledge of the end times, but before long he is hopelessly lost in lengthy explanations of unfamiliar words.

It reminds me of the little boy whose father was a preacher. All his life he'd heard his dad preach on justification, sanctification, and all the other "ations." So he was ready when his Sunday school teacher asked if anyone knew what the word *procrastination* meant. The boy replied, "I'm not sure what it means, but I know our church believes in it!"

That's the way many people are when it comes to Bible prophecy. They're not sure what these big words mean, but they know that they must believe in it.

The Bible prophecy novice begins to hear words like premillennial, postmillennial, pretribulational, posttribulational, dispensational, and covenantal. In a short period he'll see enough charts and time lines to last him a lifetime. Chances are he'll finally adopt the position of the panmillennial—it will all "pan out" in the end—and not worry about it anymore.

How can we hope to make sense out of all the conflicting views? Is it possible to boil it down to the basics so we can understand at least the main views or systems people hold regarding the last days? The answer is a resounding "Yes!" In the next few pages, I will present the three main views of the last days in a clear, easy-to-follow format.

Broadly speaking, within evangelical circles there are three main theories of the end times: amillennialism, premillennialism, and postmillennialism. As you can see, the main word in each of these terms is the word *millennial*. This is because the crucial element that each of these views interprets differently is the timing of the thousand-year reign of Christ on earth, a period called the Millennium, and its relation to the second coming of Christ.

I've given a full discussion of the Millennium in section 7, but for now it's enough that you understand the relationship between the Millennium and Jesus' second coming. Premillennialism says the Second Coming will occur before the Millennium begins. Postmillennialism says the Second Coming will come after the Millennium ends. And amillennialism says we're in the Millennium now and it will conclude with the Second Coming.

TWO MAIN POINTS OF AGREEMENT

As with most differing views in theology, there are points on which these views agree. Two of these points of agreement are essential:

1. All three of these views believe that Jesus Christ is King of kings and Lord of lords and that He rules or will rule over a glorious kingdom.
2. All three of these views hold that Jesus Christ will one day return to this world literally, physically, visibly, and gloriously as the judge of all the earth.

It is important not to overlook these points of agreement. After all, these are part of the essentials that bind us together as believers in Jesus Christ. No matter what view you may hold concerning the end times, if you know Jesus Christ as your personal Savior and are looking for His coming, then we are in agreement about the essential points that bind us together as brothers and sisters in Christ.

However, we must also recognize that there are significant differences between these views. These differences affect how we understand almost every key event of the end times. Each of these systems has a very different picture of what will happen both before and after Jesus returns to earth.

This is not just some study in irrelevant theory. Which of these views you hold will determine how you interpret the characters, chronology, and consummation of the end times. Will there be a literal kingdom on earth? Will there be a literal seven-year tribulation period before Christ returns? Will there really be an individual called the Antichrist? Will the church succeed in Christianizing the world before Christ returns? All of these are colored by your beliefs about the Millennium and the Second Coming.

THREE MAIN POINTS OF DISAGREEMENT

While there are numerous differences between these three views of the last days, three main points of disagreement are most important.

The difference between these views revolves around three key issues:

1. *When* will Jesus reign? (the timing of His reign)
2. *How* will Jesus reign? (the nature of His reign)
3. *Where* will Jesus reign? (the place of His reign)

I will present only the general framework of these three end-time views or systems. For more information on this topic, see the recommended reading list in the appendix.

THE AMILLENNIAL VIEW

The prefix *a* before the word *millennium* denotes a negation of the word. Amillennium literally means "no millennium." However, this is not exactly what this view believes. Amillennialists do believe in a period in which Christ reigns, just not a literal thousand-year kingdom.

The amillennial position is the dominant view of modern Christendom. It is the view held by the Roman Catholic church, the Greek Orthodox church, and a large portion of Protestantism. The genesis of this view is usually traced back to St. Augustine (A.D. 354–430). This was the view of reformers John Calvin and Martin Luther.

When Will Jesus Reign?

Amillennialists believe that the kingdom of Christ is happening now: between Jesus' first and second comings. Therefore, the Millennium is not a literal period of one thousand years, but is symbolic of a "long period of time." Amillennialists teach that Satan was bound at the first coming of Christ as a result of the death and resurrection of Christ (Revelation 20:1–3).

How and Where Will Jesus Reign?

Amillennialists believe that the reign of Jesus (the Millennium) will not be a literal, physical thousand-year kingdom on earth. Rather, amillennialists hold that Christ reigns on earth in the hearts of believers and in the church ("the kingdom of God is within you"). They believe that Christ will return someday—at the end of the church age—to overthrow Satan, to judge all men, and to bring in the eternal state.

Amillenialists do not hold to either a literal seven-year period of tribulation before the second coming of Christ or a literal thousand-year period of reign after His second coming.

FUTURE EVENTS ACCORDING TO THE AMILLENNIAL SYSTEM

1. A parallel development of both good (God's kingdom) and evil (Satan's kingdom) during this present age.
2. The second coming of Christ.
3. The general resurrection of all people.
4. A general judgment of all people.
5. Eternity.

THE TIMELINE OF AMILLENNIALISM

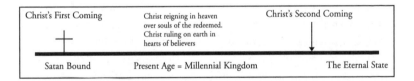

Christ's First Coming	Christ reigning in heaven over souls of the redeemed. Christ ruling on earth in hearts of believers	Christ's Second Coming
Satan Bound	Present Age = Millennial Kingdom	The Eternal State

THE PREMILLENNIAL VIEW

Premillennialists hold that the millennial kingdom will be a physical, earthly kingdom of one thousand literal years in which Jesus Christ will rule and reign over the earth from His earthly throne in Jerusalem.

Premillennialism was the view of the early church. It was the view held by such early church fathers as Papias, Clement of Rome, Barnabas, Ignatius, Polycarp, and Justin Martyr. After the third century, it began to wane and was replaced by amillennialism as the prevailing view. It began to make a comeback in the mid-nineteenth century, and is currently a popular way of understanding the last days.

Some modern premillennialists are Charles Ryrie, John Walvoord, J. Dwight Pentecost, James Montgomery Boice, Hal Lindsey, John MacArthur, Tim LaHaye, and Charles Swindoll.

Let's take a closer look at the specifics of this view.

When Will Jesus Reign?

Premillennialism teaches that the second coming of Jesus Christ will occur before (*pre*) the millennial kingdom. In fact, the millennial kingdom is inaugurated by the return of Christ to the earth. He will return at the end of a literal seven-year period of terrible judgment (the Tribulation).

How and Where Will Jesus Reign?

According to this view, the kingdom will not be established by the conversion of souls over an extended period of time but suddenly and powerfully by the glorious coming of Christ from heaven to earth. Satan will be bound for one thousand years, the duration of Christ's reign (Revelation 20:1–3); the curse will be reversed; the Jewish people will be restored to their ancient land; and Christ will reign over the earth in righteousness, peace, and joy.

It is important to note that most premillennialists would agree that Jesus is ruling over the church during this present age as its head and that He certainly reigns over the hearts of His people. He was, is, and always will be the sovereign of the universe. However, premillennialists would contend that this is not to be confused with the millennial kingdom that Christ will rule over for one thousand years as described in Revelation 20:1–6. They believe that the rule of Christ will be literally fulfilled in the future.

It should also be noted that premillennialists disagree among themselves over the timing of the Rapture. This issue will be discussed in section 2.

FUTURE EVENTS ACCORDING TO THE PREMILLENNIAL SYSTEM

1. Increase of religious apostasy (turning away from the truth) as the church age draws to a close.
2. The rapture of the church (resurrection of dead saints/translation of living saints).
3. Seven-year tribulation period on earth.
4. The second coming of Christ to earth.
5. The campaign of Armageddon.
6. The millennial reign of Christ on earth.
7. The Great White Throne Judgment.
8. The creation of a new heaven and new earth.
9. Eternity.

THE TIMELINE OF PREMILLENNIALISM

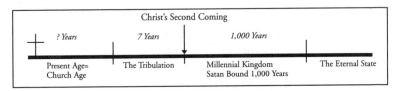

THE POSTMILLENNIAL VIEW

Postmillennialism is very similar to amillennialism in that both of these systems maintain that the Millennium is the period between the first and second comings of Christ and is not a literal one thousand years. The primary difference between these views is in the nature and scope of the kingdom in this present age. Postmillennialists believe that the church will "Christianize" the world during this present kingdom age, thus paving the way for the return of Christ.

This view was first propagated by the Unitarian teacher Daniel Whitby (1638–1726). In spite of its late arrival on the scene, postmillennialism enjoyed great popularity when it was introduced. It become the prevailing millennial view of the eighteenth and nineteenth centuries.

With advances in technology and science and the Industrial Revolution, the idea that man could himself usher in the kingdom of God made perfect sense. However, the outbreak of World War I, followed closely by World War II, dealt postmillennialism a blow from which it has never fully recovered.

When Will Jesus Reign?

Postmillennialists maintain that Jesus Christ will return to earth after (*post*) the Millennium. Consequently, the Millennium is the entire period of time between the first and second comings of Christ.

How and Where Will Jesus Reign?

For postmillennialists, Jesus' reign is spiritual and political. This view teaches that the millennial kingdom is not a literal thousand years but a golden age that will be ushered in by the church during this present age by the preaching of the gospel.

This golden age will arrive by degrees as the gospel spreads throughout the earth until the whole world is eventually Christianized. Jesus' reign will grow on earth as believers in Christ exercise more and more influence over the affairs of this earth. Ultimately, the gospel will prevail, and the earth will become a better and better place, after which Christ will appear to usher in eternity.

The best known advocate of postmillennialism in recent years is Loraine Boettner. He summarizes the postmillennial view well:

> The millennium to which the postmillennialist looks forward is thus a golden age of spiritual prosperity during this present dispensation, that is, the church age. This is to be brought about through forces now active in the world. It is to last an indefinitely long period of time, perhaps much longer than a literal one thousand years. The changed character of individuals will be reflected in an uplifted social, economic, political, and cultural life of mankind. The world at large will then enjoy a state of righteousness which up until now has been seen only in relatively small and isolated groups: for example, some family circles, and some local church groups and kindred organizations.
>
> This does not mean that there will be a time on this earth when every person will be a Christian or that all sin will be abolished. But it does means that evil in all its many forms eventually will be reduced to negligible proportions, that Christian principles will be the rule, not the exception, and that Christ will return to a truly Christianized world.[3]

FUTURE EVENTS ACCORDING TO THE POSTMILLENNIAL SYSTEM

1. Progressive improvement of conditions on earth as the end draws near, culminating in a golden age in which the world is completely Christianized.
2. The second coming of Christ.
3. The general resurrection of all people.
4. A general judgment of all people.
5. Eternity.

THE TIMELINE OF POSTMILLENNIALISM

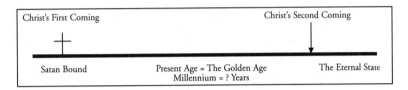

Christ's First Coming

Christ's Second Coming

Satan Bound

Present Age = The Golden Age
Millennium = ? Years

The Eternal State

SUMMARY OF THE THREE MILLENNIAL VIEWS

VIEWS	WHEN WILL CHRIST REIGN	HOW AND WHERE WILL CHRIST REIGN?
Amillennial	Between the First and Second Comings (present reign)	Christ rules over a spiritual kingdom in the hearts of believers on earth and over the souls of the redeemed in heaven (spiritual reign)
Premillennial	Immediately after the Second Coming (future reign)	Christ will rule personally for one thousand years over a literal, physical, earthly kingdom with Satan bound and the curse of the Fall removed.
Postmillennial	Between the First and Second Comings, but arriving by degrees (present reign)	Christ rules in the hearts of believers as the church brings in the kingdom by the triumph of the gospel in this world (spiritual reign)

Six

WHICH OF THESE VIEWS IS BEST AND WHY?

As you can see, these three systems are very different in their interpretation of the end times. Whichever of these systems you hold to determines how you will interpret hundreds of passages in the Bible. Therefore this is not a trivial matter. However, all of these views have points in their favor and Scriptures that can be used for support.

Which view is *best* depends on how you believe that the most pertinent Scriptures should be understood. Good and godly scholars disagree on which of these systems best reflects the teaching of Scripture.

In *101 Answers to the Most Asked Questions about the End Times,* I'm going to go with the premillennial view. In this chapter, I'll explain why I feel this is the best of the three systems. However, my goal is not to make you agree with me but to challenge you to prayerfully consider God's Word on this topic so that you will develop your own conclusions based on His Word.

WHY I BELIEVE PREMILLENNIALISM IS THE BEST VIEW

I hold the premillennial view for six main reasons. To make these easier to remember, I've developed the acronym PREMIL:

- Promises of God;
- Resurrection in Revelation 20:4–6;
- Earliest View;
- Most Natural Reading of Revelation 20:1–6;
- Imprisonment of Satan;
- Literal One Thousand Years in Revelation 20:1–6.

Now we'll look at each of the six parts of this acronym to explain why I hold the premillennial view.

P: Promises of God

Premillennialism is the only one of these systems that allows for the literal fulfillment of God's promises or covenants with Abraham and David. Let's examine these two covenants.

God unconditionally promised Abraham three things in Genesis 12:1–3 and 15:18:

1. That God would bless Abraham personally and that the whole world would be blessed through him;
2. That God would give Abraham many descendants; and
3. That God would give Abraham and his descendants a specific piece of land forever (the boundaries of this land are described in Genesis 15:18).

The first two components of God's promise have been literally fulfilled. God gave Abraham many descendants, and God has blessed the world through Abraham via the Jewish Scriptures and the Jewish Savior.

If the first two parts of the covenant have been fulfilled literally, it seems logical to conclude that the third part, the promise of land, will also be fulfilled literally. And since this promise has never been fulfilled in history, the promise must be in the future.

The land promised to Abraham fits perfectly with the idea of a thousand-year reign of Christ on earth (ruling from Jerusalem) in which Israel will occupy all the land promised in Genesis 15:18.

Now let's look at God's covenant with David. In 2 Samuel 7:12–16, God promised King David that one of his descendants would sit on his throne and reign over his kingdom forever. While God did not promise that this rule would continue uninterrupted, He did promise that David's dynasty would maintain the right to rule and that one of David's descendants would rule forever. This promise was applied specifically to Jesus when He was born (Luke 1:32–33).

Amillennialists and postmillennialists argue that this covenant is completely fulfilled in the present age as Christ sits on His throne in heaven ruling over the church. Premillennialists, on the other hand, contend that Christ must literally sit on David's throne on earth and rule over David's kingdom, the nation of Israel, in order for this covenant to be fulfilled.

This literal interpretation of the kingdom is borne out in the New Testament. In Acts, Jesus reaffirmed that the kingdom would be restored to Israel in the future.

> So when they had come together, they were asking Him, saying, "Lord, is it at this time You are restoring the kingdom to Israel?" He said to them, "It is not for you to know times or epochs which the Father has fixed by His own authority." (Acts 1:6–7)

Jesus had promised the disciples that in His kingdom they would sit on twelve thrones judging the twelve tribes of Israel (Matthew 19:28). Acts 1:3 says that Jesus had been teaching His disciples for forty days "of the things concerning the kingdom." This may be what triggered their question about future restoration of the kingdom to Israel. Evidently, Jesus had been teaching about a future restored kingdom for Israel. Understandably, they wanted to know when this great event was on God's time schedule.

If the disciples had been mistaken about a future kingdom for Israel, their question provided a perfect opportunity for Jesus to correct them. However, Jesus did not correct their statement that the kingdom would be restored to Israel. He simply pointed out that they were not to be concerned about the timing of that event.

Just before His ascension, Jesus confirmed to His disciples the fact that the kingdom would be restored to Israel. A future, millennial kingdom of Christ is the only possibility mentioned in Scripture when the Davidic covenant can be literally, completely fulfilled.

R: Resurrection in Revelation 20:1-6

Revelation 19:11–19 records John's vision of the second coming of Jesus Christ back to planet earth. The next section, Revelation 20:1–6, discusses the resurrection of the dead after Jesus has returned. Revelation 20:4b states, "And they came to life and reigned with Christ for a thousand years." This millennial reign, then, begins *after* Christ's return and the resurrection of the dead.

Amillennialists and postmillenialists argue that this resurrection refers to spiritual resurrection or conversion. However, of the forty-two times the Greek word used here for resurrection (*anastasis*) is used in the New

Testament, forty-one times it refers to bodily resurrection. It stands to reason that this is what it means here as well.

Since this resurrection and reign follow the Second Coming in Revelation 19:11–21, it stands to reason that they would follow the Second Coming in reality, too. This appears to argue for a future thousand-year period after the return of Christ—not a present kingdom as amillennialists and postmillennialists maintain.

E: EARLIEST VIEW

Premillennialism was the view of the early church for the first two centuries of church history. Papias, the bishop of Hierapolis, was a companion of Polycarp and a disciple of the apostle John (who, incidentally, wrote the book of Revelation). Papias believed in a literal thousand-year reign of Christ on the earth.

All of the other noted second- and third-century Christian scholars promulgated the tradition of a literal, earthly millennium: Irenaus, Apollinarius, Tertullian, Victorinus, and Lactantius. An early second-century writing called *The Epistle of Barnabas* takes the one thousand years literally. The eminent second-century scholar Justin Martyr (100–165) stated:

> But I and every other completely orthodox Christian feel certain that there will be a resurrection of the flesh, followed by one thousand years in the rebuilt, embellished, and enlarged city of Jerusalem, as was announced by the prophets Ezekiel, Isaiah, and others.

Premillennialism is the historic view of the church.

M: MOST NATURAL READING

In my opinion, the premillennial position is the clearest, most natural reading of Revelation 20:1–6. This is the only passage in the Bible that specifically mentions the thousand-year reign of Christ. It occurs in Revelation immediately after the second coming of Christ (Revelation 19:11–21). In Revelation 19–20, Christ's coming is clearly before (pre) the Millennium or thousand-year reign.

I: Imprisonment of Satan

Both amillennialists and postmillennialists contend that the binding of Satan in Revelation 20:1–3 occurred at the first coming of Christ and that Satan is bound right now during this present age. This seems to contradict the way Satan is pictured in the New Testament. Notice how Satan is described.

- "the ruler of this [the] world" (John 12:31; 14:30).
- "the god of this world" (2 Corinthians 4:4).
- "an angel of light" (2 Corinthians 11:14).
- "the prince of the power of the air" (Ephesians 2:2).
- "like a roaring lion, seeking someone to devour" (1 Peter 5:8).
- scheming against believers (2 Corinthians 2:11; Ephesians 6:11).
- hindering believers (1 Thessalonians 2:18).
- accusing God's people (Revelation 12:10).
- blinding the minds of the lost (2 Corinthians 4:4).

As you can see, Satan appears to be anything but bound today. He is a defeated foe, but he has not yet been bound. God's conquest over Satan was achieved at the Cross, but it will not be consummated until the Second Coming when Satan is bound and cast into the abyss. During the present age, Satan is actively opposing the work of God and harassing the Lord's people. As someone once said, "If Satan is bound today, he must have an awfully long chain."

Notice how specific Revelation 20:1–3 is in its description of Satan's binding. It says Satan is "laid hold of," "bound," and thrown "into the abyss." The abyss is then "shut" and "sealed it over him." Nothing like this happened at the first coming of Christ. But it will happen when Christ returns.

L: Literal One Thousand Years

The premillennial position is the only position that consistently interprets Bible prophecy literally. The other two positions tend to spiritualize Old Testament prophecies and apply them to the church, which they often interpret as spiritual Israel.

The Bible itself gives the correct method for interpreting Bible prophecy. All the prophecies of Christ's first coming were fulfilled literally in the person and work of our Savior. It makes sense to believe that the prophecies of Christ's second coming will also be fulfilled literally. To spiritualize the prophecies of the last days and deny a literal tribulation period, a literal Antichrist, a literal battle of Armageddon, a literal restoration of the Jewish people to the land, and a literal, earthly millennial kingdom violates the method of interpreting Bible prophecy already established in the prophecies of the first coming of Christ.

The time period of one thousand years is specifically mentioned six times in Revelation 20—in verses 2, 3, 4, 5, 6, and 7. The fact that this time period is repeated six times in seven verses emphasizes its importance.

Moreover, all the other time-specific periods and numbers mentioned in Revelation seem to be literal: "ten days" (Revelation 2:10), "one hundred and forty-four thousand" (7:4; 14:1), "five months" (9:5, 10), "two hundred million" (9:16), "forty-two months" (11:2; 13:5), and "twelve hundred and sixty days" (11:3; 12:6). When John mentions a time period that is general or nonspecific, he identifies it as such by phrases like "a little while" (6:11) or "a short time" (12:12).

It seems best, then, to take the thousand years as a literal period of time when Jesus Christ will reign with His saints on the earth after His second coming to the earth.

The premillennial view seems to be the best way of understanding the end times. It incorporates the literal fulfillment of the promises of God; it follows Revelation's own sequence of the Second Coming and the Millennium; it was the view of the early church; it is the most natural reading of Revelation 20:1–6; it does not say that Satan is already bound; and it takes Revelation at its word when it calls for a literal thousand-year reign of Christ.

Remember, it's PREMIL.

Seven

Is America mentioned in Bible prophecy?

This may be the question about Bible prophecy that I have been asked more than any other. People here in America want to know if the Bible has anything to say about the future of our nation. Will God continue to bless America in the future? Will the United States survive?

Search though you might, you will never find America mentioned *specifically, by name,* in the Bible. However, this is true of most other modern nations as well. Many students of Bible prophecy nevertheless believe that America is referred to in the pages of Scripture.

Three main passages of Scripture are used to support this idea. The first passage is Isaiah 18:1–7. This chapter refers two times to a place "whose land the rivers divide." Some scholars interpret this as a reference to the Mississippi River and the many other rivers that divide the United States. The nation is called "a people feared far and wide, / A powerful and oppressive nation" (v. 2). This is taken as a reference to the mighty military machine of the U.S. armed forces.

The problem with this view is that the passage itself identifies the nation being described: "Alas, oh land of whirring wings / Which lies beyond the rivers of Cush, / Which sends envoys by the sea, / Even in papyrus vessels on the surface of the waters" (v. 1). The nation referred to in this passage is the ancient kingdom of Cush (modern Sudan), not the United States.

The second passage is Ezekiel 38:13:

> "Sheba and Dedan and the merchants of Tarshish with all its villages will say to you, 'Have you come to capture spoil? Have you assembled your company to seize plunder, to carry away silver and gold, to take away cattle and goods, to capture great spoil?'"

In the Old Testament era, Tarshish was the farthest western region in the known world. It corresponds to the modern nation of Spain. Tarshish could be used in this context to represent all of the western nations of the last days—including America. Some translations of Ezekiel 38:13 refer to the "young lions" of Tarshish. Young lions are often used in Scripture to refer to energetic rulers. Therefore, some view these young lions of Tarshish as a veiled reference to the United States.

While this view is certainly possible, the evidence seems too tenuous to make any certain statements about this being a reference to America.

A third passage that is often cited as referring to the United States is Revelation 17–18, in which "Babylon the Great" is discussed. Babylon is called "the great city" in Revelation 17, a fact that has led some to say that Babylon is a reference to New York City.

Once again, while some of the description in Revelation 17–18 could be stretched to indicate New York City as the Babylon of the end times, I don't believe that's what it is referring to, as you will see in question 16. I believe it is much better to interpret Babylon in Revelation 17–18 as the literal Babylon on the river Euphrates.

Having carefully examined the most frequently cited passages that are used to support the idea that America is mentioned in Bible prophecy, I have concluded that America is *not* mentioned in Bible prophecy.

However, this raises another interesting question: Why *isn't* America mentioned in Bible prophecy? Israel is mentioned by name and most scholars believe that Europe is the reunited Roman empire of the last days. So why isn't America mentioned?

Perhaps it is a kind of shortsighted egocentrism that makes us think that the United States should be mentioned in Scripture. In some senses, of course, it could be argued that the United States is the greatest nation in the history of the world. For instance, we have more military firepower than has ever been possible before. But historians would argue that America, which only became a superpower just over half a century ago, is not greater politically, economically, or even militarily than the centuries-long empires of Rome, Spain, or Britain.

Nevertheless, I am asked this question all the time: "Why doesn't the Bible mention the United States?" I have identified four basic options to explain this prophetic silence.

Option 1

America will still be a powerful nation in the last days, but the Lord simply chose not to mention her specifically. After all, it is important to recognize that most modern nations are not mentioned in the Bible: Scotland isn't mentioned, nor is India, Australia, Canada, or Japan. It shouldn't surprise us that America isn't mentioned.

This view is possible, but seems unlikely to me. It would seem that if America were still the greatest nation in the world during the Tribulation, God would mention her in Scripture. As John Walvoord, one of the world's leading prophecy scholars, observes:

> Although conclusions concerning the role of America in prophecy in the end time are necessarily tentative, the Scriptural evidence is sufficient to conclude that America in that day will not be a major power and apparently does not figure largely in either the political, economic, or religious aspects of the world.[4]

Option 2

America is not mentioned specifically because she will be destroyed by other nations. In other words, she will experience a fall from the outside before the end times.

Option 3

America is not mentioned in Bible prophecy because she will have lost her influence as a result of moral and spiritual deterioration. She will experience a fall from the inside before the end times.

Option 4

While any of these first three options are possible, there is a fourth option that I feel best explains the silence concerning America in the Scriptures: America will become a third-rate nation overnight at the Rapture. The Rapture will be God's judgment on America.

Consider this fact. If the Rapture were to happen today, the United States would probably lose more people per capita than any other nation in the world. At the Rapture, the Islamic nations in the Middle East would feel almost no effect at all. But the U.S. could become a third-world nation overnight. Millions of home mortgages would go unpaid, the stock market would crash, and millions of productive workers would be suddenly removed from the workforce.

It may be that America is not mentioned because she will not be a key player on her own but rather only a part of the Antichrist's Western confederacy of nations. In a weakened economic and military condition, America might seek refuge with her NATO allies in Europe and be absorbed into the Antichrist's emerging Western coalition.

If that were the case, then America is not mentioned specifically in the Bible because after the Rapture she is merely one of the pawns in Antichrist's Euro-American empire.

Several eminent prophecy scholars and theologians support this view. John Walvoord notes:

> Although the Scriptures do not give any clear word concerning the role of the United States in relationship to the revived Roman Empire and the later development of the world empire, it is probably that the United States will be in some form of alliance with the Roman ruler.... Actually a balance of power in the world may exist at that time not too dissimilar to the present world situation, namely, that Europe and the Mediterranean area will be in alliance with America in opposition to Russia, Eastern Asia, and Africa. Based on geographic, religious, and economic factors such an alliance of powers seems a natural sequence of present situations in the world.[5]

The amalgamation of America into the Antichrist's European empire after the Rapture makes perfect sense in the current political climate. The United States is slowly but relentlessly being drawn away from national sovereignty and into a globalist order. NATO, the UN, GATT, NAFTA, the WTO, and many other acronyms signal what many view as a startling trend away from U.S. sovereignty and toward submission to multinational treaties, organizations, and courts of law.

When the Rapture occurs and the U.S. is reduced to a third-rate power, she will find her place with the other nations of the reunited Roman Empire in Antichrist's kingdom.

As to why America is not mentioned in Scripture, theologian Ed Dobson reminds us that the last days are not, after all, about America but about Israel:

> The United States will most likely be part of that coalition because it is a Western superpower. But the primary focus of end-time prophecies is on the Middle East and Europe. The

rest of the world, including the United States, will be involved, but the spotlight is over there—not on the New World.[6]

EIGHT

WHAT IS THE NUMBER ONE SIGN THAT THESE ARE THE END TIMES?

The Bible gives us numerous signs to watch for, signs that indicate whether or not we are living in the end times. However, I believe the number one sign—the "supersign"—is the modern nation of Israel (which became an independent nation in 1948).

That Israel would be regathered and restored in the last days is predicted in many places in Scripture (see Isaiah 43:5–6; Jeremiah 30:3; Ezekiel 34:11–13; 36:34; 37:1–14; and Romans 11:25–27). Students of Bible prophecy no longer have to say that this will happen someday. It began in 1948 and continues to be fulfilled today as the Jews are being brought back to their land.

Israel must exist as a sovereign nation for many prophecies in Scripture to be fulfilled. Here are just a few examples:

1. Antichrist will make a seven-year covenant with Israel (Daniel 9:27).
2. Antichrist will invade Israel and desecrate the temple (Daniel 11:40–41; Matthew 24:15–20).
3. Gog and his allies will invade the nation of Israel when it is at peace (Ezekiel 38–39).
4. All the nations of the earth will invade Jerusalem (Zechariah 12:1–9; 14:1–2).
5. The people of Israel will flee into the wilderness to escape the wrath of Satan (Revelation 12:13–17).

It's interesting to me that Israel seems to be in the news every day, either on radio or TV or in the newspaper. All eyes are on this tiny piece of real estate and the perpetual peace process that swirls around it. Even R. C. Sproul, who is a prominent amillennialist theologian, sees the current situation in Israel as significant for the fulfillment of Bible prophecy:

I remember sitting on my porch in Boston in 1967, and watching on television the Jewish soldiers coming into Jerusalem, dropping their weapons and rushing to the Wailing Wall, and weeping.... I don't know what the significance of it all is. But I will tell you this: we should be watching very carefully. It is a remarkable event in history that the city of Jerusalem is now back in Jewish hands, under Jewish control.[7]

John Walvoord highlights the unequaled significance of Israel as a sign of the last days:

Of the many peculiar phenomena which characterize the present generation, few events can claim equal significance as far as Bible prophecy is concerned with that of the return of Israel to their land. It constitutes a preparation for the end of the age, the setting for the coming of the Lord for His church, and the fulfillment of Israel's prophetic destiny.[8]

Now that the Jews are back in their land, the hammer of the endtimes' gun has been cocked. All that remains is for God to pull the trigger to set the end in motion.

Nine

WHAT IS THE NUMBER TWO SIGN THAT THESE ARE THE END TIMES?

After the regathering of Israel to her land, the most significant sign of the end times is the reuniting of the Roman Empire.

The Bible predicts that when Jesus returns, the ruling power on earth will be a ten-kingdom confederation of nations reunited from the old Roman Empire and ruled over by Antichrist. It will be "Rome II."

In the great prophecies of Daniel 2 and 7, the Bible previews the course of world history from the time of Nebuchadnezzar and his kingdom (Babylon) to Christ's kingdom. These passages reveal that five Gentile world empires will rule the world in succession from 605 B.C. until the second coming of Christ. In retrospect we now know that the first four of these world empires were Babylon, Medo-Persia, Greece, and Rome. From history we know that these empires did in fact rule the world successively in the exact order predicted by Daniel, who received the prophecy in about 530 B.C.

However, in the visions in both Daniel 2 and 7 there is a fifth and final form of Gentile world dominion that has yet to be fulfilled. This final world empire will be Rome reunited—Rome II—because it arises from the countries that made up the old Roman Empire. It will be the kingdom of Antichrist.

Daniel 2 depicts these five great world empires using the symbolism of a great statue of a man built from five kinds of material.

THE METALLIC MAN OF DANIEL 2

Gold	Babylon
Silver	Medo-Persia
Brass	Greece
Iron	Rome
Iron and Clay	Rome II (Antichrist's kingdom)

Five Kingdoms

Gold	BABYLON
Silver	MEDO-PERSIA
Brass	GREECE
Iron	ROME
Iron & Clay	KINGDOM OF ANTICHRIST

THE BEASTS OF DANIEL 7

Daniel 7 presents the same five world empires in the form of great beasts that devour and destroy the earth.

Lion with the wings of an eagle	Babylon
Lopsided bear with three ribs in its mouth	Medo-Persia
Leopard with four wings and four heads	Greece
Terrible beast with teeth of iron and claws of bronze	Rome
Ten horns and the little horn	Rome II (Kingdom of Antichrist—"the little horn")

PARALLELS BETWEEN DANIEL 2 AND 7

It is interesting to consider that, unlike its predecessors, the Roman Empire was never really destroyed: It fell apart. Rome was simply divided up, and part of it eventually became the modern nations of Europe. The Bible predicts that in the last days, the old Roman Empire will be reunited in the form of a ten-kingdom confederation led by the

Antichrist (Daniel 7:8, 23–25). This will be the fifth and final world empire.

World Empire	Daniel 2	Daniel 7
Babylon	Head of Gold	Lion
Medo-Persia	Chest and Arms of Silver	Bear
Greece	Belly and Thighs of Bronze	Leopard
Roman Empire	Legs of Iron	Terrible Beast
Rome II (Reunited Roman Empire)	Feet and Toes of Iron and Clay (10 toes)	Ten Horns and the Little Horn

There are three key points that prove that this fifth great empire will be ruling the world when Christ returns.

First, in Daniel 2 the ten toes on the feet made of iron and clay are an extension of the iron legs, which represent the ancient Roman Empire. In Daniel 7 the ten horns and the little horn (Antichrist) are on the head of the fourth beast, which also represents the ancient Roman Empire. Since the original Roman Empire never existed in a ten-kingdom form, it seems to me that this is picturing a new form of the Roman Empire: Rome II.

Second, the stone that strikes the statue, destroying the ten toes, is considered by most Bible scholars to represent Jesus' return. If that is so, it must mean that the kingdom that is in power when Jesus returns will be the ten-nation confederacy that arises out of the Roman Empire (see Daniel 2:34, 44–45).

Third, the little horn in Daniel 7:8, which is usually understood to be the Antichrist, rules over the ten horns on the fourth beast. Since Antichrist will rule over the world at the time Christ returns, it must mean that the fifth beast, the final kingdom, is the future kingdom of Antichrist that will be forged together out of the nations of the Roman Empire.

The current rise of the European Union seems to be a direct fulfillment of Daniel's prophecy. Most of the member nations were part of the Roman Empire at the height of its glory. Amazingly, it has taken under fifty years to bring about that amalgamation of nations. Here are some of the key events and dates of what appears to be the reuniting of the Roman Empire in our time.

1957	Birth of the modern EU (Treaty of Rome), six nations join: Belgium, Germany, Luxembourg, France, Italy, and the Netherlands (total of 220 million people).
1973	EEC (European Economic Community) formed; Denmark, Ireland, and Great Britain join, bringing in 66 million more people. Greece joins the EEC in 1981, becoming the tenth member.
1986	Portugal and Spain join the EEC.
1995	Austria, Finland, and Sweden join the EU (European Union), bringing the total population to 362 million in 15 members.
January 1, 1999	Monetary union of the EU; currency called the Euro.

I'll never forget seeing a copy of a European magazine after the Maastricht Treaty was ratified (this treaty scheduled the permanent linkage of European nations). The magazine headline read, "Back Together Again." When had the nations of Europe ever been together? Only during the days of the Roman Empire.

It appears that the broken iron empire from Nebuchadnezzar's dream is beginning to come together again, just as Daniel predicted. The EU now has an elected representative legislative body (the European Commission), a 518 member advisory board (the European Parliament), and a presidency that rotates among the member countries. The European Community Conference on Security and Cooperation has even called for a new collective security organization to replace NATO. All this seems to be paving the way for a united government to go along with the united economy.

The feet of iron and clay are making every effort to adhere to one another. All that remains is for ten of the nations in the mix to rise to the top and form a consolidated common government. When this happens, Rome will truly live again, and out of this Western confederacy the Antichrist will rise to rule the world during the great Tribulation.

For me, this event and the regathering and rebirth of Israel are the two key signs of the end times.

Ten

Will the Earth be Destroyed in a Nuclear Holocaust?

According to a *Time* magazine poll (10-26-98), 51 percent of Americans believe that a man-made disaster will wipe out civilization during the next century. Probably the number one threat on that list would be nuclear weaponry.

Ever since the dawn of the nuclear age in the 1940s, people have wondered if the world will end in a nuclear nightmare. This fear has been heightened by the recent proliferation of nuclear weapons. Nations such as Pakistan, North Korea, India, and China have nuclear weapons. It's only a matter of time until rogue states like Iran and Iraq and terrorist organizations also have access to "the bomb."

Several passages of Scripture have been used to support the idea that the world will be destroyed by nuclear weapons: Isaiah 24:18–20; Zechariah 14:12; and 2 Peter 3:7, 10–14. Here's a sample:

> But by His word the present heavens and earth are being reserved for fire, kept for the day of judgment and destruction of ungodly men.... But the day of the Lord will come like a thief, in which the heavens will pass away with a roar and the elements will be destroyed with intense heat, and the earth and its works will be burned up. Since all these things are to be destroyed in this way, what sort of people ought you to be in holy conduct and godliness, looking for and hastening the coming of the day of God, because of which the heavens will be destroyed by burning, and the elements will melt with intense heat! But according to His promise we are looking for new heavens and a new earth, in which righteousness dwells. Therefore, beloved, since you look for these things, be diligent to be found by Him in peace, spotless and blameless. (2 Peter 3:7, 10–14)

I have heard several sermons in which this passage has been used to graphically describe a great nuclear explosion that blows up the earth. Zechariah 14:12 describes the flesh of people rotting off the body where they stand: eyes rotting in their sockets, tongues rotting in their mouths. This sometimes describes what happens to people when a nuclear weapon is detonated.

I don't believe that the Bible tells us specifically whether nuclear weapons will be used in the future on this earth. Many of the passages that are cited as referring to a nuclear detonation seem to refer to divine judgment directly from the hand of God rather than a nuclear explosion (see Revelation 8:6–12).

Nevertheless, however one interprets those passages, the Bible is clear that the world will not be destroyed by man or any man-made disaster. The Bible states in Genesis 1:1 that God created the heavens and the earth and in 2 Peter 3:5–7 that God will someday destroy the present heaven and earth with fire. Only God could make it, and only God will destroy it.

For when they maintain this, it escapes their notice that by the word of God the heavens existed long ago and the earth was formed out of water and by water, through which the world at that time was destroyed, being flooded with water. But by His word the present heavens and earth are being reserved for fire, kept for the day of judgment and destruction of ungodly men. (2 Peter 3:5–7)

This passage makes it clear that it is God Himself who will "push the button" to destroy this world, not some Middle Eastern madman. The God who created this world is in total control of His creation. There's not a maverick molecule in this vast universe. No man will ever destroy this earth. God has reserved that right for Himself.

Eleven

Is the recent explosion of knowledge a sign of the Last Days?

Daniel 12:4 says, "But as for you, Daniel, conceal these words and seal up the book until the end of time; many will go back and forth, and knowledge will increase."

These words have often been cited to prove that people will travel at great speeds ("go back and forth") and that there will be a great increase of knowledge in the last days. On the basis of this verse, Isaac Newton predicted that the day would come when the volume of knowledge would be so increased that man would be able to travel at speeds of up to fifty miles per hour. In response to this suggestion, the atheist Voltaire cast great ridicule on Newton and the Bible.

Undoubtedly, knowledge has exploded in the last forty years. It continues to expand at a dizzying pace. All the new technology related to the computer industry alone is incredible.

Before attending seminary I worked as an attorney at the Oklahoma Court of Criminal Appeals. Right before I left the Court in 1988, we purchased a state-of-the-art mainframe computer that filled an entire room. Thirteen years later my personal laptop computer will blow that mainframe away in speed, function, and capacity.

According to published reports, 90 percent of all the scientists who have ever lived are alive today. Fifty percent of the world's inventions have been created in the last ten years. The Internet is currently doubling in size every seven months.

Consider these figures on the growth of knowledge in our world:

From 1750 to 1900	250 years	Knowledge doubled
From 1900 to 1950	50 years	Knowledge doubled
From 1950 to 1960	10 years	Knowledge doubled
From 1960 to 1968	8 years	Knowledge doubled
From 1968 to 1990	every 3 years	Knowledge doubled
From 1990 to 2001	every 18 months	Knowledge doubled

One estimate I read suggested that since 1990, total human knowledge may have doubled as much as sixty times. By 2005, knowledge may be doubling every year or less.

These numbers are staggering. Nevertheless, I do not believe this increase in general knowledge is a sign of the end times. Daniel 12:4 does not describe a last days explosion of knowledge in general, but an increase of a particular kind of knowledge: knowledge of God's plan for the end.

The phrase "many will rush here and there" is used in the Bible to mean movement in search of something, often information (see Amos 8:12; Zechariah 4:10). Therefore, I believe that Daniel 12:4 is talking about men who, in the last days, will run to and fro studying the book of Daniel and other prophetic books in the Bible to find answers about what in the world is going on.

And we see this being fulfilled today, don't we? We understand Daniel's book better today than we did in times past—perhaps even better than Daniel himself understood it. We have the Olivet discourse of Jesus in Matthew 24, the book of Revelation, and twenty-five hundred years of history to help us better understand Daniel's prophecies. As we get closer to the end, knowledge of the end times will continue to increase. For the final generation during the Tribulation period, the end-time prophecies of Scripture will read like the daily newspaper.

As we approach the end of all things, it seems that the book of Daniel is being unsealed. God urges us to "rush here and there," searching its pages diligently to gain greater knowledge of God's prophetic program.

This is the knowledge explosion God wants us to experience in our lives.

Twelve

Will the temple be rebuilt in Jerusalem in the end times?

The temple mount in Jerusalem is the most sacred thirty-five-acre piece of land in the world. Three major world religions—Judaism, Islam, and Christianity—claim it as one of their most holy sites. Not surprisingly, this location will play a part in the end times. God's Word mentions four Jewish temples that have stood or will stand in the future on this sacred site:

- The Temple of Solomon—Constructed in 960 B.C. by Solomon; destroyed in 586 B.C. by the Babylonians.
- The Temple of Zerubbabel and Herod—Originally constructed by Zerubbabel in 538–515 B.C.; embellished and expanded by Herod the Great beginning in 19 B.C.; destroyed by the Romans in A.D. 70.
- The Tribulation Temple—future.
- The Millennial Temple—future.

There are five passages in the Bible that indicate that a temple will exist in Jerusalem during the future tribulation period: Daniel 9:27; 12:11; Matthew 24:15; 2 Thessalonians 2:4; and Revelation 11:1–2.

1. Daniel 9:27a: "And he will make a firm covenant with the many for one week, but in the middle of the week he will put a stop to sacrifice and grain offering."

According to this verse, the Antichrist will make a seven-year covenant (one week of years) with Israel, allowing the Jewish people to offer sacrifices in the temple. Then, after three and a half years, he will rescind the covenant. If sacrifices and offerings are to be offered by the Jewish people, it seems clear that there must be a rebuilt temple in Jerusalem.

2. Daniel 12:11: "From the time that the regular sacrifice is abolished and the abomination of desolation is set up, there will be 1,290 days."

Once again, if there is to be a regular daily sacrifice in Israel, it must be in a rebuilt temple.

3. Matthew 24:15: "Therefore when you see the ABOMINATION OF DESOLATION which was spoken of through Daniel the prophet, standing in the holy place."

If "the holy place" refers to a part of the temple (as most Bible scholars agree), and if the Antichrist's sacrilegious idol (the abomination of desolation) is placed there, we can only conclude that the temple will be rebuilt at some point.

4. Second Thessalonians 2:4: "[The man of lawlessness] opposes and exalts himself above every so-called god or object of worship, so that he takes his seat in the temple of God, displaying himself as being God."

This is another verse that indicates that the Antichrist will sit in the rebuilt temple in Jerusalem during the Tribulation, proclaiming himself to be God.

5. Revelation 11:1–2: "Then there was given me a measuring rod like a staff; and someone said, 'Get up and measure the temple of God and the altar, and those who worship in it. Leave out the court which is outside the temple and do not measure it, for it has been given to the nations; and they will tread under foot the holy city for forty-two months.'"

There will be a future temple in Jerusalem. It will be trampled underfoot by the nations led by Antichrist for the final forty-two months (three and a half years) of the Tribulation.

These passages clearly indicate that the Jewish people will rebuild the temple in Jerusalem before the coming Tribulation period. In fact, preparations are currently underway in Israel to bring this to fruition.

The main impediment to the rebuilding of a temple in Jerusalem is the presence of the Muslim Dome of the Rock—the mosque of Omar—on the place where the temple must be rebuilt. Also on the temple mount is the Al-Aqsa Mosque, which was built in A.D. 715 and is regarded as the third holiest place in Islam (after Mecca and Medina). Muslims consider the Dome of the Rock to be the crown of the temple mount.

But how will the Jews ever be able to rebuild their temple with the Dome of the Rock on the same piece of real estate without triggering World War III? To me, this is one of the thorniest problems in all of Bible prophecy.

There are four possible solutions to this problem. First, some believe that it may be possible to rebuild the temple without disturbing the Dome of the Rock. The Jewish temple and Muslim Dome of the Rock could stand side by side on the temple mount.

This is very unlikely for two reasons. One, the best archaeologists, including Israeli scholars, concur that the Dome of the Rock stands on the site where the first and second Jewish temples once stood. Two, even if the temple could be rebuilt next to the Dome of the Rock, this would be anathema to both the Jews and the Muslims.

A second solution that has been proposed is that God will send some great disaster such as an earthquake that will destroy the Muslim structures on the temple mount.

Third, some believe that when the Antichrist comes to power, he will broker a peace treaty between Israel and the Arabs. Part of that plan would include giving Israeli sovereignty over the temple mount area.

It is true that the Antichrist will be able to do what no one has been able to do up to that point. It is conceivable that he would bring a comprehensive peace plan to the Middle East. If he is able to convince the Muslims to give up control of the temple mount and return it to the Jews, he certainly would be hailed as the greatest diplomat in human history. This may, in fact, be the event that catapults him onto the international political scene as the world's messiah.

A fourth possibility is that the annihilation of Russia and her Muslim allies (as detailed in Ezekiel 38–39) will eliminate the Muslim threat to the Jews, thus allowing them to tear down the Dome of the Rock and Al-Aqsa Mosque and rebuild their temple without fear of reprisal.

The Bible doesn't tell us how the temple will be rebuilt. Any of the scenarios in views two, three, or four above could be right—or God could bring about the rebuilding of the temple through some other means. But one thing is sure: The temple will be rebuilt in Jerusalem just as God's Word predicts!

Preparations for the rebuilding of the third Jewish temple are underway now among the Jewish people. The Temple Institute in Jerusalem is vigorously working to construct needed objects and utensils for renewed worship in the third temple, including the Menorah, the pure gold crown worn by the high priest, firepans and shovels, the mitzraq (vessel used to transport the blood of sacrifical offerings), the copper laver, linen garments of the priests, and stone vessels to store the ashes of the red heifer. Efforts continue to produce an unblemished red heifer to fulfill the purification requirements of Numbers 19:1–10.

Randall Price, the foremost evangelical authority on the temple, concludes his excellent book on the temple with these timely words:

> What does this say to you and me? It says that not only have the Jews already begun the ascent to their goal, but they are only one step away from accomplishing it! As this book has shown, the current conflict over the Temple Mount and the resolve of the Jewish activists to prepare for the conclusion of this conflict have provided the momentum for the short distance that remains of the climb. We live in a day that is on the brink of the rebuilding effort, and with it the beginning of the fulfillment of the prophecies that will move the world rapidly to see as a reality the coming Last Days Temple.[9]

THIRTEEN

ARE THERE HIDDEN BIBLE CODES?
AND IF SO, DO ANY RELATE TO THE END TIMES?

In the early 1990s a Jewish man from Hollywood called me to ask me if I knew anything about the hidden codes in the Old Testament. When I confessed my ignorance, he offered to send me a video on the subject.

On the video, a Jewish rabbi taught about the various codes that he claimed lie hidden in the text of the Old Testament. The rabbi's presentation was long and boring. I threw the video away and forgot all about Bible codes. Little did I know that a few years later the whole subject of Bible codes would be such a big issue.

In recent years there has been an explosion of popular books dealing with hidden codes in the Bible. These books have been written by Jewish rabbis, Messianic Jews, and Bible prophecy teachers. The best known of these books is Michael Drosnin's *The Bible Code*. A movie titled *The Omega Code* used the unraveling of hidden Bible codes as the key to its end-times plot.

These teachers claim that the alleged codes in the Hebrew text of the Old Testament can be discovered by using computers to search for the letters of specific words that occur at a specific interval or spacing. The process is referred to as equidistant letter sequencing (ELS) or "the skip process." The sequencer finds a Hebrew letter, skips a certain number of letters, then skips the same number of letters again, and so on, until the hidden word is revealed. The skip can be of any length as long as the skips are equal, and the word can be spelled forward, backward, vertically, horizontally, or diagonally.

Bible code enthusiasts claim to have found references to Hitler, the Holocaust, the assassinations of John F. Kennedy and Israeli Prime Minister Yitzhak Rabin, the Gulf War, man's landing on the moon, and many references to *Yeshua* (Jesus) in Messianic passages.

While this idea sounds ingenious, the whole notion of Bible codes should be approached with great caution. I have six reasons for saying this. First, some of the skip distances can be up to one thousand letters.

This incredible separation in the letters makes this whole process suspect.

Second, in the Torah alone (the first five books of the OT), scholars using the ELS process have also found 2,328 references to Mohammed, 104 references to Krishna, and the name Koresh (as in David Koresh) encoded 2,729 times.[10] In other words, it seems you can find whatever you want to find.

Third, the uniqueness of these codes to the Scripture is yet to be proven. One of the key arguments of Bible code enthusiasts is that the existence of these hidden codes validates the uniqueness and inspiration of Scripture. However, many excellent biblical scholars strongly contend that these codes are much ado about nothing. The same principles used for finding Bible codes have been used on other books, and references to world figures and world events have been found in these secular writings.

Michael Drosnin, author of *The Bible Code,* issued this challenge: "When my critics find a message about the assassination of a prime minister encrypted in *Moby Dick,* I will believe them."[11]

Accepting that challenge, Professor Brendan McKay, a mathematician at the Australian National University, used the ELS technique to search Herman Melville's *Moby Dick* for encrypted messages. He discovered thirteen predicted assassinations of public figures including Indira Gandhi, Martin Luther King, Sirhan Sirhan, JFK, Abraham Lincoln, and Yitzhak Rabin.

Fourth, there is absolutely no biblical support for this practice. Neither Jesus nor the apostles ever utilized any such technique, even though they quoted or alluded to the Old Testament hundreds of times.

Fifth, even if these hidden codes can be proven to be valid, they still will not provide any information about the last days. The whole Bible code explosion is an exercise in "Monday morning quarterbacking." We already know all of the information that has been revealed in these codes. We already know about Hitler and JFK. The only way these codes can possibly be validated is after the fact, because if the method discovered a name no one had ever heard of, it wouldn't have any meaning for the finder. If something can be proven to be a prediction only after it has already happened, then it is no longer a future event and the method isn't worth much.

Sixth, the Bible is full of straightforward prophecies. We would be much better off to turn to these passages and study their clear meaning rather than searching for some hidden codes. J. Paul Tanner, who has studied Bible codes extensively, provides a helpful warning:

> People do not need some "biblical crossword puzzle." Instead they need to read and meditate on the revealed truths of God's holy Word. They need to be engaged in Bible study to learn the marvelous truths God has revealed, rather than being diverted by the speculative counting of letters (for which there is no divine sanction or apostolic precedent).[12]

FOURTEEN

IS THE MORAL DECAY OF MODERN SOCIETY A SIGN OF THE END TIMES?

There is little doubt for most people that our society is declining morally and that the downward slide is picking up speed. The extent and viciousness of crime, the abuse of drugs, the number of unwed mothers (many of whom are still children themselves), the rate of divorce, the proliferation of pornography, and the open acceptance of homosexuality as an acceptable lifestyle all signal a major moral downgrade in our society. This causes many people to wonder if these are signs that the end is near.

However, this may not necessarily be so. Most of the passages in the New Testament that discuss the moral and spiritual trends in the last days focus on the spiritual apostasy that will occur in the church, not in society in general.

The familiar passage in 2 Timothy 3:1–9 that lists the kinds of behavior that will characterize "the last days" is primarily describing apostasy or falling away that will take place within the church (notice the context in verses 5 and 8). Apostasy (departure from the faith) within the church is a clear sign of the last days (1 Timothy 4:1–4; 2 Peter 3:3–4; Jude 18–19). Of course, we can safely assume that spiritual apostasy in the church will translate into moral decline in society as a whole.

The only passage that specifically mentions the increase of lawlessness in society as a whole as a sign of the last days is Matthew 24:12. "Because lawlessness is increased, most people's love will grow cold." God's Word is clear that as the end draws near, the sinfulness of man will reach a fever pitch, and man's love for his fellow man will grow cold.

We must be careful, however, in applying this sign of Christ's coming. It is difficult to quantify the sinfulness of man. Sin has always been rampant in our world. At every point in history, people believed that the wickedness of their day was worse than it had ever been before. But no matter how bad things get, they can always get worse. Therefore, we should be careful not to point to every incidence of moral decay in our society as a clear sign of the last days.

What we should do is recognize that as the end draws near, sin will run rampant in society, and love of people for one another will grow cold.

Fifteen

Is the army of 200 million in Revelation 9:16 a reference to China?

Revelation 9:15–16 describes a massive army of 200 million mounted troops who destroy one-third of all the people on earth. The most common interpretation of this passage is that it describes a great Chinese invasion of Israel. This conclusion is based on three main points:

1. The army of 200 million is viewed as parallel with the kings from the east in Revelation 16:12 who cross the dried-up Euphrates River to come into Israel.
2. The modern nation of China could amass an army of this magnitude.
3. The description of the weapons used by this army is similar to a scene of modern warfare; the images could be describing tanks, helicopters, artillery, rocket launchers, and missiles.

Revelation vividly describes the weaponry:

And this is how I saw in the vision the horses and those who sat on them: the riders had breastplates the color of fire and of hyacinth and of brimstone; and the heads of the horses are like the heads of lions; and out of their mouths proceed fire and smoke and brimstone. A third of mankind was killed by these three plagues, by the fire and the smoke and the brimstone which proceeded out of their mouths. For the power of the horses is in their mouths and in their tails; for their tails are like serpents and have heads, and with them they do harm. (Revelation 9:17–19)

Ray Stedman, former pastor of Peninsula Bible Church in Palo Alto, California, believes that these verses are describing all the armies of the world invading Israel at Armageddon with modern weaponry:

The lions' mouths which spouted fire and smoke suggests can-
nons, mortars, rocket launchers, and missiles killing great masses
of people with fire, radiation, and even poison gases.... Another
intriguing image is that of the horses' tails, described as being like
snakes, having heads that inflict injury. These words could apply
to various kinds of modern armament—helicopter gunships
with rotors mounted on their long tail assemblies, or perhaps
missiles which leave a snake-like trail of smoke in their wake and
inflict injury with their warheads. Perhaps it is a description of
weapons that are yet to be invented.[13]

Although it is possible that these verses describe modern weapons of
war—and although it is possible that these warriors will be from China—I
believe that it is better to view this massive army as an armada of demonic
invaders that assault the earth during the Tribulation. I prefer this view for
five reasons:

1. This army's unleashing is the sixth trumpet judgment (see
    Revelation 9). The fifth and sixth trumpets go together: They are
    the first two of three "woes" (v. 12). Because the fifth trumpet
    judgment is clearly a demonic invasion of earth, it would stand
    to reason that the sixth trumpet judgment would imply a
    demonic army, too.
2. This armada is led by fallen angels, as is the army of the fifth
    trumpet judgment. Since the leaders are four fallen angels, it
    makes sense that the troops they are leading are also demons
    (Revelation 9:15). Demons do gather human armies for
    Armageddon (Revelation 16:13–16), but here they don't just
    gather them: They lead them in their destruction.
3. The fearsome description in Revelation 9:17–19 would better
    apply to supernatural beings than to modern warfare.
4. The Bible has other examples of supernatural cavalry. Horses of fire
    swept Elijah up to heaven (2 Kings 2:11). Horses and chariots of
    fire protected Elisha at Dothan (2 Kings 6:13–17). Horses and
    horsemen from the celestial realm introduce the reign of Christ
    (Revelation 19:14). The Lord Himself will return riding on a white
    horse (Revelation 19:11). It seems logical that Satan would resist
    the coming of the kingdom with his own infernal cavalry.

5. The weapons that are mentioned—fire, brimstone, and smoke—are always supernatural weapons in the Bible. In Revelation, they are associated with hell four times (14:10–11; 19:20; 20:10; 21:8).

For these reasons, I believe the army of 200 million in Revelation 9:16 is not a human army at all (from China or anywhere else) but an invasion of earth by demonic cavalry—hellish horsemen riding Satanic steeds! During the tribulation period, the earth will be overrun with demons who afflict men with great pain (Revelation 9:10) and ultimately slay one-third of the people on earth (9:15, 18).

Sixteen

WILL THE LITERAL CITY OF BABYLON BE REBUILT IN THE LAST DAYS?

Revelation 17–18 describes a great city "Babylon" that will be prominent in the end times. There are seven clues in these chapters that help identify this city.

1. Babylon is specifically identified as a city (Revelation 17:18).
2. Babylon is described as a city of worldwide importance and influence; possibly it will be the capital city of the world in the end times (17:15, 18).
3. Babylon and the Antichrist are very closely connected with one another. The woman (Babylon) is pictured riding on the Beast (Antichrist).
4. Babylon is a center of false religion (17:4–5; 18:1–2).
5. Babylon is the center of world commerce (18:9–19). These two systems, religion and commerce, will share the same geographical location under Antichrist's domain.
6. Babylon persecutes the Lord's people (17:6; 18:20, 24).
7. Babylon will be destroyed suddenly and completely at the end of the Tribulation, never to rise again (18:8–10, 21–24).

Putting these clues together reveals that Babylon will be the great religious, economic capital of the Antichrist's kingdom in the last days. But what city is represented by Babylon?

Babylon, this great harlot of the end times, has been variously identified with the Roman Catholic church and the Vatican, apostate Christendom, New York City, Jerusalem, and Rome. I believe the best view, however, is that Babylon is the literal city of Babylon on the Euphrates in modern Iraq. I believe it will be rebuilt in the last days. There are seven main points that favor this identification of Babylon in Revelation 17–18.

First, in Revelation the great city that is described as the last days capital of Antichrist is specifically called "Babylon" six times in Revelation (14:8; 16:19; 17:5; 18:2, 10, 21). Although it is possible that the name Babylon is a code name for Rome, New York, Jerusalem, or some other city, since there is no indication in the text that it is to be taken figuratively or symbolically, it is probably best to take it as referring to literal Babylon. Geographical locations throughout Revelation seem to be literal (with one clear exception, and in that case it is clear in the text that the reference isn't literal—see below).

The cities of the seven churches in Revelation 2–3 are almost universally understood as the literal locations mentioned. The Euphrates river is mentioned twice in Revelation; it too is usually taken literally. Armageddon in Revelation 16:16 is a literal place in northern Israel.

The one time John wants to identify a location using symbolic language, he tells the reader that it is nonliteral. In Revelation 11:8 he refers to Jerusalem as "Sodom and Egypt," but he makes it clear that he is not speaking literally: "the great city which mystically is called Sodom and Egypt." The fact that John is careful to let the reader know when he is not speaking literally of a geographical location leads me to believe that when he leaves that part out, he intends for us to take it at face value.

Second, Babylon is the second most mentioned city in the Bible (behind Jerusalem). Babylon is referred to nearly three hundred times in Scripture. Throughout the Bible, Babylon is depicted as the epitome of evil and rebellion against God. Babylon is Satan's capital city on earth.

1. Babylon is the city where man first began to worship himself in organized rebellion against God (Genesis 11:1–11).
2. Babylon was the capital city of the first world ruler, Nimrod (Genesis 10:8–10; 11:9).
3. Nebuchadnezzar, who destroyed the city of Jerusalem and the temple in 586 B.C., was the king of Babylon.
4. Babylon was the capital city of the first of four Gentile world empires to rule over Jerusalem.

Since Babylon is pictured throughout Scripture as Satan's capital on earth, it makes sense that in the end times he will once again raise up this city as the capital of the final world ruler.

In Charles Dyer's excellent book *The Rise of Babylon*, he says:

Throughout history, Babylon has represented the height of rebellion and opposition to God's plans and purposes, so God allows Babylon to continue during the final days. It is almost as though he "calls her out" for a final duel. But this time, the conflict between God and Babylon ends decisively. The city of Babylon will be destroyed.[14]

Third, the city of Babylon fits the criteria as described in Revelation 17–18. As Robert Thomas notes, "Babylon on the Euphrates has a location that fits this description politically, geographically, and in all the qualities of accessibility, commercial facilities, remoteness of interferences of church and state, and yet centrality in regard to the trade of the whole world."[15]

Fourth, the Euphrates river is mentioned by name twice in Revelation (9:14; 16:12). Revelation 9:14 says that four fallen angels are being held at the Euphrates river awaiting the appointed time for them to lead forth a host of demons to destroy one-third of mankind. In Revelation 16:12, the sixth bowl judgment is poured out and dries up the Euphrates river to prepare the way for the kings of the east.

These references to the Euphrates point to the fact that something important and evil is occurring there. If Babylon on the Euphrates had been rebuilt and was functioning as a religious and political center for Antichrist, it would be a good explanation for this emphasis on the Euphrates river in Revelation.

Fifth, the prophet Zechariah records an incredible vision that pertains to the city of Babylon in the last days:

Then the angel who was talking with me came forward and said, "Look up! Something is appearing in the sky."

"What is it?" I asked.

He replied, "It is a basket for measuring grain, and it is filled with the sins of everyone throughout the land."

When the heavy lead cover was lifted off the basket, there was a woman sitting inside it. The angel said, "The woman's name is Wickedness," and he pushed her back into the basket and closed the heavy lid again.

Then I looked up and saw two women flying toward us, with wings gliding on the wind. Their wings were like those of a stork, and they picked up the basket and flew with it into the sky.

"Where are they taking the basket?" I asked the angel.

He replied, "To the land of Babylonia, where they will build a temple for the basket. And when the temple is ready, they will set the basket there on its pedestal." (Zechariah 5:5–11, NLT)

The parallels between Zechariah 5:5–11 and Revelation 17–18 are striking.

Zechariah 5:5–11	Revelation 17–18
Woman sitting in a basket	Woman sitting on the Beast, seven mountains and many waters (17:3, 9, 15)
Emphasis on commerce (a basket for measuring grain)	Emphasis on commerce (merchant of grain 18:13)
Woman's name is Wickedness	Woman's name is "Babylon the Great, Mother of all Prostitutes and Obscenities in the World"
Focus on false worship (a temple is built for the woman)	Focus on false worship (18:1–3)
Woman is taken to Babylon	Woman is called Babylon

God's Word teaches that in the end times wickedness will return to the place where it began—Babylon. John's prostitute will fulfill the prophecy of Zechariah 5 when Babylon is established as the end-time city of evil.

Sixth, since the city of Babylon was never destroyed suddenly and completely as predicted in Isaiah 13 and Jeremiah 50–51, these passages must refer to a future city of Babylon, one that will be totally destroyed in the Day of the Lord.

Seventh, Jeremiah 50–51 clearly describe the geographical city of Babylon on the Euphrates. The many parallels between this passage and Revelation 17–18 suggest that they are both describing the same city.

PARALLELS BETWEEN JEREMIAH 50-51 AND REVELATION 17-18

BABYLON	JEREMIAH 50–51	REVELATION 17–18
Compared to a golden cup	51:7a	17:3–4 & 18:6
Dwelling on many waters	51:13a	17:1
Involved with nations	51:7b	17:2
Named the same	50:1	18:10
Destroyed suddenly	51:8a	18:8
Destroyed by fire	51:30b	17:16
Never to be inhabited	50:39	18:21
Punished according to her works	50:29	18:6
Fall illustrated	51:63–64	18:21
God's people flee	51:6, 45	18:4
Heaven to rejoice	51:48	18:20[16]

The city of Babylon will be rebuilt in the last days to serve as the religious and commercial capital for the Antichrist's empire. Wickedness will return to this place for its final stand. Then, with the seventh bowl judgment at the end of the Tribulation, God will put it in Antichrist's heart to fulfill His purpose by destroying the great city of Babylon with fire (Revelation 17:16–17; 18:8). Babylon will fall, never to rise again!

The recent rise of Iraq on the world political and economic scene is not an accident. In spite of the Gulf War and tremendous worldwide pressure, Iraq remains a formidable foe. I believe this current rise of Babylon is a key part of God's plan for the last days.

Seventeen

Does Russia play a role in the end times?

One of the great prophecies in the Bible is found in Ezekiel 38–39. These chapters predict that in the last days a vast confederation of nations from north of the Black and Caspian Seas, extending down to Iran in the east and North Africa to the southwest, will join together in a great offensive against Israel after its return to the land. The leader of this offensive is called Gog, who is identified as the prince of Rosh.

Three times in Ezekiel 38–39 the prophet says that Gog will lead his army from "the remote parts of the north" (38:6, 15; 39:2). Could this prophecy be a reference to the nation we today know as Russia?

Let's begin by seeing if there is any connection between Rosh and Russia.

Rosh: Proper Name or Title?

The word *rosh* in Hebrew simply means head, top, summit, or chief. It is a very common word and is used in all Semitic languages. It occurs approximately seven hundred fifty times in the Old Testament, along with its root and derivatives. The problem is that the word rosh in Ezekiel can be translated as either a proper noun (making Rosh the name of a place) or an adjective (simply meaning chief or head).

Many Bible translations take the second route, understanding rosh as an adjective meaning "chief." *The King James Version, Revised Standard Version, New American Bible,* and *New International Version* all adopt this translation. However, the *Jerusalem Bible, New English Bible,* and *New American Standard Bible* all translate rosh as a proper name indicating a geographical location. I believe the weight of evidence favors taking rosh as a proper name. There are five arguments in favor of this view.

First, eminent Hebrew scholars C. F. Keil and Wilhelm Gesenius both held that the better translation of rosh is as a proper noun referring to a specific place.[17]

Second, the Septuagint, the Greek translation of the Old Testament, translates rosh as the proper name Ros. This is significant since the Septuagint was translated only three centuries after Ezekiel was written (obviously much closer in time to the original than our modern translations).

Third, many Bible dictionaries and encyclopedias, in their articles on Rosh, support taking it as a proper name. Some examples: *New Bible Dictionary, Wycliffe Bible Dictionary,* and *International Standard Bible Encyclopedia.*

Fourth, rosh is mentioned the first time in Ezekiel 38:2 and then repeated in Ezekiel 38:3 and 39:1. If rosh were simply a title, it would probably be dropped in these two places because in Hebrew when titles are repeated they are generally abbreviated.

Fifth, the most impressive evidence in favor of taking rosh as a proper name is simply that this translation is the most accurate. G. A. Cooke, a Hebrew scholar, translates Ezekiel 38:2, "the chief of Rosh, Meshech and Tubal." He calls this "the most natural way of rendering the Hebrew."[18]

If the word rosh in Ezekiel 38–39 is to be understood as a proper name, the next task is to determine what nation is meant, since it's such a significant power in the end times.

IS ROSH RUSSIA?

An ancient group of people known as the Sarmatians (not to be confused with the Samaritans) lived in the area around the Caspian Sea from the tenth century B.C. At the time Ezekiel was writing, the Sarmatians were known as the Rashu, Rasapu, Ros, and Rus. In 200 B.C. they poured into what today is southern Russia.

Based on the background of the term *rosh,* the Hebrew scholar Gesenius says that rosh is "undoubtedly the Russians, who are mentioned by the Byzantine writers of the tenth century, under the name *Ros,* dwelling to the north of Taurus…as dwelling on the river Rha (*Wolga*).[19]

Moreover, Ezekiel 38–39 says three times that Gog, the leader of Rosh, comes from "the remote parts of the north" (38:6, 15; 39:2). Assuming that this means the nation farthest north from Israel, a glance at a globe will reveal that this is Russia.

I believe, therefore, that Rosh is Russia, and that the Scripture predicts that the great Russian bear will rise in the last days to mount a furious invasion of Israel.

Many people thought that when the Soviet Union was dissolved the bear went into permanent hibernation. But Russia today is much more dangerous than ever before. Her economy is in shambles—she is a starving bear and her great Soviet Union has been dissolved—she is a mother bear robbed of her cubs. The fulfillment of God's prophecies concerning Russia seems more imminent than ever before.

As we track the bear in the end times, we discover that her footprints lead right to the land of Israel. Let's consider four key points: 1.) Russia's allies; 2.) Russia's activity; 3.) Russia's annihilation; and 4.) the aftermath of Russia's destruction.

RUSSIA'S ALLIES

When Russia makes her great push to the south into the land of Israel in the last days, she will be led by a power-crazed madman called Gog. Gog, mentioned eleven times in Ezekiel 38–39, is probably not the leader's name, but a title like Pharaoh, Caesar, or President. *Gog* means a high mountain, high, supreme, or a height. Ezekiel calls him the prince or leader of Rosh three times (Ezekiel 38:2, 3; 39:1).

Gog will be joined by "a vast and awesome horde" of allies (Ezekiel 38:9, NLT). These allies will come from the areas around Russia. Eight locations are mentioned in Ezekiel 38:1–6.

ANCIENT NAME	MODERN NATION
Magog southern (Ancient Scythians)	**Modern Central Asia** (Islamic republics of the former Soviet Union)
Meshech (Ancient Muschki and Musku in Cilicia and Cappadocia)	**Turkey**
Tubal (Ancient Tubalu in Cappadocia)	**Turkey**
Persia (Name changed to Iran in 1935)	**Iran**
Ethiopia (Ancient Cush, south of Egypt)	**Sudan**
Put (Ancient nation west of Egypt)	**Libya**

ANCIENT NAME	MODERN NATION
Gomer (Ancient Cimmerians— from seventh century to first century B.C. in central/western Anatolia)	**Turkey**
Beth-togarmah (Til-garimmu— between ancient Carchemish and Haran) Southern Turkey	**Southern Turkey**

From this list, it seems that Russia will have five key allies: Turkey, Iran, Libya, Sudan, and the nations of Central Asia. Amazingly, all of these are Muslim nations. Many of them are forming or strengthening their ties with one another as these words are being written. What's more, Iran, Libya, and Sudan are three of Israel's most aggressive opponents. It's not too difficult to imagine these nations conspiring together to invade Israel in the near future.

RUSSIA'S ACTIVITY

Ezekiel says that these nations, led by Russia, will come against Israel "in the last days" at a time when the people of Israel are living in peace and prosperity (38:8–12). This probably describes the first half of the Tribulation, when Israel will be living under her peace treaty with Antichrist. Near the middle of the Tribulation, Russia and her Islamic allies will descend upon the nation of Israel "like a storm and cover the land like a cloud" (38:9, NLT).

There are four main reasons why I believe Russia and her allies will invade Israel:

1. To cash in on the wealth of Israel (Ezekiel 38:11–12).
2. To control the Middle East.
3. To crush Israel (Islamic nations hate Israel).
4. To challenge the authority of Antichrist (Daniel 11:40–44).[20]

Israel will be under her peace treaty with Antichrist at this time, so an attack against Israel would be a direct challenge to Antichrist. After the armies of Ezekiel 38 are destroyed, Antichrist will break his covenant with Israel and invade her himself (Daniel 11:41–44).

RUSSIA'S ANNIHILATION

When these nations invade Israel, it will look like the biggest mismatch in history. Gog's assault force "will come like a storm" and "will come up against My people Israel like a cloud to cover the land" (Ezekiel 38:9, 16). Gog's assault will make the Arab invasions of Israel in 1967 and 1973 pale in comparison.

When Russia assembles this last days strike force, it will look like Israel is finished. But, as always, God will be in control of the entire situation. He will mount up in His fury to destroy these godless invaders.

> "It will come about on that day, when Gog comes against the land of Israel," declares the Lord GOD, "that My fury will mount up in My anger. In My zeal and in My blazing wrath I declare that on that day there will surely be a great earthquake in the land of Israel." (Ezekiel 38:18–19)

When God comes to rescue His helpless people, He will use four means to destroy the invaders:

1. A great earthquake (38:19–20).
2. Infighting among the troops of the various nations (38:21). In the chaos after the powerful earthquake, the armies of each of the nations represented will turn against each other. This will be the largest case of death by friendly fire in human history.
3. Disease (38:22).
4. Torrential rain, hailstones, fire, and burning sulfur (38:22). The famous Six-Day War occurred in Israel in June, 1967. This will be the "One-Day War" or even the "One-Hour War," when God will supernaturally destroy this Russian-Islamic horde.

THE AFTERMATH OF RUSSIA'S DESTRUCTION

There are four key events that occur in the aftermath of this invasion.

1. The Birds and the Beasts (Ezekiel 39:4–5, 17–20)

The carnage that results from this slaughter will provide a great feast for the birds of the air and the beasts of the field. God refers to the carnage as "My sacrifice" and "My table" to which He invites the birds and the beasts as His guests. (Compare this to Revelation 19:17–18.)

2. The Seven-Month Burial of the Dead (Ezekiel 39:11–12, 14–16)

Cleanup squads will be assembled to go through the land. They will set up markers wherever they see a human bone. When the grave diggers come behind them, they will see the markers and take the remains to the Valley of Gog's Hordes for burial. The cleansing will be so extensive that a town will be established in the valley at the grave sites to aid those who are cleansing the land. The name of the town will be Hamonah (horde).

3. The Seven-Year Burning of the Weapons (Ezekiel 39:9–10)

It will take seven years to dispose of the weapons and armor left by Gog's demolished army. Since this event occurs at the midpoint of the Tribulation, the Israelites will continue to burn these weapons on into the millennial kingdom for three and a half years.

4. The Blessing of Salvation (Ezekiel 39:21–22)

In the midst of His wrath, God will also pour out His grace and mercy. God will use the awesome display of His power against Russia and her allies to bring many—both Jews and Gentiles—to salvation.

> "I will not let My holy name be profaned anymore. And the nations will know that I am the LORD, the Holy One in Israel.... And I will set My glory among the nations; and all the nations will see My judgment which I have executed and My hand which I have laid on them. And the house of Israel will know that I am the LORD their God from that day onward." (Ezekiel 39:7, 21–22)

Many of those who turn to the true God as a result of this demonstration of His power will undoubtedly be among the vast group of the redeemed in Revelation 7:9–14.

In my opinion, this is one of the most amazing prophecies in all of Scripture. And everything seems to be getting ready for its fulfillment in the near future.

Russia is a key place to watch as the coming of Christ draws near.

Eighteen

Can anyone really understand the book of Revelation?

The book of Revelation may be the most neglected book in the Bible. There are undoubtedly many reasons for this, but one of the chief reasons I've heard is that no one can really understand what it means. All its symbols and imagery cause people to throw their hands up and give up ever trying to understand the meaning of Revelation.

But Revelation is the capstone of God's disclosure to man. To neglect it would be tragic. Revelation gives us the end of the story just as Genesis gives us the beginning. Failure to understand Revelation would be like reading an engrossing, mesmerizing novel but skipping the end without ever reading how the story ends.

Making Sense of Revelation

Let me give you five practical keys to unlocking the meaning of this great book. I hope it will turn into "Apocalypse Wow" in your life.

The Lord Meant for Us to Understand the Book of Revelation

The first key is to recognize that God wants us to "get" Revelation. To say that it can't be understood by believers is to deny the truth behind the title of the book: "The Revelation of Jesus Christ." The word *Revelation* is a translation of the Greek word *apokalupsis,* which means to uncover, to unveil, or to take the lid off something. In other words, the purpose of this book is not to hide the truth from us or make it confusing, but for Jesus Christ to take the lid off the future so we can know about the end times.

Moreover, in Revelation 1:3, the Lord promises a special blessing to those who study and apply the book's message to their lives: "God blesses the one who reads this prophecy to the church, and he blesses all who listen to it and obey what it says" (NLT). This is the only book in the Bible that contains such a promise about itself. Notice the threefold impact of this blessing:

Who Is Blessed	Explanation
The one who reads	In the early church, not everyone had a copy of the Scriptures so someone would read them aloud to the people. Today this blessing extends to all who read Revelation in our own Bibles.
The one who listens	Just to hear the book of Revelation (and other prophecies of the Bible) read is a great blessing in troubled times—like today.
The one who obeys	Not only is it important to read and hear Bible prophecy, but a blessing will come if we observe and obey what it says. After being taught by Revelation, we should diligently watch for the events of the last days to come to pass.

If we are supposed to obey what Revelation says, doesn't it stand to reason that God expects us to understand it, at least generally?

It's about the Second Coming

A second key to unlocking the meaning of Revelation is to understand that the main theme of the book is the second coming of Jesus Christ and the events that immediately precede and follow it.

Chapters 4–18 give the events that lead up to the Second Coming, chapter 19 describes the Second Coming, and chapters 20–22 relate the events that follow it.

Revelation 1:7 gives the theme of the book:

BEHOLD, HE IS COMING WITH THE CLOUDS, and every eye will see Him, even those who pierced Him; and all the tribes of the earth will mourn over Him. So it is to be. Amen.

Past, Present, and Future

The third key to understanding Revelation is to grasp the structure of the book. Revelation 1:19 gives the divinely inspired outline: "Therefore write the things which you have seen, and the things which are, and the things which will take place after these things." This verse divides the book in three sections:

1. The things that John had just seen (Revelation 1:9–20),
2. The things that are now happening (Revelation 2–3),
3. The things that will take place after these things (Revelation 4–22).

Key Verse: Revelation 1:19	"The things which you have seen Revelation 1	"The things which are" Revelation 2–3	"The things which shall take place after all these things" Revelation 4–22		
Topic	The Lord of the Churches	The Letters to the Churches	Tribulation (4–19)	Millennium (20)	Eternity (21–22)
Content	John's vision of the glorified	•Ephesus (loveless) •Smyrna (suffering) •Pergamum (compromising) •Thyatira (tolerant) •Sardis (dead) •Philadelphia Sardis (dead) (faithful) •Laodicea (lukewarm)	•Seals (7) •Trumpets (8–9) •Key Figures 10–15 (10–15) •Bowls (16–19)	•Satan Chained •Saints Reign	•New heavens and earth (21:1) •New Jerusalem (21:2–22:5)
Theme	The Christ	The Church	The Consummation		
Depiction of Jesus	Christ in the Cosmos	Christ in the Churches	Christ in Conquest (19–20)		Christ in Consummation (21–22)
Ages of Revelation	The Present Age ("Church Age") (Revelation 1–3)		Tribulation Age (7 years)	Millennial Age (1,000 years)	Eternal State

Revelation Is Review

The fourth key to unlocking the meaning of Revelation is to realize that most of what is in the book is not really new information. There's an old saying that Revelation is the Grand Central Station of the Bible because it's where all the trains of thought from the whole Bible meet. While it is certainly true that Revelation looks ahead and reveals the future, it also looks back and brings together all the threads from the first sixty-five books of the Bible.

Revelation has 404 verses. Of these, 278 allude to the Old Testament. Though Revelation has no direct quotations from the Old Testament, it contains a total of 550 references to the Old Testament. Revelation therefore is not so much giving us new information as it is putting all the scattered pieces from the Old Testament into a comprehensive sequence of events.

Understanding the Symbols

The fifth and final key to understanding Revelation is to correctly interpret the symbols in the book. Revelation obviously contains many symbols, so many that people sometimes feel like Alice in Wonderland when they step into the book of Revelation.

This has led to two extremes in interpretation. Some say that the presence of all the symbols means that the book cannot be understood at all. They say that the book just gives us an overview of the cosmic struggle between good and evil but that none of the specific details can be understood. The other extreme is unchecked speculation that manipulates the symbols to fit all kinds of current events, basically making Revelation mean whatever the writer wants it to mean.

We need a middle ground. We cannot throw Revelation away because it uses symbolism, nor can we make its symbols mean whatever we want them to mean.

Most Bible scholars believe that the best way to discover what the symbols in Revelation mean is to search Revelation itself. Since God is the author of all Scripture, we can be assured that the symbols will be explained either in Revelation itself or in other parts of the Bible. The infallible guide to the meaning of these symbols is God's Word.

Arnold Fruchtenbaum, a recognized expert in prophetic interpretation, notes:

So there are symbols. But the Bible itself will explain what these symbols mean either by direct statement or through a comparison of the usage of the symbol elsewhere in the Scriptures. The meaning of the symbols will not be determined by speculation. While the Bible does use symbols, it is consistent in the usage of symbols. A specific symbol will mean the same thing throughout the Old and New Testaments in the vast majority (though not all) cases.[21]

Don't be afraid or intimidated by Revelation. God wants you to understand and apply the truths of this book to your life. He has promised a blessing to you if you do. Follow these five keys, and ask the Lord to open your heart and mind to the precious truth of our coming King!

NINETEEN

WHAT SHOULD WE DO IF WE BELIEVE JESUS IS COMING SOON?

Believers in the early church were consistently told to be on the lookout for the coming of Christ. They were also given clear, practical instructions on what they should be doing in light of this imminent event. The most straightforward passage in the New Testament concerning what we should be doing if we believe Jesus is coming soon is in Peter's first letter:

> The end of all things is near; therefore, be of sound judgment and sober spirit for the purpose of prayer. Above all, keep fervent in your love for one another, because love covers a multitude of sins. Be hospitable to one another without complaint. As each one has received a special gift, employ it in serving one another as good stewards of the manifold grace of God. (1 Peter 4:7–10)

Notice the word *therefore* in verse 7. Peter is saying that the end of the world is coming, *therefore* here's what we should be doing. This passage emphasizes four things we should do if we believe that the end is coming soon.

KEEP YOUR HEAD CLEAR: PRAY FOR OTHERS

As we approach the coming apocalypse, more and more people are going to get caught up in the prophetic frenzy. People will be tempted to quit their jobs, sell all their possessions, and go wait on a mountaintop in their pajamas for Jesus to come.

But the Word tells us that in view of the end of all things we are to be "earnest." This word literally means "not drunk." In other words, we are to be sober-minded, clearheaded, and mentally alert for the purpose of prayer. Believing that Christ could come back today should spur us on to a sober, disciplined prayer life.

KEEP YOUR HEART WARM: LOVE OTHERS

The badge of Christianity is love (John 13:34–35). As we see the end approaching we are to love one another with a "deep love." The word translated *deep* was used in ancient times of a horse at full gallop when its muscles were stretched to the limit. Peter is saying that our love for one another is to be stretched out but never reaching its breaking point.

KEEP YOUR HOME OPEN: SHOW HOSPITALITY TO STRANGERS

One of the signs of the second coming of Christ according to Jesus is that "the love of many will grow cold" (Matthew 24:12, NLT). In light of this, believers are called to show their love in a concrete way by reaching out in Christian love to strangers.

This beautiful Christian virtue is mentioned specifically six times in the New Testament (Romans 12:13; 1 Timothy 3:2; 5:9–10; Titus 1:8; Hebrews 13:1–3; 1 Peter 4:9). As this world becomes a colder and more isolated place, we are to keep our homes open and show the warmth of Christ to strangers.

KEEP YOUR HANDS BUSY: USE YOUR SPIRITUAL GIFTS

Every believer in Jesus Christ has at least one spiritual gift. Spiritual gifts are supernatural empowerments that God has given to His children to serve the body of Christ.

As we see the curtain about to rise on the final act of history, we hear the Lord calling us to keep our hands busy, using for His service the gifts He has given us.

TWENTY

HOW CLOSE ARE WE TO THE END?

At every prophecy conference Q&A session I have ever attended, someone has asked this question. After all, this is the big one, isn't it? How close are we to the end? How much longer will it be until Jesus comes back?

This question reminds me of the man who was sitting downstairs reading late one night after his wife had already gone to bed. He heard the grandfather clock begin to chime in the hallway and started counting the chimes to see what time it was. The clock chimed nine, ten, eleven, twelve, then thirteen. Upon hearing the thirteenth bell, he ran upstairs to his wife: "Honey, wake up—it's later than it's ever been!"

That's the one sure answer to this question I can give: We are now closer to the end than we've ever been. However, the ultimate answer to this question is that no one except the Lord knows for sure how close we are to the end.

We can point to various signs the Lord has given—such as the regathering of Israel to her land, the European Union as the possible reuniting of the Roman Empire, the continued heightening of tensions in the Middle East, the unstable conditions in Russia, and the development of a one-world economy that could easily be controlled by the Antichrist. And it does appear that these signs point to the soon coming of Christ to earth. So the Rapture must be even nearer. But how near? We just don't know.

These signs indicate that the *general* time of the Second Coming is near. But we still must confess that we don't know the *specific* day or hour of His coming for His church. We can confidently say, "Jesus may come today." But at the same time we must also admit that He may not come in the next decade. He may not come in my lifetime or yours.

One passage that is often used to pinpoint the coming of Christ is Matthew 24:34: "Truly I say to you, this generation will not pass away until all these things take place." This verse is used by some to prove that once the signs of the last days begin, Christ will return within one generation (usually calculated to be about forty years). However, this verse probably means that the generation that personally witnesses the signs in Matthew 24:4–30, that is, the tribulation period, will not pass away before Christ returns. Thus, this verse should not be used to establish a date for the coming of Christ.

For those of us today who see the storm clouds of some of these signs gathering on the horizon, all we can say is that we believe we are in the end times in a general sense.

My grandfather was a pastor who loved the prophetic Scriptures. When Israel became a nation in 1948, he recognized the prophetic significance. He commented on numerous occasions that he believed Jesus would come in his lifetime. He lived his life looking for the Rapture, believing the end was near. However, the Lord called him home in 1963.

Was my grandfather wrong? No, he wasn't wrong. He didn't miss the Rapture. His spirit is presently with the Lord. At the Rapture, his body will be resurrected to join the Lord and His saints in the air. The precious hope of the Rapture added unspeakable joy to his life.

The point of prophecy in Scripture is that we are to live as if He could come at any moment. That's all we can do. We must leave the timing of this event with the Lord.

The Rapture

Two men walking up a hill
One disappears
One's left standing still
I wish we'd all been ready
LARRY NORMAN

In the early 1970s, everyone in my home church was talking about Hal Lindsey's blockbuster book *The Late Great Planet Earth*. I was about eleven years old at the time. Around that same time a movie about the Rapture was produced called *A Thief in the Night*. One Wednesday night at church they showed the movie in our youth meeting. One of the final scenes in the movie portrays people disappearing at the Rapture and those who were left behind.

One sunny afternoon shortly afterward I arrived home from school and discovered that my mother was not in the house. This was very unusual. My mom, older sister, and younger brother were always home when the bus dropped me off. I began to call her name and look around in the house. I walked out on the patio to see if anyone was in the back-yard. They were nowhere to be found. I rushed out in the front yard and looked up and down the street in vain.

Suddenly, the thought hit me: *I've missed the Rapture! My family has gone without me!*

Then, in a final act of desperation, I decided to head back into the house to call my dad at work. If my dad was there, then everything was okay because I knew there was no way he would miss the Rapture.

As I started back into the house, I heard one of the greatest sounds in my life: my mom calling my name. She and my sister and brother had run next door to visit our neighbor.

I have never forgotten that day. The truth of the Rapture of the church was as real to me that day as it has ever been.

Let's consider some of the questions we all have about this next great event on God's prophetic timetable.

TWENTY-ONE

WHAT IS THE RAPTURE?

The Rapture is that future event when Jesus Christ will descend from heaven and, in a moment of time, resurrect the bodies of departed believers, transform the bodies of living believers immediately into His glorious presence, and then escort them to heaven to live with Him forever. The Rapture is the blessed hope of the church.

There are seven key points in 1 Thessalonians 4:13–18 that summarize the precious truth of the rapture.

1. The Realization

First, Paul makes it clear that he wants us to understand the Rapture.

> But we do not want you to be uninformed, brethren, about those who are asleep, so that you will not grieve as do the rest who have no hope. For if we believe that Jesus died and rose again, even so God will bring with Him those who have fallen asleep in Jesus. (1 Thessalonians 4:13–14)

The Lord wants every believer to know the truth of the Rapture. In the King James Version, verse 13 begins, "But I would not have you to be ignorant, brethren." Someone once said that the fastest growing denomination in America is the "church of the ignorant brethren." But the Lord doesn't want us to be ignorant about the truth of the Rapture.

The first thing the Lord wants us to realize about the Rapture is that our believing loved ones who have passed away will not miss out on the Rapture. When Jesus comes, He will bring the perfected spirits of departed believers with Him. Knowing this truth is to bring us comfort and hope and to soften our grieving when loved ones pass away. When believers die, it is not goodbye, but only good night. We will see them again at the Rapture.

2. The Revelation

Paul also wants us to know without any doubt that what he is saying is directly from the Lord: "For this we say to you by the word of the Lord"

(v. 15a). What Paul is recording is divinely revealed. It's not something he made up on his own.

3. The Return

At the Rapture, the Lord Himself will come again in the clouds. He will return accompanied by three things: a commanding shout, the call of the archangel, and the trumpet call of God.

> We who are alive and remain until the coming of the Lord, will not precede those who have fallen asleep. For the Lord Himself will descend from heaven with a shout, with the voice of the archangel and with the trumpet of God, and the dead in Christ will rise first. (vv. 15b–16)

This commanding shout is the last of three great cries or commands of the Savior. Notice that at each of these cries the dead are resurrected (see also John 5:28–29).

1. The cry from the cemetery when Lazarus was raised (John 11:43–44);
2. The cry from the cross when the dead came to life (Matthew 27:50–53);
3. The cry from the clouds when the dead are raised at His coming (1 Thessalonians 4:16).

4. The Resurrection

When Christ comes down from heaven, the first thing that will happen is that the bodies of deceased believers will be resurrected and reunited to their perfected spirits that have returned with the Lord: "The dead in Christ will rise first" (1 Thessalonians 4:16b).

These resurrected bodies will be glorified, incorruptible bodies fit for the heavenly realm (1 Corinthians 15:35–56; 2 Corinthians 5:1–5; Philippians 3:20–21). The nature of these new bodies will be discussed in question 92.

5. The Removal

As soon as the dead have been raised, living believers will immediately be transformed and translated into the presence of Christ without ever tasting physical death: "Then we who are alive and remain will be caught up together with them in the clouds" (v. 17a).

Though 1 Corinthians 15:51 is often mounted over church nurseries, it is an apt description of what some of us will experience at the Rapture: "We will not all sleep, but we will all be changed." Millions of believers will never know the sting of death. They will be raptured instantly into the presence of the Lord in the clouds in the blink of an eye (1 Corinthians 15:52).

6. The Reunion

The dead in Christ and the living saints will all be raptured together: "Then we who are alive and remain will be caught up together with them in the clouds to meet the Lord in the air, and so we shall always be with the Lord" (v. 17).

What a glorious reunion we will have as all the saints of this age meet the dear Savior!

7. The Reassurance

Knowing that there is a rapture brings comfort and hope to all of God's people, especially when a believing loved one dies: "Therefore comfort one another with these words" (v. 18).

Twenty-two

Is the word "rapture" found in the Bible?

A few years ago I was in a restaurant having lunch with a man who had just started attending our church. He was asking me some questions about the last days, and I was telling him about the Rapture. In the middle of our conversation a man at the table next to us, who had obviously been listening in on our discussion, told me in no uncertain terms that the Rapture is an unbiblical doctrine because the word *rapture* is not even in the Bible.

While he was dead wrong in denying the doctrine of the Rapture, he was correct in stating that the word rapture is not in the English translations of the Bible. If you were to read all of the 727,747 words in the KJV of the Bible or in any other well-known translation, you would discover that the word rapture is not there. However, you would not find the words *Trinity* or *Bible* either. And yet we know those things are very real.

We get the word rapture from Latin. In 1 Thessalonians 4:17, the Greek word *harpazo* (which means to snatch, to seize, or to take away) was translated in the Latin versions of Scripture with the word *rapturo*, which was brought over to English as *rapture*.

So while it is true that the word rapture does not occur in most English translations, the doctrine of a catching away of living believers to meet the Lord is clearly present (1 Corinthians 15:51–55; 1 Thessalonians 4:17). This doctrine could just as well be called the "catching away of the church," the "snatching away of the church," the "translation of the church" or the *"harpazo* of the church." But since the phrase "rapture of the church" is an excellent description of this event and has become the most common title, there is no reason to change the terminology.

Twenty-three

What are the main passages in the Bible that deal with the Rapture?

While the catching up of the church is alluded to many times in the New Testament, there are three passages that most fully describe the Rapture of the church: John 14:1–3; 1 Corinthians 15:50–57; and 1 Thessalonians 4:13–18.

> "Do not let your heart be troubled; believe in God, believe also in Me. In My Father's house are many dwelling places; if it were not so, I would have told you; for I go to prepare a place for you. If I go and prepare a place for you, I will come again and receive you to Myself, that where I am, there you may be also." (John 14:1–3)

> Now I say this, brethren, that flesh and blood cannot inherit the kingdom of God; nor does the perishable inherit the imperishable. Behold, I tell you a mystery; we will not all sleep, but we will all be changed, in a moment, in the twinkling of an eye, at the last trumpet; for the trumpet will sound, and the dead will be raised imperishable, and we will be changed. For this perishable must put on the imperishable, and this mortal must put on immortality. But when this perishable will have put on the imperishable, and this mortal will have put on immortality, then will come about the saying that is written, "DEATH IS SWALLOWED UP IN VICTORY. O DEATH, WHERE IS YOUR VICTORY." "O DEATH, WHERE IS YOUR STING?" The sting of death is sin, and the power of sin is the law; but thanks be to God, who gives us the victory through our Lord Jesus Christ. (1 Corinthians 15:50–57)

> But we do not want you to be uninformed, brethren, about those who are asleep, so that you will not grieve as do the rest who have no hope. For if we believe that Jesus died and rose again,

even so God will bring with Him those who have fallen asleep in Jesus. For this we say to you by the word of the Lord, that we who are alive and remain until the coming of the Lord, will not precede those who have fallen asleep. For the Lord Himself will descend from heaven with a shout, with the voice of the archangel and with the trumpet of God, and the dead in Christ will rise first. Then we who are alive and remain will be caught up together with them in the clouds to meet the Lord in the air, and so we shall always be with the Lord. Therefore comfort one another with these words. (1 Thessalonians 4:13–18)

Now that you've read the key scriptural passages on the Rapture, let's dig a little deeper into the meaning of this exciting end-time event.

Twenty-four

Why is the Rapture called a mystery?

In 1 Corinthians 15:51, the apostle Paul refers to the Rapture as a mystery. When we think of a mystery, we most often think of something that is difficult to understand or solve. While so many things about the end times seem mysterious, that's not the Bible's meaning of the word. In the New Testament, a *mystery* is a truth that is being revealed by God for the first time.

The mystery of the Rapture is that some people will go to heaven and receive new, glorified bodies without ever dying. They will do an end run around the grave: "Behold, I tell you a mystery; we will not all sleep, but we will all be changed" (1 Corinthians 15:51). This was a totally new truth that had never been disclosed by God until He inspired Paul to record it in his first letter to the Corinthians.

If you read your Bible from Genesis 1 to Corinthians 14, you would correctly conclude that the only way to get to heaven and obtain your glorified body would be to die. But in 1 Corinthians 15, all that changes. There the Lord unveils the glorious truth that a whole generation of believers will be transformed without feeling the sting of physical death.

May we be that generation!

Twenty-five

What are the major views on the timing of the Rapture?

Every evangelical Christian I've met believes that Jesus will return for His people. But there is wide disagreement about the timing of this event in relation to the tribulation period. Will the church go through any or all of the Tribulation before the Rapture occurs? In the minds of most believers, this is the big question about the Rapture. This is clearly the most often debated issue about the rapture of the church.

There are five main theories today on the timing of the Rapture:

1	**The Pretribulational Rapture**	The Rapture will occur before the tribulation period begins.
2	**The Midtribulational Rapture**	The Rapture will occur at the midpoint of the Tribulation.
3	**The Posttribulational Rapture**	The Rapture will occur at the end of the Tribulation right before the second coming of Christ back to earth; believers will be raptured up to meet Christ in the air and then will return immediately with Him back to the earth.
4	**The Partial Rapture**	Faithful, devoted believers will be raptured before the Tribulation, but the rest of believers will be left to go through the purging of the Tribulation.
5	**The Prewrath Rapture**	The Rapture will occur about three-fourths (five and a half years) of the way through the Tribulation, when the wrath of God begins to be poured out on the earth at the seventh seal.

Of these, the two views that are the most commonly held today are the pretrib and posttrib views.

VARIOUS VIEWS OF THE TIMING OF THE RAPTURE

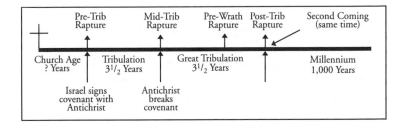

TWENTY-SIX

WHICH OF THESE VIEWS IS BEST AND WHY?

I believe the pretrib view is the most scriptural regarding the timing of the Rapture. There are seven key points that have brought me to this conclusion. I have arranged them in a handy acronym that spells out the word *PRETRIB*.

P—Place of the church in the book of Revelation;
R—Removal of the restrainer;
E—Exemption from divine wrath;
T—Twenty-four elders;
R—Rapture of the church versus the return of Christ;
I—Imminence;
B—Blessed hope.

P: PLACE OF THE CHURCH IN REVELATION

None of the key New Testament passages that deal with the Tribulation mention the presence of the church.

The primary section of the Bible that describes the tribulation period is Revelation 4–19. In these chapters there is a curious silence about the church. In Revelation 1–3 the church is specifically mentioned nineteen times. It is again mentioned in Revelation 22:16. But between those two points, the church of Jesus Christ is strangely absent from the biblical account of events on earth. To me this is strong evidence that the church will not be present on earth during the Tribulation.

R: REMOVAL OF THE RESTRAINER

Second Thessalonians 2 outlines three important ages that take us from the present age to eternity:

The Present Age (Before the Rapture)	The Age of Restraint	2 Thessalonians 2:6
The Tribulation Age (After the Rapture)	The Age of Rebellion	2 Thessalonians 2:7–9
The Messianic Age (After the Second Coming)	The Age of Revelation	2 Thessalonians 2:8*b*

Though it may be hard to believe, the age in which we now live is described as the age of restraint. Something or someone is holding back the full blast of evil that is to come when the Antichrist is unleashed.

Think about it for a moment. If this evil world we live in now is described as the time of restraint, what in the world will it be like when the restrainer is removed? It will be like removing a dam from a lake—evil will overflow this world, swamping everything in its path.

Who or What Is the Restrainer?

The key question in this discussion is this: Who or what is this person or entity that is restraining the appearance of the Antichrist? Down through the centuries many candidates have been suggested:

- The Roman Empire.
- The Jewish state.
- The apostle Paul.
- The preaching of the gospel.
- Human government.
- Elijah.
- Some unknown heavenly being.
- Michael the archangel.
- The Holy Spirit.
- The church (believers).

The greatest minds of Christian history have wrestled with this question and given up in frustration. St. Augustine said, "I frankly confess I do not know what He means."

I can sympathize with Augustine, but I believe there are several points that can help us identify the restrainer. Only one conclusion satisfies all four of the following requirements:

1. The Greek word used here, *katecho* (translated "what is holding him back" or "the one who is holding it back" [2 Thessalonians 2:6–7]), means "to hold back or restrain."

2. The word describing the one who is holding back or restraining is used in both the neuter and masculine forms:

   - Neuter: "you know what restrains him now"—a principle (2 Thessalonians 2:6).

- Masculine: "he who now restrains"—a person (2 Thessalonians 2:7).
3. Whatever the restrainer is, he or it must be removable.
4. He or it must be powerful enough to hold back the outbreak of evil under Antichrist.

Here's a question for you: Who is able to restrain evil and hold back the appearance of Antichrist? The answer, of course, is God. But what is God's instrument for accomplishing His will on earth? The church.

I believe, therefore, that the restrainer should be understood as *God's Holy Spirit working in and through the church.* It's not just the Holy Spirit and not just the church. It's both, working together.

Here's why I think this:

1. This restraint requires omnipotent power.
2. This view adequately explains the change in gender in 2 Thessalonians 2:6–7. In Greek the word *pneuma* (Spirit) is neuter. But the Holy Spirit is also consistently referred to by the masculine pronoun *he,* especially in John 14–16.
3. The Holy Spirit is spoken of in Scripture as restraining sin and evil in the world (Genesis 6:3) and in the heart of the believer (Galatians 5:16–17).
4. The church and its mission of proclaiming the gospel is the primary instrument the Holy Spirit uses to restrain evil in this age. We are the salt of the earth and the light of the world (Matthew 5:13–16). Salt holds off decay and light holds back the dark.

Donald Grey Barnhouse, one of the greatest Bible teachers of this century, summarizes this view.

Well, what is keeping the Antichrist from putting in his appearance on the world stage? *You* are! You and every other member of the body of Christ on earth. The presence of the church of Jesus Christ is the restraining force that refuses to allow the man of lawlessness to be revealed. True, it is the Holy Spirit who is the real restrainer. But as both 1 Corinthians 3:16 and 6:19 teach, the Holy Spirit indwells the believer. The believer's body is the temple of the Spirit of God. Put all believers together then, with the Holy Spirit indwelling each of us, and you have a formidable restraining force.

For when the church is removed at the rapture, the Holy Spirit goes with the church insofar as His restraining power is concerned. His work in this age of grace will be ended. Henceforth, during the Great Tribulation, the Holy Spirit will still be here on earth, of course—for how can you get rid of God?—but He will not be indwelling believers as He does now. Rather, he will revert to His Old Testament ministry of "coming upon" special people.[22]

At the Rapture, the Spirit-indwelt church and its restraining influence will be removed. Thus the way will be cleared for Satan to put his plan into full swing by bringing his man onto center stage to take control of the world.

E: Exemption from Divine Wrath

The Bible promises that God's people are exempt from the coming wrath of the tribulation period (1 Thessalonians 1:9–10; 5:9; Revelation 3:10). The nature of the entire tribulation period is one of pounding judgment against a rebellious world. The judgment of God begins with the first seal that is opened in Revelation 6:1 and continues all the way until the Second Coming in Revelation 19:11–21.

To say that God's wrath is confined to the very end of the Tribulation (as the prewrath rapture view maintains), one must overlook the fact that all of the seal judgments are opened by the Lamb (Revelation 6:1). They are the wrath of God against sinful man, and they are opened at the beginning of the Tribulation. The very nature of the tribulation period demands that Christ's bride be exempt from this time of trouble.

Genesis 18–19, which records the rescue of Lot and his family from Sodom, seems to indicate that it is against God's character to destroy the righteous with the wicked when He pours out His judgment. The rapture of Enoch to heaven before the Flood is another illustration of this principle (Genesis 5:24).

In Revelation 3, the Lord's promise of deliverance from the tribulation period is very specific:

"Because you have kept the word of My perseverance, I also will keep you from the hour of testing, that hour which is about to come upon the whole world, to test those who dwell on the earth. I am coming quickly." (Revelation 3:10–11a)

Notice two important things about this promise. First, the Lord promises to keep His people not just from the hardships of worldwide testing but also from the hour of testing itself. What is the hour of worldwide testing? Since John only mentions one period of worldwide testing in the book of Revelation (chapters 6–19), he must mean the tribulation period.

Second, notice the means of this protection: "I am coming quickly" (v. 11a).

If we put these two points together, it seems that the Lord will protect His people from the time of worldwide testing by coming for them at the Rapture.

T: Twenty-Four Elders

In Revelation there are twelve references to a group of beings called the "twenty-four elders" (Revelation 4:4, 10; 5:5, 6, 8, 11, 14; 7:11, 13; 11:16; 14:3; 19:4). The fact that they are mentioned twelve times makes them key players in Bible prophecy.

There are four main views concerning the identity of the twenty-four elders. People have suggested that they are: angelic beings, Israel, the church, or all of the redeemed—Israel and the church. I favor the third. Eight clues in Revelation lead me to believe that the twenty-four elders represent the raptured church.

The Title

They are called elders (*presbuteros*). We get our English word *Presbyterian* from this word.

I am reminded of the little girl who came home from her Presbyterian Sunday school class, and her mother asked her what the lesson was about. The little girl replied, "We talked about heaven."

"Well," her mother asked, "What did they say about it?"

The little girl said, "The teacher told us that only twenty-four presbyterians made it to heaven."

In the New Testament, a church's elders are a few members who represent the rest of the body. I believe that these twenty-four elders represent the glorified church in heaven.

The Number

The Levitical priesthood in the Old Testament numbered in the thousands (1 Chronicles 24). Since all of the priests could not worship in the temple at the same time, the priesthood was divided into twenty-four groups, and a representative of each group served in the temple on a rotating basis. Though there were only twenty-four priests at the temple at all times, they represented the larger group.

Christians are called a holy priesthood (1 Peter 2:5). I believe that the twenty-four elders of Revelation represent the larger group of priests—the whole church of Jesus Christ.

The Position

These elders are seated on thrones. Enthronement with Christ is promised only to the church (Revelation 3:21).

The Crowns

The elders cannot be angels because angels are never pictured in Scripture as wearing crowns. Church age believers, on the other hand, are promised crowns at the judgment seat of Christ (Revelation 2:10).

This is also why I believe that the twenty-four elders cannot represent saved Israel: Old Testament believers will not be resurrected and rewarded until after the Tribulation is over (Daniel 12:1–3), yet these elders are shown with crowns while the Tribulation is still under way.

The Clothing

The white clothing of the elders is the clothing of the redeemed in the church age (Revelation 3:5, 18; 19:8)

The Praise

Only the church can sing the song the elders sing in Revelation 5:9–10. Only in this age have people been saved from every tribe, tongue, people, and nation.

The Distinction

The elders are clearly distinguished from angels in Revelation 5:11.

Location

Where does the Bible say these elders are? Are they on earth getting ready for the Tribulation? No! They are in heaven worshiping Him who sits on the throne and the Lamb. From their first mention in Revelation 4:4, the twenty-four elders are in heaven, raptured, judged, rewarded, and enthroned.

If the elders do represent the church, as I believe, then the fact that they are in heaven in Revelation 4 is another indication that the church must be raptured to heaven before the first judgment of the Tribulation is unleashed in Revelation 6:1. The only place you find the church in Revelation 4–19 is in heaven, represented by the twenty-four elders who are seated on thrones, dressed in white, crowned with crowns, and worshiping the Lamb (Revelation 4:4, 10; 5:5–6, 8, 11, 14).

R: Rapture of the Church Versus Return of Christ

Some students of Bible prophecy strongly object to the notion that the rapture of the church and the second coming of Christ are distinct events separated by seven years. They contend that this is teaching two future comings of Christ although the Bible only presents one event.

The only way to resolve this issue is to set what the Bible says about these events side by side to see if they are describing the same occurrence. You be the judge. (Please refer to the chart on page 97.)

The differences between the passages describing the Rapture and those describing Jesus' second coming suggest that they are not the same event. This conclusion would lend support to the pretrib view, since it also treats the two as separate events.

I: Imminence

The Rapture is presented in the New Testament as an event that from man's viewpoint could occur at any moment, and believers are to be looking for it all the time (1 Corinthians 1:7; 16:22; Philippians 3:20; 4:5; 1 Thessalonians 1:9–10; Titus 2:13; Hebrews 9:28; Jude 1:21). Only the pretrib position allows for an imminent, any moment, signless coming of Christ for His own.

Only those who believe in a pretrib rapture can honestly say, "Jesus may come today!" For midtribbers, the Rapture must be at least three and a half years away since they believe that the Rapture comes halfway through the Tribulation, which hasn't yet begun. For prewrathers, it must be at least five and a half years away, since they believe that the Rapture will happen that deep into the yet-to-begin Tribulation. For a similar reason, the Rapture is still at least seven years away for posttribbers.

The Bible indicates that the any moment coming of Christ should fill believers with hope, anticipation, and motivation for godly living. Any day might be *the* day. Only pretrib believers can experience this joy, since they are the only group for whom the Rapture is imminent.

B: Blessed Hope

The truth of the Rapture is intended to be a comfort and a blessing to the Lord's people. It is our "blessed hope" (Titus 2:13). In 1 Thessalonians 4:18, after describing the Rapture, Paul concludes with this command: "Therefore comfort one another with these words."

Think about this for a moment. If Paul had taught a midtrib, prewrath, or posttrib rapture, would the truth of the Rapture really be that comforting? If God's people knew they would have to endure three and a half years, five and a half years, or all seven years of horrible Tribulation to get to the Rapture, how much of a comfort would the thought of rapture be?

The blessed hope of the Rapture is that Jesus will come and take us to be with Him—before the time of worldwide devastation is unleashed. And what a comfort and blessing it is!

I believe in a pretribulation rapture of the church because of:

P—Place of the church in the book of Revelation;
R—Removal of the restrainer;
E—Exemption from divine wrath;
T—Twenty-four elders;
R—Rapture of the church vs. the return of Christ;
I—Imminence;
B—Blessed hope.

The timing of the Rapture is *PRETRIB*.

The Rapture	The Return (Second Coming)
Christ comes in the air (1 Thessalonians 4:16–17)	Christ come to the earth (Zechariah 14:4)
Christ comes *for* His saints (1 Thessalonians 4:16–17)	Christ come *with* His saints (1 Thessalonians 3:13; Jude 14)
Christ claims His bride	Christ comes with His bride
Not in the Old Testament (1 Corinthians 15:51)	Predicted often in the Old Testament
There are no signs—it is imminent	Portended by many signs (Matthew 24:4–29)
It is a time of blessing and comfort (1 Thessalonians 4:18)	It is a time of destruction and judgment (2 Thessalonians 2:8–12)
Involves believers only (John 14:1–3; 1 Corinthians 15:51–55; 1 Thessalonians 4:13–18)	Involves Israel and the Gentile nations (Matthew 24:1–25:46)
Will occur in a moment, in the time it takes to blink; only His own will see Him (1 Corinthians 15:51–52)	Will be visible to the entire world (Matthew 24:27; Revelation 1:7)
Signals the beginning of the Tribulation	Signals the beginning of the Millennium
Christ comes as the bright morning star (Revelation 22:16)	Christ comes as the sun of righteousness (Malachi 4:2)

TWENTY-SEVEN

ISN'T THE PRETRIB RAPTURE A RECENT VIEW?

One of the charges often leveled against the pretrib view is that it can't be right because it was developed quite late compared to the other views. It only came into being around 1830 through the ministry of J. N. Darby. On other topics, I myself have argued that a certain view is to be preferred because it is the earliest one—see my arguments in favor of premillennialism (question 6), for instance.

But in this case, I believe that what is thought to be a later view is the best. I have two reasons for feeling this way. First, the fact that a specific interpretation has been recently circulated does not necessarily mean it is false. The great doctrines of justification by faith alone (*sola fide*) and the sufficiency of Scripture alone (*sola Scriptura*) were "rediscovered" in the sixteenth and seventeenth centuries by the Reformers. Certainly no true believer would deny these doctrines, yet they were relatively unknown for many centuries.

Second, the pretrib rapture position may not be so new after all. The doctrine actually does have historical precedent—from as early as the fourth to the seventh century A.D. A sermon delivered by the Byzantine leader Pseudo-Ephraem entitled *On the Last Times, the Antichrist, and the End of the World* or *Sermon on the End of the World* includes a concept very similar to the pretrib rapture, though it was delivered more than one thousand years before the writings of John Nelson Darby.

The sermon contains just under fifteen hundred words, yet it is considered "one of the most interesting apocalyptic texts of the early Middle Ages."[23] The sermon was so popular in its day that it was quickly translated into several languages.

In one place the sermon reads: "All the saints and elect of God are gathered together before the Tribulation, which is to come, and are taken to the Lord, in order that they may not see at any time the confusion which overwhelms the world because of our sins."

According to prophecy scholars Timothy Demy and Thomas Ice:

Pseudo-Ephraem clearly presents at least three important features found in modern pretribulationism: (1) there are two distinct comings: the return of Christ to rapture the saints, followed later by Christ's Second Advent to the earth, (2) a defined interval between the two comings, in this case three and one-half years, and (3) a clear statement that Christ will remove the church from the world before the tribulation.[24]

Therefore, we can say that the pretrib rapture position is not a recent view, after all. It was held and preached possibly as early as A.D. 373.

TWENTY-EIGHT

WHO WILL TAKE PART IN THE RAPTURE?

The Bible limits the participants in the Rapture to church-age believers, that is, those who have trusted in Christ as their Savior between the Day of Pentecost and the day of the Rapture. This is why the Rapture is often more specifically called "the rapture of the church."

Believers who are alive on earth when the trumpet sounds will be immediately transformed and transported to heaven. All these living believers will obviously be from the church age. Then there are "the dead in Christ" who are resurrected at the Rapture (1 Thessalonians 4:16). These too are Christians from the church age. Old Testament believers are not "in Christ."

OLD TESTAMENT BELIEVERS

Since it is true that only Christians will take part in the Rapture, people often wonder what will happen to Old Testament believers. When will they be resurrected and receive their glorified bodies?

God has a plan for His Old Testament saints as well. They will be resurrected at the *end* of the tribulation period. There are two Old Testament passages that suggest this. Notice that each of these passages specifically places the resurrection after the Tribulation.

O LORD, they sought You in distress;
They could only whisper a prayer,
Your chastening was upon them.
As the pregnant woman approaches the time to give birth,
She writhes and cries out in her labor pains,
Thus were we before You, O LORD.
We were pregnant, we writhed in labor,
We gave birth, as it seems, only to wind.
We could not accomplish deliverance for the earth,
Nor were inhabitants of the world born.
Your dead will live;
Their corpses will rise.

You who lie in the dust, awake and shout for joy,
For your dew is as the dew of the dawn,
And the earth will give birth to the departed spirits.
(Isaiah 26:16–19)

A great tribulation will come upon the earth, one that is in some ways equivalent to giving birth. Yet after that time, the dead will "awake and shout for joy" and "the earth will give birth to the departed spirits."

> "Now at that time Michael, the great prince who stands guard over the sons of your people, will arise. And there will be a time of distress such as never occurred since there was a nation until that time; and at that time your people, everyone who is found written in the book, will be rescued. Many of those who sleep in the dust of the ground will awake, these to everlasting life, but the others to disgrace and everlasting contempt." (Daniel 12:1–2)

Once again, the dead will arise, but only after the time of great distress. God has a separate resurrection program for Old Testament believers. He will resurrect them only after the Tribulation has run its seven-year course.

I believe that only church-age believers will be part of the Rapture before the Tribulation.

Twenty-nine

At the Rapture, what will happen to babies and young children who have not believed?

As you might imagine, this question is frequently asked by parents with small children. Believing parents want to know if their young children who have not yet trusted Christ will be left behind at the Rapture.

It is important at the outset to note that there is no specific Scripture that addresses this subject. Nevertheless, I believe we can find an answer that is both biblically sound and satisfying for loving parents. Theologians have developed three main views on this issue.

View #1: No Children Will Be Included in the Rapture

Those who hold this view would emphasize that the Rapture is only for believers and that if a person has not personally believed in Christ, he is not eligible for the Rapture. They would point out that in both the flood of Noah's time and the destruction of the inhabitants of Canaan during the conquest, small children were not excluded from the judgment.

View #2: All Infants and Young Children Will Be Raptured before the Tribulation

Those who hold this view point out that Scripture implies that when young children die they go to heaven. Several passages in the Bible seem to support this position: 2 Samuel 12:20–23; Matthew 19:1–15; Mark 10:1–16. Since, as many believe, all young children go to heaven when they die even if they have never put saving faith in Christ, many would argue that all children alive at the time of the Rapture will likewise be taken so that they may be exempted from the horrors of the Tribulation.

While I agree that infants and small children who die go to heaven to be with Christ, I do not believe that this necessarily means that they will participate in the Rapture. These are two different issues.

View #3: Infants and Young Children of Believers Will Be Raptured to Heaven before the Tribulation

This is a mediating view between the first two positions. While it's wise to avoid dogmatism on this issue, I believe this is the best view for two reasons.

First, Paul reminds us in 1 Corinthians 7:14 that in a Christian family the children are "set apart for Him" (NLT). It seems inconceivable to me that the Lord would rapture believing parents to heaven and leave their defenseless children alone in the world for the tribulation period. Parents are commanded to raise and protect their children (Proverbs 22:6; Ephesians 6:4; 1 Timothy 5:8). If God were to rapture the parents and leave the children behind, He would be preventing the parents from obeying His own command.

Second, I believe there is biblical precedent for this view. When the Lord sent the Flood on the earth during the days of Noah, it is true that all the world was destroyed—including unbelieving men, women, and children. But God delivered Noah, his wife, and his three sons and their wives.

When God destroyed Sodom and Gomorrah, He destroyed all the inhabitants of the cities, including the children of unbelievers. The only ones to escape were Lot and his two daughters.

In Egypt at the first Passover, the homes of the faithful—including their young children—were protected from the judgment of God by the blood of the lamb on the doorpost.

In each of these cases, the believer and his children were delivered from the time of judgment. Only unbelievers and their children were destroyed.

While I recognize that Noah's three sons and Lot's daughters were not infants or small children and were probably believers themselves, I believe that these incidents provide biblical precedent for the position that when God sends cataclysmic judgment, He rescues both the believer and his children but allows unbelievers and their children to face judgment.

I believe that during the Tribulation the young children of unbelievers will have the opportunity to believe in Christ as they come of age. Those who die during the Tribulation before they are old enough to understand the claims of the gospel will be taken to heaven to be with Christ.

Regardless of which view we hold, the one fact we can all rest in is that God is a God of love, compassion, mercy, and justice. Whatever He does when the Rapture occurs will be wise, righteous, and just.

God loves our children more than we do. They are precious in His sight.

THIRTY

IS IT EVER RIGHT TO SET A DATE FOR THE RAPTURE?

The following personal ad appeared in a newspaper: "Yesterday in this space I predicted that the world would come to an end. It did not, however. I regret any inconvenience this may have caused."

Unfortunately, setting specific dates for events in the end times often does more than cause inconvenience. When the predicted date comes and goes—which so far has happened every time—people discredit the Bible and lead others to become more disillusioned with its teachings.

The Bible strictly prohibits date setting for the coming of Christ:

- "Therefore be on the alert, for you do not know which day your Lord is coming" (Matthew 24:42).
- "For this reason you also must be ready; for the Son of Man is coming at an hour when you do not think He will" (Matthew 24:44).
- "Be on the alert then, for you do not know the day nor the hour" (Matthew 25:13).
- "It is not for you to know times or epochs which the Father has fixed by His own authority" (Acts 1:7).

The book of Revelation, which is our most complete source of information for the last days, never mentions any specific date for Christ's coming or any other event. All Jesus tells us in the last book of the Bible about the timing of His coming is that it will occur "quickly" (Revelation 1:1, 3; 3:11; 22:7, 12, 20).

Jesus claimed during His earthly ministry that even He did not know the day of His coming: "But of that day and hour no one knows, not even the angels of heaven, nor the Son, but the Father alone" (Matthew 24:36).

Anyone who claims to know the specific time of Christ's coming is claiming to know something that the Father didn't even tell the Son while He was on earth nor the angels who are in His presence. This is the height of arrogance and folly.

If you hear someone setting a date for the Rapture, you can know two things right away: He is wrong, and he is disobeying the Bible.

Thirty-one

Are there any more prophecies that must be fulfilled before the Rapture can occur?

I have often heard prophecy teachers say, "There are no more prophecies that must be fulfilled for the Rapture to occur." While this statement is true, it is also misleading because it implies that there are or were signs or prophecies that must be fulfilled before the Rapture can take place.

The Bible teaches that the Rapture is both signless and imminent. At least from the human point of view, the Rapture comes without sign or warning—He will come "like a thief in the night."

None of the key rapture passages in the New Testament mention any signs that must occur before the Rapture. All that has to happen for Jesus to come is for Jesus to come.

It is true that there are many signs listed in Scripture: in the books of Daniel, Matthew, and Revelation, for instance. But all of these relate to the second coming of Christ to earth, not the Rapture. This is a very important distinction.

As we see the prophetic signs in Scripture lining up, we must remember that these are the signs not of the imminent Rapture but of the approaching Tribulation and second coming of Christ to establish His kingdom. However, the fact that we already see the signs of these events obviously indicates that the Rapture is probably not far away.

THIRTY-TWO

WILL BELIEVERS WHO HAVE BEEN RAPTURED TO HEAVEN BE ABLE TO WATCH THE EVENTS OF THE TRIBULATION UNFOLD ON EARTH?

This is a question that every believer has probably asked at one time or another. We are curious about what we will know and be able to see when we get to heaven.

The main passage that is used to support the idea that departed believers in heaven are watching the events on earth is Hebrews 12:1. Following the inspiring list of faithful believers from the past, the writer of Hebrews concludes:

> Therefore, since we have so great a cloud of witnesses surrounding us, let us also lay aside every encumbrance and the sin which so easily entangles us, and let us run with endurance the race that is set before us. (12:1)

You may have heard this huge cloud of witnesses described as an audience in a huge heavenly stadium watching us here on earth. But in this passage we are to be motivated not because they see us but because we see them. As we look back on the patient endurance and faithfulness in their lives, their examples motivate us to emulate them.

The Bible does reveal that when we get to heaven, we will be aware of at least some events that are transpiring on earth. For instance, when Samuel the prophet appeared to King Saul after his death, he was aware of some of the events surrounding Saul and his kingdom (1 Samuel 28:16–18).

The rejoicing in heaven over the salvation of a sinner on earth may include believers already in heaven as well as angels (Luke 15:7, 10). The martyrs in heaven in Revelation 6:9–10 are aware that their persecutors are still alive on earth. The multitude in heaven in Revelation 19:1–6 is aware of the destruction of Babylon on earth.

Whether our knowledge of events on earth is limited by God or if we will know everything that transpires is not specifically stated. What can be safely said is that those who are in heaven know at least some of what is happening on this earth and may even follow these events with intense interest.

However, once we get to heaven, we may not be as interested in watching earthly events as we might think. While we will certainly know at least some of the main events that are occurring on earth during the Tribulation, it is clear from Revelation that when we get to heaven, we will be primarily consumed with worshiping the Lamb on the throne, not watching the Tribulation on earth.

THIRTY-THREE

HOW WILL PEOPLE WHO ARE LEFT BEHIND EXPLAIN THE RAPTURE?

The Rapture will be an astonishing event. Think about it: In a split second, millions of people will disappear from the earth without a trace (except maybe millions of little piles of clothes). The world will be left in total chaos. Cars will be driverless, planes pilotless, classrooms teacherless, and factories workerless. Missing persons reports will flood the phone lines.

One has to wonder how people who are left behind will explain this unparalleled event.

I believe there will be two main explanations: a natural explanation and a supernatural explanation. The natural explanation will be the most popular. The pundits will flood the airwaves with their theories. *Geraldo Rivera Live* will have dozens of guests debating their hypotheses. Conspiracy theories will abound. *Nightline* will have a two-week special to investigate the possible explanations.

Who knows what kind of bizarre ideas will be presented: a massive UFO abduction, a time warp, a new weapon of mass destruction created by the Russians. Thanks to the current climate in America, one thing we can know for sure is that there won't be any lack of theories.

Then there will be the spiritual explanations. In view of who gets taken it will probably be explained as some kind of spiritual event—possibly a judgment on those taken. Some New Age groups might explain the Rapture as a "cleansing" of the earth as Mother Gaia purifies herself from the toxins of all those narrow-minded religious fanatics.

Some of those left behind will suddenly remember what they had been told by a believer about the Rapture. Unsaved church members will remember a sermon on the Rapture. The Rapture may turn out to be the greatest evangelistic event of all time. Millions of people who have heard about the Rapture but never received Christ will suddenly realize that everything they'd been told was true and they've been left behind. While the so-called experts crow their theories, people by the thousands will realize what has happened and will humbly bow their knees to Christ.

These "tribulation saints" will be persecuted and even martyred for their faith (Revelation 6:9; 7:13–14; 20:4). But when they leave this life, they will join the mighty company of the redeemed—together we will come before the throne to worship the Lamb.

THIRTY-FOUR

WILL PEOPLE WHO REJECT THE GOSPEL AND MISS THE RAPTURE HAVE ANOTHER OPPORTUNITY TO BE SAVED DURING THE TRIBULATION?

Recently I was talking with a friend who has written several prophecy books and speaks all over the country at prophecy conferences. He told me that this is the number one prophecy question that people ask him.

Much of the interest in this issue probably stems from the fact that all of us have friends and loved ones who have heard the truth about Christ but have rejected His free offer of salvation. We wonder if they will have an opportunity to receive Christ if the Rapture comes before they change their minds.

I am not aware of any prophecy scholar who doesn't agree that people will be saved during the tribulation period. In fact, the salvation of the lost seems to be one of the chief purposes of the tribulation period:

"And it will come about that whoever calls on the name of the LORD
Will be delivered;
For on Mount Zion and in Jerusalem
There will be those who escape,
As the LORD has said,
Even among the survivors whom the LORD calls." (Joel 2:32)

In Revelation 7:9 the apostle John sees "a great multitude which no one could count, from every nation and all tribes and peoples and tongues, standing before the throne and before the Lamb." Revelation 7:14 identifies this great multitude as: "the ones who come out of the great tribulation, and they have washed their robes and made them white in the blood of the Lamb." I believe there may be a massive revival during the great Tribulation.

However, there are many respected students of Bible prophecy who contend that anyone who openly rejects the gospel and is left behind at the Rapture will be prevented by God from being saved during the

Tribulation. They hold that these people have made their choice and now they must live with it. They say that God will send a strong deception upon those who heard the truth and rejected God's offer of mercy before the Rapture. Support for this view comes from 2 Thessalonians 2:

> Then that lawless one will be revealed whom the Lord will slay with the breath of His mouth and bring to an end by the appearance of His coming; that is, the one whose coming is in accord with the activity of Satan, with all power and signs and false wonders, and with all the deception of wickedness for those who perish, because they did not receive the love of the truth so as to be saved. For this reason God will send upon them a deluding influence so that they will believe what is false, in order that they all may be judged who did not believe the truth, but took pleasure in wickedness. (2 Thessalonians 2:8–12)

While this verse could be used to support this position, to me it does not seem to be referring to people who reject the truth before the Rapture, but rather those who reject the truth and receive the Antichrist after the Rapture. This entire passage is describing what happens during the tribulation period when Antichrist is present. It refers to those who witness the deception of the Antichrist, believe his message, and reject the truth. This passage says that those who do this will be condemned by God.

Many who have rejected the gospel before the Rapture will undoubtedly continue to reject it after the rapture. However, to say, based on this verse, that no one who has clearly heard the claims of Christ before the Rapture and rejected them can receive God's mercy during the Tribulation is making this verse say much more than the context allows.

God will use the horror of the tribulation period to bring millions of sinners to faith in His Son. There will be great revival during the Tribulation. Among this numberless crowd there will certainly be some who have been given a second opportunity by our gracious Lord.

THIRTY-FIVE

WHAT EFFECT SHOULD KNOWING ABOUT THE RAPTURE HAVE ON OUR LIVES TODAY?

Every key passage on the Rapture contains a practical application. Prophecy was not given just to stir our imaginations; prophecy is intended to change our attitudes and actions to be more in line with God's Word and character. Charles Dyer, who has authored two excellent prophecy books, emphasizes this purpose of Bible prophecy:

> God gave prophecy to change our hearts, not to fill our heads with knowledge. God never predicted future events just to satisfy our curiosity about the future. Every time God announces events that are future, He includes with His predictions practical applications to life. God's pronouncements about the future carry with them specific advice for the "here and now."[25]

There are at least six life-changing effects or influences that understanding the Rapture is to have on our hearts.

1. The Rapture Has a Converting Influence on Seeking Hearts

On a human level, no one knows how much time he has left to live. We are painfully aware of our mortality. We have no guarantee that we will see tomorrow.

On a prophetic level, too, we don't know how much time we have. Christ could come at any moment to take His bride, the church, to heaven, and all unbelievers will be left behind to endure the horrors of the Tribulation. With this in mind, the most important question for every reader to face is whether he has a personal relationship with Jesus Christ as Savior.

The message of salvation through Jesus Christ contains both bad news and good news. The bad news is that the Bible declares that all people, including you and me, are sinful and therefore separated from the Holy God of the universe (Isaiah 59:2; Romans 3:23). God is holy and cannot simply overlook sin. A just payment for the debt must be made. But we are spiritually bankrupt and have no resources within ourselves to pay the huge debt we owe.

The Good News, or gospel, is that Jesus Christ has come and satisfied our sin debt. He bore our judgment and paid the price for our sins. He died on the cross for our sins and was raised to life on the third day to prove conclusively that the work of salvation had been fully accomplished (Colossians 2:14; 1 Peter 3:18).

The salvation that Christ accomplished is available to all. Salvation is a free gift that God offers to sinful people who deserve judgment—that's all of us. Won't you receive the gift today? Place your faith in Christ for your eternal salvation. "Believe in the Lord Jesus, and you will be saved" (Acts 16:31).

Those who fail to trust Christ before the Rapture will be left behind to endure the Tribulation. Won't you respond to the invitation now?

2. The Rapture Has a Caring Influence on Soul-Winning Hearts

It is the rare Christian who can study Bible prophecy without being gripped by the awesome power and wrath of God. The Bible brings us face-to-face with what is in store for those who don't know Christ as their Savior.

We are told in 2 Corinthians 5:20 that God has called us to be ambassadors for Christ, pleading with people to be reconciled with God. Those of us who have already responded to the message of God's grace and forgiveness through Christ know where this world is headed. As we study the end times and realize the awfulness of the Tribulation and the destiny of the lost, we are motivated to redouble our efforts to plead with a perishing world.

3. The Rapture Has a Cleansing Influence on Sinning Hearts

The Word of God is clear that a proper understanding of the Rapture should produce a life of holiness and purity.

> Beloved, now we are children of God, and it has not appeared as yet what we will be. We know that when He appears, we will be like Him, because we will see Him just as He is. And everyone who has this hope fixed on Him purifies himself, just as He is pure. (1 John 3:2–3)

Focusing on Christ's coming is a surefire formula for maintaining personal purity. However, this coming must be a reality to us. It is one thing for us to hold right doctrine about Christ's coming. It is another thing for the doctrine to hold us!

In 1988 a book was published: *88 Reasons Why Christ Will Return in 1988.* In the book the author stated that he had conclusive proof that Christ would rapture the Church to heaven in early October 1988.

A pastor friend in eastern Oklahoma called me that summer to say that the book had caused quite a furor among many people in his church and other churches in the area. Of course, the Bible clearly declares that date setting concerning the coming of Christ is futile and foolish (Matthew 24:36; Luke 21:8). However, this erroneous book had caused many people to reexamine their lives just in case.

Obviously, the book was incorrect, but the point is that when people began to consider the fact that Christ might return soon, it transformed their lives. The Bible declares that we should always be looking for Christ's coming, not just when someone sets an arbitrary date: "Live sensibly, righteously and godly in the present age, looking for the blessed hope and the appearing of the glory of our great God and Savior, Christ Jesus" (Titus 2:12b–13).

The practical, cleansing effect of prophecy is also presented in 2 Peter 3:

> But the day of the Lord will come like a thief, in which the heavens will pass away with a roar and the elements will be destroyed with intense heat, and the earth and its works will be burned up. Since all these things are to be destroyed in this way, what sort of people ought you to be in holy conduct and godliness, looking for and hastening the coming of the day of God, because of which the heavens will be destroyed by burning, and the elements will melt with intense heat! (vv. 10–12)

When anyone says that studying Bible prophecy is not practical, he reveals that he doesn't understand what the Bible says about the personal impact of prophecy. In an immoral, sinful society like ours, what could be more practical than personal purity?

4. The Rapture Has a Calming Influence on Scared Hearts

Another practical effect of the Rapture is that it has a calming influence on us when our hearts get troubled. Jesus said:

"Do not let your heart be troubled; believe in God, believe also in Me. In my Father's house are many dwelling places; if it were not so, I would have told you; for I go to prepare a place for you. If I go and prepare a place for you, I will come again and receive you to Myself, that where I am, there you may be also." (John 14:1–3)

Trouble is the common denominator of all mankind. Often these difficulties can leave us distraught, distracted, and disturbed. One of the great comforts in times like these is to remember that our Lord will someday return to take us to be with Himself.

In John 14:1–3, three main points are emphasized to calm our troubled hearts: a person, a place, and a promise. The person is our Lord, the place is the heavenly city (New Jerusalem), and the promise is that He will come again to take us to be with Him forever.

5. The Rapture Has a Comforting Influence on Sorrowing Hearts

Every person who is reading these words has either faced or will probably face the grief of losing a close friend or loved one to death. When death strikes, pious platitudes do little to bring comfort. The only real, lasting comfort when death takes someone we love is the hope that we will see him again in heaven.

And now, brothers and sisters, I want you to know what will happen to the Christians who have died so you will not be full of sorrow like people who have no hope. For since we believe that Jesus died and was raised to life again, we also believe that when Jesus comes, God will bring back with Jesus all the Christians who have died. (1 Thessalonians 4:13–14, NLT)

The truth of the Rapture should transform the way we view death. God has promised that death has lost its sting, that it will ultimately be abolished, and that life will reign.

This is not to say that we shouldn't grieve when our friends or loved ones die. Jesus wept at the tomb of Lazarus (John 11:35), and Stephen's friends wept loudly over his battered body (Acts 8:2). However, the Bible declares that our weeping is not the weeping of despair. We are to find deep solace, hope, and comfort for our grieving hearts in the truth of God's Word about the future for His children.

6. THE RAPTURE HAS A CONTROLLING INFLUENCE ON SERVING HEARTS

In 1 Corinthians 15:58, after presenting the truth of the Rapture, Paul concludes with a strong admonition: "Therefore, my beloved brethren, be steadfast, immovable, always abounding in the work of the Lord, knowing that your toil is not in vain in the Lord." Paul is saying that since you know that Christ will someday come to receive you to Himself, let nothing move you; be strong and steady in your Christian service.

So many today are unstable and unsettled in Christian work. Knowing about Christ's coming and future events should cure that problem. Realizing that Christ could return at any time should make us enthusiastic about serving the Lord.

The Bible is clear: Waiters are workers. When Christ comes we are to be "dressed in readiness" with our "lamps lit" (Luke 12:35). If the Rapture is a reality to us, it will motivate us to work faithfully for our Lord.

The fact that the Rapture could happen any moment ought to be heartening news for us. But we have to be careful not to get so caught up in thinking about the end that we're no use in the here and now.

Noted Bible teacher Warren Wiersbe tells a story of when he was a young man preaching on the last days. After he'd spent the service laying out the plan of prophecy in great detail, an older gentleman came up to him and whispered in his ear, "I used to have the Lord's return planned out to the last detail; but years ago I moved from the planning committee to the welcoming committee."

Certainly we want to study Bible prophecy and know about God's plan for the future. That's what this book is all about. But we must make sure we're not so caught up in the planning that we forget the welcoming. Are you on the welcoming committee for the Lord's coming? Are you living each day to please the Master?

May God help our study of the last days to transform our lives in conformity with His Word as we wait for our Savior to return.

THE ANTICHRIST

The time comes, it is quite clear,
The Antichrist is very near.
SEBASTIAN BRANT, *THE SHIP OF FOOLS*, CIII 92–93

Other than Jesus Christ, the most important figure in Bible prophecy and all of human history is the coming world ruler—the Antichrist. Dr. Harold Willmington, a well-respected prophecy scholar, aptly describes the uniqueness of the future world dictator:

> Since the days of Adam, it has been estimated that approximately 40 billion human beings have been born upon our earth. Four and one-half billion of this number are alive today. However, by any standard of measurement one might employ, the greatest human (apart from the Son of God himself) in matters of ability and achievement is yet to make his appearance upon our planet.[26]

Who is this satanic superman who is yet to burst on the world scene? What will he do? What will he be like? Will he appear in our lifetime?

The person we refer to as the Antichrist is known by many different names and titles in Scripture. Here are the top ten aliases for the coming world dictator:

1. The little horn (Daniel 7:8).
2. A king, insolent and skilled in intrigue (Daniel 8:23).
3. The prince who is to come (Daniel 9:26).
4. The one who makes desolate (Daniel 9:27).
5. The king who does as he pleases (Daniel 11:36).
6. A foolish shepherd (Zechariah 11:15).
7. The man of lawlessness (2 Thessalonians 2:3).
8. The son of destruction (2 Thessalonians 2:3).

9. The rider on the white horse (Revelation 6:2).
10. The Beast out of the sea (Revelation 13:1–9; 17:3, 8).

There are more than one hundred passages of Scripture that describe the origin, nationality, character, career, kingdom, and final doom of the Antichrist. The goal of this section is to bring all of these scriptural passages into clear focus by providing solid, biblical answers about the coming Antichrist.

Thirty-six

Where do we get the word Antichrist?

The term *Antichrist* immediately evokes a reaction within us. It's a mysterious word, full of evil, power, and fear. Most people have heard this term but few know where it came from.

The word Antichrist (*antichristos*) is found only five times in the New Testament, all in the epistles of John (1 John 2:18, 22; 4:3; 2 John 7). When John wrote his epistles, he was primarily concerned with correcting a doctrinal error that had arisen in his day, namely that some were denying the humanity of Jesus Christ.

John states that even in his own day many "antichrists" (false teachers) had arisen who were denying the true Christ and deceiving many. John's emphasis was on these false teachers of his own day. Certainly they were not the ultimate Antichrist of the end times. But they did represent the initial stage of Satan's "antichrist program," which will come to fruition in the last days (1 John 4:3; 2 Thessalonians 2:7).

We get the term antichrist from John's epistles.

THIRTY-SEVEN

WHAT DOES THE WORD ANTICHRIST MEAN?

The prefix *anti-* can mean "against, opposed to" or "instead of, in place of." So the real question is this: Will the future Antichrist be "against" Christ or "in place of" Christ? Will he be Christ's chief adversary—His archvillain, if you will—or a false, counterfeit messiah?

The answer? Both.

Both meanings are undoubtedly included in the term *Antichrist*. He will be the Lord Jesus' ultimate opponent. He will also be a "mirror Christ," a demonic "savior" whose origin, nature, and purpose are diametrically opposed to Christ's.

The following charts are helpful in this discussion.[27] This first list of titles reveals the chasm between Christ and His adversary.

Antichrist's total opposition to Christ is seen in these contrasting descriptions:

Christ	Antichrist
The Truth	The Lie
The Holy One	The Lawless One
The Man of Sorrows	The Man of Sin
The Son of God	The Son of Destruction
The Mystery of Godliness	The Mystery of Iniquity
Cleanses the Temple	Desecrates the Temple
The Lamb	The Beast

The Antichrist will do all three of the things Satan unsuccessfully tempted Jesus to do in Matthew 4: He will perform miracles to serve his own selfish agenda; he will worship Satan; and he will grandstand for his followers. In every area that could be imagined, Antichrist will be fundamentally opposed to Christ.

The Antichrist will also be "anti" Christ in the sense of being a counterfeit messiah. He will be an amazing parody of the true Christ. In John

5:43, Jesus said, "I have come in My Father's name, and you do not receive Me; if another comes in his own name, you will receive him."

Feature	Christ	Antichrist
Origin	Heaven	Bottomless pit
Nature	The Good Shepherd	The Foolish Shepherd
Destiny	To be exalted on high	To be cast down into hell
Goal	To do His Father's will	To do his own will
Purpose	To save the lost	To destroy the holy people
Authority	His Father's Name	His own name
Attitude	Humbled Himself	Exalts himself
Fruit	The True Vine	The vine of the earth
Response	Despised	Admired

Here are eighteen ways Antichrist will mimic the ministry of the true Son of God:

Christ	Antichrist
Miracles, signs, and wonders (Matthew 9:32–33; Mark 6:2)	Miracles, signs, and wonders (Matthew 24:24; 2 Thessalonians 2:9)
Is God (John 1:1–2; 10:35)	Claims to be God (2 Thessalonians 2:4)
Is the Lion from Judah (Revelation 5:5)	Has a mouth like a lion (Revelation 13:2)
Causes men to worship God (Revelation 1:6)	Causes men to worship Satan (Revelation 13:3–4)
Followers sealed on their forehead (Revelation 7:4; 14:1)	Followers sealed on their forehead or right hand (Revelation 13:16–18)

Christ	Antichrist
Worthy name (Revelation 19:16)	Blasphemous names (Revelation 13:1)
Married to a virtuous bride (Revelation 19:7–10)	Married to a vile prostitute (Revelation 17:3–5)
Crowned with many crowns (Revelation 19:12)	Crowned with ten crowns (Revelation 13:1)
Is the King of kings (Revelation 19:16)	Is called "the king" (Daniel 11:36)
Sits on a throne (Revelation 3:21; 12:5; 20:11)	Sits on a throne (Revelation 13:2; 16:10)
Sharp sword from his mouth (Revelation 19:15)	Bow in his hand (Revelation 6:2)
Rides a white horse (Revelation 19:11)	Rides a white horse (Revelation 6:2)
Has an army (Revelation 19:14)	Has an army (Revelation 6:2; 19:19)
Violent death (Revelation 5:6; 13:8)	Violent death (Revelation 13:3)
Resurrection (Matthew 28:6)	Resurrection (Revelation 13:3, 14)
Second Coming (Revelation 19:11–21)	Second Coming (Revelation 17:8)
One-thousand-year worldwide kingdom (Revelation 20:1–6)	Three-and-a-half-year worldwide kingdom (Revelation 13:5–8)
Part of a holy Trinity: Father, Son, and Holy Spirit	Part of an unholy trinity: Satan, Antichrist, and False Prophet

J. Dwight Pentecost, author of the prophecy classic *Things to Come,* aptly summarizes both meanings of the word Antichrist: "Satan is seeking to give the world a ruler in place of Christ who will also be in opposition to Christ so that he can rule over the world, instead of Christ."[28]

Thirty-eight

What will the Antichrist be like?

What is your image of the final world ruler? Some picture him as Satan incarnate: a man in a red suit, sprouting horns and a tail. Others see him as a modern-day diabolical fanatic like the Marquis de Sade or Rasputin or Adolf Hitler. To others he is nothing but an insecure megalomaniac. Or perhaps he will be the greatest smooth talker, con man, and religious charlatan to ever live. Still others see him as a bloodthirsty, brutal butcher who spends all his time focused on genocide.

While no brief answer can fully summarize what Antichrist will be like, there are six key characteristics of the Antichrist that help us gain the overall picture of what he will be like from the time of his rise to his demise. I think you might be surprised by some of them.

1. He Will Be an Intellectual Genius (Daniel 8:23)

He will overwhelm and captivate the world with his superhuman intellect and powers of perception.

2. He Will Be an Oratorical Genius (Daniel 11:36; Revelation 13:2, 6)

The whole world will be swayed by the hypnotic spell of his words. Over and over in biblical passages about the Antichrist the focus is on his great words or speaking ability.

As theologian A. W. Pink says:

> So it will be with this daring counterfeiter: he will have a mouth speaking very great things. He will have a perfect command and flow of language. His oratory will not only gain attention but respect. Revelation 13:2 declares that his mouth is "as the mouth of a lion" which is a symbolic expression telling of the majesty and awe-producing effects of his voice. The voice of a lion excels that of any other beast. So the Antichrist will outrival orators ancient and modern.[29]

3. He Will Be a Political Genius (Daniel 9:27; Revelation 17:11-12)

The Antichrist will emerge from relative obscurity to take the world political scene by storm. He begins as a "little" horn, but soon is elected to rule over the reunited Roman Empire (Revelation 17:13).

He will be the consummate unifier and diplomat. He will assume power under the stealth of diplomacy. His platform will be peace and prosperity. He will weld opposing forces together with ease. All the dreams of the United Nations will be realized in his political policies. He may well receive the Nobel peace prize or be *Time* magazine's Man of the Year. Daniel 9:27 reveals that he will even bring such peace to the Middle East that the Temple Mount area in Jerusalem will be returned to Jewish sovereignty. He will undoubtedly be hailed as the greatest peacemaker the world has ever seen.

4. He Will Be a Commercial Genius (Daniel 11:43; Revelation 13:16-17)

He will be the CEO of the world's economy. He will set interest rates, prices, stock values, and supply levels. Under his leadership everything will be nationalized—but under his personal control. From the midpoint of the Tribulation until the second coming of Christ, no one will be able to buy or sell without his permission.

5. He Will Be a Military Genius (Revelation 6:2; 13:2).

At the midpoint of the Tribulation, the mask will come off, and the beast will replace the olive branch with the sword. He will subjugate the whole world. All the greatness of Alexander and Napoleon will be as nothing compared to him. No one will be able to stand in the way of his conquest. He will crush everything and everyone before him. He will be the final, great Caesar.

6. He Will Be a Religious Genius (2 Thessalonians 2:4; Revelation 13:8).

Satan's prodigy will be able to do what neither Mohammed, nor Buddha, nor any pope has ever been able to do: unite the world in worship. All the religions of the world will be brought together in the worship of one man. Just think what genius and power and deception it will take to pull this off!

To help us better envision what the Antichrist will be like, H. L. Willmington has provided this helpful analogy with American presidents. The coming world ruler will possess:

- The leadership of a Washington and Lincoln
- The eloquence of a Franklin Roosevelt
- The charm of a Teddy Roosevelt
- The charisma of a Kennedy
- The popularity of an Ike
- The political savvy of a Johnson
- The intellect of a Jefferson[30]

Truly the Antichrist will be hailed as the savior of the world.

THIRTY-NINE

WILL THE ANTICHRIST BE BORN OF A VIRGIN?

The Antichrist is presented in Scripture as a complete counterfeit of the true Christ. If this is so, will the parody extend to the point that he will be the product of a counterfeit "virgin birth"? Some students of Bible prophecy contend that just as Christ was the product of a human mother and the Holy Spirit (the God-man), so the Antichrist will be the product of a human mother and Satan himself (the devil-man). This was the view of Jerome in the fourth century A.D.

As the counterfeit son he would have a supernatural origin. He would literally be Satan's son. Hollywood has latched onto this idea in such movies as *The Omen* and *Rosemary's Baby.*

Support for this notion is drawn primarily from Genesis 3:15. Here the Lord cursed the serpent and said, "I will put enmity between you and the woman, and between your offspring and hers; he will crush your head, and you will strike his heel" (NIV).

The offspring of the woman in this passage is a clear reference to the coming Messiah who would crush the head of the serpent once and for all. But notice that there is a reference here to the serpent's offspring, too, the one who would be the arch-adversary of the woman's offspring. Those who hold to a supernatural origin for the Antichrist say that Genesis 3:15 is the first prophecy of the coming Antichrist.

While the supernatural origin of the Antichrist is certainly possible, it seems better to view the Antichrist not as Satan's literal son but as a man who is totally controlled by Satan. The Antichrist is consistently presented in the Bible as a man.

In 2 Thessalonians 2:9 we read about the person and work of the coming Antichrist. "The one whose coming is in accord with the activity of Satan, with all power and signs and false wonders." The Antichrist is described in 2 Thessalonians 2 as an "evil man" who is energized by the power of Satan to do his wicked work.

Revelation 13:4 says that the dragon (Satan) gives his power to the beast (Antichrist). These verses teach that the Antichrist is able to do what he can do not because he is Satan's offspring but because Satan energizes and empowers him as his chosen human instrument for world rule.

A man named Adso wrote a book in approximately A.D. 950 called *Letter on the Origin and Life of the Antichrist.* In this work he counters the view held by many in his day that the Antichrist will be born from a virgin and contends that he will be born from the union of a human father and mother. However, "he will be conceived wholly in sin, generated in sin, born in sin. The devil will enter the womb of his mother at the very instant of conception. He will be fostered by the power of the devil and protected in his mother's womb."

Adso's view, which became the predominant view in church history, seems to be the most consistent with the way the Antichrist is described in the Bible. Whether Satan enters the Antichrist at the moment of conception is debatable, but the main point remains—the Antichrist will be fully human, yet totally possessed by Satan.

FORTY

IS THE ANTICHRIST A JEW OR A GENTILE?

This is undoubtedly one of the most asked and debated questions about the coming Antichrist. It springs from the issue of how you take the prefix *anti-* in front of the name Christ. If anti means "opposed to" Christ as the ruler of Gentile world power, then Antichrist is probably a Gentile. However, if anti means "in place of" Christ as a false messiah, then it would seem more likely that he would be a Jew.

As far back as the second century A.D. Christian scholars were writing about this issue. Irenaeus (120–202) believed that the Antichrist would be a Jew from the tribe of Dan. He based this conclusion on Jeremiah 8:16 and the fact that Dan is omitted from the list of the tribes of Israel in Revelation 7:4–8. The consistent view of the church during the closing decades of the second century was that the Antichrist would be a Jewish false messiah from the tribe of Dan. This view was also held later by Jerome (A.D. 331–420).

The specific Scripture that is most often used to substantiate the Jewish heritage of the Antichrist is the *King James Version* translation of Daniel 11:37: "Neither shall he regard the God of his fathers." The entire argument rests on the phrase "the God of his fathers." Those who maintain that the Antichrist is a Jew believe that his rejection of "the God of his fathers" proves his Jewishness.

However, this statement could equally apply to a Gentile whose parents were followers of Christianity—or Buddhism or Islam or anything else. This verse simply says that Antichrist will totally reject whatever religion his ancestors practiced. Moreover, most of the more recent translations (ASV, RSV, NASB, and NIV) render the word *God* (*elohim*) in this passage as *gods*. The *New Living Translation* translates the verse correctly: "He will have no regard for the gods of his ancestors."

Therefore, whether you follow the KJV translation or newer translations, it is clear that the key verse used by those who believe the Antichrist is a Jew is far from conclusive. On the contrary, the Bible clearly teaches that the coming Antichrist will be a Gentile. His Gentile heritage can be discerned from four main points.

First, many Bible scholars believe that the "little horn" of Daniel 8 is a reference to the Seleucid ruler Antiochus Epiphanes (see also question 52). If so, he is the only historical person who is specifically identified in Scripture as a "type" or preview of the person and work of the Antichrist. This second-century madman's efforts to impose Greek culture on the Jews culminated in the Maccabean revolt chronicled in the apocryphal book 2 Maccabees. Therefore, if the "type" of the Antichrist is a Gentile, it follows that the Antichrist himself will be a Gentile, too.

Second, the origin of the Antichrist is symbolically described in Revelation 13:1: "Then I saw a beast coming up out of the sea." The word *sea* when used symbolically in Scripture always stands for the Gentile nations. This is confirmed in Revelation 17:15, where "the waters…are peoples and multitudes and nations and tongues."

However, in this case the word *sea* could mean the abyss since this beast is also said to have come from that bottomless pit (11:7; 17:8). If this is true, then the fact that he comes up out of the sea would be describing his satanic, demonic origin from the underworld.

Third, the Antichrist is presented in the Scripture as the final ruler of Gentile world power. He will sit on the throne over the final world empire that will raise its fist in the face of God. Since all the rulers over the Gentile world powers in Daniel 2 and 7 were Gentiles, it is logical that the final ruler of the final form of Gentile world power will also be a Gentile.

Fourth, one of the primary activities of the Antichrist will be his violence against the Jews. He will persecute the Jewish people, invade Israel, and desecrate the rebuilt Jewish Temple (Daniel 7:25; 9:27; 11:41, 45; 2 Thessalonians 2:4; Revelation 11:2; 12:6; 13:7). It seems highly unlikely that a Jew would be the great persecutor of his own people. Gentiles have always led the way in the persecution of the Jews.

For these four reasons, I believe the Antichrist will be a Gentile.

FORTY-ONE

FROM WHAT NATION WILL THE ANTICHRIST ARISE?

As we have seen, the Scriptures indicate that the coming world ruler will be a Gentile. But is the Bible more specific? Can we know his nation of origin?

Daniel 9:26 tells us that Antichrist will be of the same nationality as the people who destroyed the Jewish temple, an event that was still in the future when Daniel wrote. With the benefit of hindsight, we know that in A.D. 70 the temple was destroyed by the Romans.

Therefore, it appears that the Antichrist will be of Roman origin. I believe he will arise from the reunited Roman Empire (by which I mean Western Europe).

FORTY-TWO

COULD THE ANTICHRIST COME FROM AMERICA?

As I have shown, I believe that the Antichrist will arise out of the reunited Roman Empire. Many have taken this to mean that he will come out of one of the nations of Europe that formed the nucleus of the old Roman empire, possibly even Rome itself. However, since the United States came from European nations that constituted the Roman Empire and has language and laws derived from Rome, is it possible that the Antichrist could come from America? Could he even be an American president?

No one can say for sure. Although he could be an American, it seems best to hold that the Antichrist will come out of Europe. This was the western portion of the Roman Empire that existed in John's day when he prophesied Antichrist's coming from a future form of the Roman Empire.

No matter where he comes from, one things is sure: He is coming. And he will do exactly what the Bible predicts.

FORTY-THREE

WHAT WILL THE ANTICHRIST DO?

All this talk about who the Antichrist will be and where he will come from can sometimes cloud the more important issue: What will he do? Let's take a look.

Here is what I feel is a fairly complete list of the twenty-six main activities of the coming Antichrist:

1. He will appear in "the time of the end" of Israel's history (Daniel 8:17).
2. His manifestation will signal the beginning of the Day of the Lord (2 Thessalonians 2:1–3).
3. His manifestation is currently being hindered by the "restrainer" (2 Thessalonians 2:3–7).
4. His rise to power will come through peace programs (Revelation 6:2). He will make a covenant of peace with Israel (Daniel 9:27). This event will signal the beginning of the seven-year Tribulation. He will break that covenant at its midpoint.
5. Near the middle of the Tribulation, the Antichrist will be assassinated or violently killed (Daniel 11:45; Revelation 13:3, 12, 14).
6. He will descend into the abyss (Revelation 17:8).
7. He will be raised back to life (Revelation 11:7; 13:3, 12, 14; 17:8).
8. The whole world will be amazed and will follow after him (Revelation 13:3).
9. He will be totally controlled and energized by Satan (Revelation 13:2–5).
10. He will subdue three of the ten kings in the reunited Roman Empire (Daniel 7:24).
11. The remaining seven kings will give all authority to the Beast (Revelation 17:12–13).
12. He will invade the land of Israel and desecrate the rebuilt temple (Daniel 9:27; 11:41; 12:11; Matthew 24:15; Revelation 11:2).

13. He will mercilessly pursue and persecute the Jewish people (Daniel 7:21, 25; Revelation 12:6).

14. He will set himself up in the temple as God (1 Thessalonians 2:4).

15. He will be worshiped as God for three and a half years (Revelation 13:4–8).

16. His claim to deity will be accompanied by great signs and wonders (2 Thessalonians 2:9–12).

17. He will speak great blasphemies against God (Daniel 7:8; Revelation 13:6).

18. He will rule the world politically, religiously, and economically for three and a half years (Revelation 13:4–8, 16–18).

19. He will be promoted by a second beast who will lead the world in worship of the Beast (Revelation 13:11–18).

20. He will require all to receive his mark (666) in order to buy and sell (Revelation 13:16–18).

21. He will establish his religious, political, and economic capital in Babylon (Revelation 17).

22. He and the ten kings will then destroy Babylon (Revelation 18:16).

23. He will kill the two witnesses (Revelation 11:7).

24. He will gather all the nations against Jerusalem (Zechariah 12:1–2; 14:1–3; Revelation 16:16; 19:19).

25. He will fight against Christ when He returns to earth. In this campaign he will suffer total defeat (Revelation 19:19).

26. He will be cast alive into the lake of fire (Daniel 7:11; Revelation 19:20).

FORTY-FOUR

IS THE ANTICHRIST A HOMOSEXUAL?

In some translations of the Bible, such as the *King James Version, New American Standard,* and *New King James Version,* Daniel 11:37 says that the coming Antichrist will "show no regard...for the desire of women." Many students of Bible prophecy have interpreted this as meaning that the Antichrist will be a homosexual.

Since the Antichrist is a man who is totally controlled by Satan, he will probably live his life in complete disobedience to God in every area of life. It makes sense, then, that this might apply also to his sexual orientation. The Antichrist may be sexually polluted, perverted, and profane.

While this is certainly a possible interpretation, the verse may mean something else entirely. "The desire of women" may refer to a false god worshiped by women. Or the phrase might simply mean that the Antichrist will not have a natural desire for women—not that he will have sexual desire for men. The context of this passage seems to indicate that the Antichrist will be so intoxicated with his love for power that it will totally consume all of his passion. The next two verses go on to explain verse 37:

> "But instead he will honor a god of fortresses, a god whom his fathers did not know; he will honor him with gold, silver, costly stones and treasures. He will take action against the strongest of fortresses with the help of a foreign god; he will give great honor to those who acknowledge him and will cause them to rule over the many, and will parcel out land for a price. (vv. 11:38–39)

It is certainly possible that the Antichrist will be a homosexual. It would be in character for what may be the most corrupt of men. Yet the passage in Daniel seems to be intending to say that he will be so enraptured with the god of military might, conquest, and political power that this obsession will eclipse his normal desire for women.

FORTY-FIVE

IS THE ANTICHRIST A RESURRECTED INDIVIDUAL FROM THE PAST?

As we have already observed, the Antichrist will be Satan's complete counterfeit of the true Christ. Part of Satan's masterful trickery will be to parody the greatest event of Christianity: the death and resurrection of Christ (see Daniel 11:45; Revelation 13:3, 12–14, 17:8).

In the early church a very well-accepted theory concerning the identity of the Antichrist was the *Nero redivivus,* that is, that Antichrist would be the Roman Emperor Nero raised back to life. Nero died by suicide in A.D. 68, and a series of imposters pretending to be Nero returned in A.D. 69 and 80. In A.D. 88 a serious Nero imposter appeared in Parthia.

Another popular theory is that the Antichrist will be Judas Iscariot brought back from the grave. There are three main arguments that are used to support this view. First, Luke 22:3 says that "Satan entered into Judas who was called Iscariot." John says it even stronger:

> Jesus answered them, "Did I Myself not choose you, the twelve, and yet one of you is a devil?" Now He meant Judas the son of Simon Iscariot, for he, one of the twelve, was going to betray Him. (John 6:70–71)

Second, in John 17:12 our Lord refers to Judas Iscariot as the "son of perdition" or the "one doomed to destruction" (NIV). The only other place this title is used in the New Testament is in 2 Thessalonians 2:3—in reference to the Antichrist.

Third, Acts 1:25 states that Judas went "to his own place" when he died. Some interpret this to mean that when Judas died he went to a special place to await the time when he would be brought back as the final Antichrist. People who hold to this view then compare Acts 1:25 to Revelation 17:8—"The beast that you saw was, and is not, and is about to come up out of the abyss and go to destruction"—and say that Judas is waiting in the abyss for his resurrection as Antichrist.

While it is certainly possible that the Antichrist will be Nero, Judas Iscariot, or some other nefarious individual from the past brought back to life, the Bible never clearly identifies any person from the past as the future Antichrist. It is true that the Antichrist will die and be resurrected (see next question), but that doesn't mean he must be someone who has already lived and died. Therefore, without any direct biblical proof, it seems best to view the Antichrist as a future world ruler who will be under the total control of Satan and not any resurrected character from the past.

FORTY-SIX

WILL THE ANTICHRIST BE ASSASSINATED AND COME BACK TO LIFE?

As we discovered in answering the previous question, there are several passages in Revelation that clearly speak of the death and resurrection of the Antichrist. Having concluded that the Antichrist is not a resurrected individual from the past, the answer must be that he will be a future individual who will be violently killed (probably assassinated) and miraculously raised from the dead during the Tribulation.

Just think of the overwhelming impact this will have on the world: At the climax of history a great ruler will be cut down, only to experience a healing that will inevitably be compared to the death and resurrection of Jesus Christ. Revelation 13:3–4 and 17:8 record the worldwide amazement at the resurrection of the Beast.

> I saw one of his heads as if it had been slain, and his fatal wound was healed. And the whole earth was amazed and followed after the beast; they worshiped the dragon because he gave his authority to the beast; and they worshiped the beast, saying, "Who is like the beast, and who is able to wage war with him?" (Revelation 13:3–4)

> The beast that you saw was, and is not, and is about to come up out of the abyss and go to destruction. And those who dwell on the earth, whose name has not been written in the book of life form the foundation of the world, will wonder when they see the beast, that he was and is not and will come. (Revelation 17:8)

This will be the greatest event in history as far as the people of this world are concerned. Imagine the assassination of the most charismatic leader the world has ever seen. All of mankind will be in mourning. It will be like combining into one package of angst the world's grief over the deaths of JFK, Princess Di, and the crew of the *Challenger* space shuttle.

Everyone will watch the funeral procession on television. Networks will show nothing else. The decorated hearse will arrive at the cemetery, and the coffin will be removed. As the pallbearers take their first solemn steps toward the gravesite, the most incredible thing the world has ever seen will transpire—before the eyes of billions of people.

The body rises out of the casket. The pallbearers recoil in terror and drop the coffin. The Antichrist stands up, walks calmly to the nearest microphone, looks right into the camera, and addresses a dumbfounded world.

It is this great event that will catapult the Antichrist to worldwide rule.

Revelation 17:8 says that when the Antichrist is killed, he will go to the bottomless pit for a period of time before coming back to life. I believe that it is during this time in the bottomless pit that he is completely energized by Satan. He will receive his orders and strategy from Satan, literally selling his soul to the devil. Then he will come back to earth with hellish ferocity to establish his world domination over a completely awestruck earth.

CAN SATAN RESURRECT ANYONE?

Any discussion of the Antichrist's resurrection inevitably raises at least one other question: Does Satan have the power to raise a dead person back to life?

Many maintain that he does not. They believe that the Antichrist will only appear to die and will then fake a resurrection to deceive the world. However, the words used in Revelation 13:3 to describe the "death" of the Antichrist are always used in other places to describe a violent death. In Revelation 5:6, for instance, the same word is used of the death of Jesus Christ. Moreover, Revelation 17:8 says that after the Antichrist is killed he will go to the abyss for a time before reappearing on earth. This doesn't seem to be describing someone who is faking his death.

I cannot explain every detail of how this death and resurrection occur, but I do believe these passages lead us to a startling conclusion: God will permit Satan to perform this marvelous feat to further his nefarious parody of Christ and further deceive the world.

For once, at least, Satan will have the power to raise someone from the dead.

Forty-seven

How long will Antichrist's kingdom last?

According to Scripture, the worldwide kingdom of Antichrist will last three and a half years. He will be on the world scene as a key player for several years leading up to his seizure of power, but his period of world rule will last only three and a half years. This period is stated in various ways in Scripture, but it always equals the same time period.

Term	Comment	Reference
42 months	3 years (36 months) + half a year (6 months) = 42 months	Revelation 11:3; 13:5
Time, times, and half a time	"time" (1 year) + "times" (2 years) + "half a time" (half a year) = 3 $1/2$ years	Daniel 7:25, 12:7; Revelation 12:14
1,260 days	Using the prophetic system of 360 days in a year, 1260 days equals 3 $1/2$ years	Revelation 11:3; 12:6

The Antichrist will reign for three and a half years, the second half of the seven-year-long tribulation period. He will rule during the great Tribulation.

FORTY-EIGHT

WILL BELIEVERS IN CHRIST KNOW WHO THE ANTICHRIST IS BEFORE WE ARE RAPTURED TO HEAVEN?

In recent times some people have become obsessed with trying to identify the Antichrist. Many interesting names have appeared on lists of candidates: Napoleon, various Catholic popes, Benito Mussolini, Adolf Hitler, Henry Kissinger, Mikhail Gorbachev, Juan Carlos and his son Philippe, Bill Clinton, and any other person the list maker didn't especially like.

These attempts to identify the Antichrist often draw a great deal of attention for a while. But the fact that they've all been wrong so far highlights the danger of trying to figure it out. The New Testament teaches that believers will not know who the Antichrist is before we are raptured to heaven. Paul says:

> Now we request you, brethren, with regard to the coming of our Lord Jesus Christ and our gathering together to Him, that you not be quickly shaken from your composure or be disturbed either by a spirit or a message or a letter as if from us, to the effect that the day of the Lord has come. Let no one in any way deceive you, for it will not come unless the apostasy comes first, and the man of lawlessness is revealed, the son of destruction.
> (2 Thessalonians 2:1–3)

Paul was writing to the Thessalonian believers to clear up some confusion they had about the coming Day of the Lord (which I believe begins with the tribulation period). Evidently someone had taught them that they were already in the Tribulation. Paul corrects this error by pointing out that the Day of the Lord can't come until two things happen: a great apostasy or rebellion and the revelation of the Antichrist or man of lawlessness.

Since, as I believe, the Antichrist will be revealed at the beginning of the Day of the Lord (tribulation period) and the church will be raptured before this time, it doesn't appear that Christians will know the identity of the Antichrist before we are taken to heaven. If you ever do figure out who the Antichrist is, then I've got bad news for you—you've been left behind!

Having said that, however, I do believe that as we see the last days develop, we may be able to recognize certain individuals who could fit the picture of the Antichrist given in the Bible. But believers should always stop short of specifically identifying any person as the coming Antichrist. Satan's superman will be unveiled at the beginning of the Day of the Lord after the church as been translated to glory, not before.

Christians should not become fixated with trying to discover who the Antichrist will be. After all, we are supposed to be looking for *Christ,* not Antichrist.

FORTY-NINE

WHAT IS THE MARK OF THE BEAST (666)?

There has probably been more wild speculation about this subject than almost any other aspect of Bible prophecy. As my friend Dr. Harold Willmington says, "There's been a lot of sick, sick, sick about 666."

As you will recall from the introduction to this section, another name for the Antichrist is the beast out of the sea. In Revelation 13:18, this beast is given a strange designation: "The number of the beast…is that of a man; and his number is six hundred and sixty-six."

In the movie *The Omen,* Damien was born on June 6, at 6:00 (666) to symbolize his identification as the coming Antichrist. Almost everyone, including the most biblically illiterate people, have heard something about 666—also known as the mark of the beast.

Revelation 13:16–18 is the key passage on this mysterious number:

And he causes all, the small and the great, and the rich and the poor, and the free men and the slaves, to be given a mark on their right hand or on their forehead, and he provides that no one will be able to buy or to sell, except the one who has the mark, either the name of the beast or the number of his name. Here is wisdom. Let him who has understanding calculate the number of the beast, for the number is that of a man; and his number is six hundred and sixty-six.

One popular explanation of 666 is that the triple six refers to "man's number." Since six is one short of seven, a number associated with God, six could just be a designation for God's greatest creation: man. John Walvoord advocates this position:

Probably the simplest explanation here is the best, that the triple six is the number of a man, each digit falling short of the perfect number seven. Six in the Scripture is man's number. He was to work six days and rest on the seventh. The image of Nebuchadnezzar was sixty cubits high and six cubits broad.

Whatever may be the deeper meaning of the number, it implies that this title referring to the first beast, Satan's masterpiece, limits him to man's level which is far short of the deity of Christ.[31]

This explanation of 666 is good, but probably doesn't explain the full significance of the mark of the beast.

Another approach some have used to try to decrypt this number is a process called *gematria*. In gematria, a numerical value is attributed to each of the letters of the alphabet. If you want to find the numerical total of a word or name, you add together the values of each of its letters.

Hebrew, Latin, Greek, and English all have numerical value for each letter in the alphabet. For the Hebrew language, each of the twenty-two letters in its alphabet is assigned a numerical value as follows: 1, 2, 3, 4, 5, 6, 7, 8, 9, 10, 20, 30, 40, 50, 60, 70, 80, 90, 100, 200, 300, and 400. Therefore, every word, every place, and every person's name in Hebrew has a numerical value. As prophecy expert Arnold Fruchtenbaum notes:

> In this passage whatever the personal name of the Antichrist will be, if his name is spelled out in Hebrew characters, the numerical value of his name will be 666. So this is the number that will be put on the worshippers of the Antichrist. Since a number of different calculations can equal 666, it is impossible to figure the name out in advance. But when he does appear, whatever his personal name will be, it will equal 666. Those who are wise (verse 18) at that time will be able to point him out in advance.[32]

When the Antichrist begins to appear on the world scene at the beginning of the Tribulation, those who have an understanding of God's Word will be able to identify him by the number of his name. If they use gematria, they will discover that the numerical value of his name will be 666.

Unfortunately, many have applied gematria to the names of modern leaders to see if they could be the Antichrist. The names Henry Kissinger, Lyndon Johnson, JFK, Mikhail Gorbachev, Ronald Reagan, and Bill Gates III all work out to 666. So do "MS DOS 6.21," "Windows 95," and "System 7.0."

All such foolish speculation should be avoided. The Antichrist will not be exposed until after the Rapture. At that time those who come to know Christ after the Rapture will be able to determine who he is as he comes on the scene because the number of his name will be 666.

FIFTY

CAN PEOPLE WHO TAKE THE MARK OF THE BEAST BE SAVED?

When the beast seizes power at the middle of the Tribulation, every person on earth will be faced with a monumental decision: Will I take the mark of the beast?

Everyone who wishes to buy or sell anything during the Tribulation will be required to take the mark—either on his right hand or forehead. The word *mark* in Greek (*charagma*) means a brand or tatoo. It signifies ownership, loyalty, or protection. The technology is certainly available today to tatoo, brand, or embed a number on or under the skin of every person alive to regulate world commerce.

As Henry Morris observes:

> The nature of the mark is not described, but the basic principle has been established for years in various nations. The social security card, the draft registration card, the practice of stenciling an inked design on the back of the hand, and various other devices are all forerunners of this universal branding. The word itself ("mark") is the Greek *charagma*. It is used only in Revelation, to refer to the mark of the beast (eight times), plus one time to refer to idols "graven by art and man's device" (Acts 17:29). The mark is something like an etching or a tattoo which, once inscribed, cannot be removed, providing a permanent (possibly eternal) identification as a follower of the beast and the dragon.[33]

The issue for each person alive during the Tribulation will be this: Will I swear allegiance to the man who claims to be god? Will I give up ownership of my life to him by taking his mark, or will I bow the knee to the true God and lose my right to buy and sell and even face beheading (Revelation 20:4)? The Antichrist's economic policy will be very simple: Take my mark and worship me, or starve.

It will certainly be bad for those who refuse to take the mark. But it will be far worse for those who choose to receive it. By receiving that mark, a person forfeits eternal life.

> Then another angel, a third one, followed them, saying with a loud voice, "If anyone worships the beast and his image, and receives a mark on his forehead or on his hand, he also will drink of the wine of the wrath of God, which is mixed in full strength in the cup of His anger; and he will be tormented with fire and brimstone in the presence of the holy angels and in the presence of the Lamb. And the smoke of their torment goes up forever and ever; they have no rest day and night, those who worship the beast and his image, and whoever receives the mark of his name." (Revelation 14:9–11)

Don't take the mark.

FIFTY-ONE

WHO IS THE FALSE PROPHET?

There have always been false prophets and false teachers. One of Satan's chief methods of operation is to corrupt the true message of God through his false messengers. But in the end times Satan will increase this strategy dramatically.

The Bible says that in the last days there will be many false prophets who will perform great signs and wonders and spew out deceiving lies (Matthew 24:24). In this era of deception one false prophet will rise high above all the rest in his ability to capture the world's attention. He is called the "false prophet" in Revelation 16:13; 19:20; and 20:10. He is the second beast of Revelation (see 13:11–18).

He is the final person in the unholy trinity of the end times (Revelation 16:13; 19:20–20:2; 20:10).

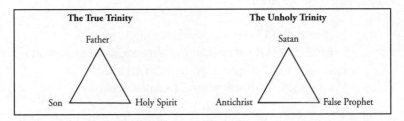

THE UNHOLY TRINITY OF THE END TIMES

Just as the Holy Spirit's ministry is to glorify Christ and lead men to worship Him, so the false prophet's chief ministry will be to glorify the Antichrist and lead people to worship him. Here are five key ways the false prophet counterfeits the ministry of the Holy Spirit.

Holy Spirit	False Prophet
Points men to Christ	Points men to Antichrist
Instrument of divine revelation	Instrument of satanic revelation
Seals believers in God	Marks unbelievers with the number of Antichrist
Builds the body of Christ	Builds the empire of Antichrist
Enlightens men with the truth	Deceives men by miracles

The first beast of Revelation (the Antichrist) will primarily be a military and political figure. The second beast will be a religious figure. He will be a kind of "Satanic John the Baptist" preparing the way for the coming of the Antichrist. The false prophet will be the beast's chief propagandist, right-hand man, and closest colleague and companion.

The Antichrist and the false prophet are mentioned together four places in the New Testament:

1. In Revelation 13:1–18, they share a common goal.
2. In Revelation 16:13, they share a common agenda for the world.
3. In Revelation 19:20, they share a common sentence.
4. In Revelation 20:10, they share a common destiny.

Revelation 13:11–18 emphasizes three key facts about the false prophet: His deceptive appearance, his devilish authority, and his deadly activity.

HIS DECEPTIVE APPEARANCE

The false prophet won't be your average man on the street:

> Then I saw another beast coming up out of the earth; and he had two horns like a lamb, and he spoke as a dragon. (Revelation 13:11)

He has the *nature* of a wild beast. He is hostile to God's flock. He ravages God's people. He has the *appearance* of a lamb. He looks gentle, mild, and harmless. And he has the *voice* of a dragon. He is the voice of hell itself belching forth the fiery lies of Satan. When he speaks, he is Satan's mouthpiece.

Bible commentator John Phillips summarizes the deceptive appearance and deadly appeal of the false prophet:

> The role of the false prophet will be to make the new religion appealing and palatable to men. No doubt it will combine all the features of the religious systems of men, will appeal to man's total personality, and will take full advantage of his carnal appetite.
>
> The dynamic appeal of the false prophet will lie in his skill in combining political expediency with religious passion, self-interest with benevolent philanthropy, lofty sentiment with blatant sophistry, moral platitude with unbridled self-indulgence. His arguments will be subtle, convincing, and appealing. His oratory will be hypnotic, for he will be able to move the masses to tears or whip them into a frenzy.
>
> He will control the communication media of the world and will skillfully organize mass publicity to promote his ends. He will be the master of every promotional device and public relations gimmick. He will manage the truth with guile beyond words, bending it, twisting it, and distorting it. Public opinion will be his to command. He will mold world thought and shape human opinion like so much potter's clay. His deadly appeal will lie in the fact that what he says will sound so right, so sensible, so exactly what unregenerate men have always wanted to hear.[34]

His Devilish Authority

Like the Antichrist, the false prophet will be empowered by Satan himself.

> He exercises all the authority of the first beast in his presence. And he makes the earth and those who dwell in it to worship the first beast, whose fatal wound was healed. (Revelation 13:12)

His Deadly Activity

Revelation 13:13–18 delineates seven deadly activities of the false prophet. This is what he will be doing during the great Tribulation.

1. He Will Come up out of the Earth

The false prophet is "earthly" in the fullest sense of the word.

> Then I saw another beast coming up out of the earth; and he had
> two horns like a lamb and he spoke as a dragon. (Revelation 13:11)

Many students of Bible prophecy have taken this to mean that the
false prophet will be a Jew since the first beast comes up out of the sea,
which in the Bible usually symbolizes Gentile nations. They say the land
out of which this beast rises could refer to Israel.

In my opinion, though, it is better to see the false prophet as a Gentile
just like the first beast. Because he will help the first beast persecute the
Jewish people, it seems doubtful that he will be Jewish himself. His coming up out of the earth may be meant to contrast him with the Holy Spirit
who comes down from heaven.

2. He Will Perform Miracles
The false prophet will be a wonder-working master showman.

> He performs great signs, so that he even makes fire come down
> out of heaven to the earth in the presence of men. And he
> deceives those who dwell on the earth because of the signs which
> it was given him to perform in the presence of the beast, telling
> those who dwell on the earth to make an image to the beast who
> had the wound of the sword and has come to life. (Revelation
> 13:13–14)

He will mimic the miracles of the two witnesses just as the Egyptian
magicians once counterfeited the miracles of Moses (Exodus 7:11–13, 22;
8:7; Revelation 11:4–6).

3. He Will Erect an Image to the Antichrist for All the World to Worship
Just as the Holy Spirit urges believers to worship Jesus Christ, so the false
prophet will compel people to worship the Antichrist.

> He deceives those who dwell on the earth because of the signs
> which it was given him to perform in the presence of the beast,
> telling those who dwell on the earth to make an image to the
> beast who had the wound of the sword and has come to life.
> (Revelation 13:14)

This image, the abomination of desolation (Daniel 11:31; 12:11; Matthew 24:15), will undoubtedly be placed in the temple in Jerusalem. Antiochus Epiphanes prefigured this sacrilege when he erected an altar of Zeus in the temple (see questions 40 and 52). As with Nebuchadnezzar's image in Daniel 3, all will have to bow before it or die.

4. He Will Raise the Antichrist from the Dead

While this is not stated explicitly in the text, it is strongly implied. The death and resurrection of the Antichrist is mentioned three times in Revelation 13 (vv. 3, 12, 14). Since the false prophet is a miracle worker who deceives the world, it seems probable that Satan will use the false prophet as his human instrument to raise the Antichrist back to life.

5. He Will Give Life to the Image of the Beast

Somehow the false prophet will animate the statue or likeness of the Antichrist.

> And it was given to him to give breath to the image of the beast, so that the image of the beast would even speak and cause as many as do not worship the image of the beast to be killed. (Revelation 13:15)

If the false prophet will have the power to raise the dead, perhaps it should not be too surprising that he will have the power to give life to an inanimate object.

6. He Will Force Everyone to Take the Mark of the Beast

> And he causes all, the small and the great, and the rich and the poor, and the free men and the slaves, to be given a mark on their right hand or on their forehead. (Revelation 13:16)

7. He Will Control World Commerce on Behalf of the Beast

> He provides that no one will be able to buy or to sell, except the one who has the mark, either the name of the beast or the number of his name. (Revelation 13:17)

The false prophet will take his place alongside the Antichrist to lead the final great deception of man. Through the power of the modern media and the continuing development of a "world community," we can begin to see how the false prophet will be able to dupe the world.

FIFTY-TWO

ARE THERE ANY HISTORICAL FIGURES THAT HELP US SEE WHAT ANTICHRIST WILL BE LIKE?

There have been many men in history who have been "types" or pictures of what the coming Antichrist will be like. These seven provide the clearest parallels with the coming man of sin.

NIMROD

In Genesis 10:9–12, Nimrod is depicted as the first world ruler. He also established the first worldwide, organized rebellion against God. If we put Genesis 10:10 together with 11:1–9, it seems that he was the leader in the rebellion at the tower of Babel.

PHARAOH

The ruler of Egypt to whom Moses appealed is a type of the Antichrist. He oppressed God's people and openly defied God. He also had magicians who performed miracles to counter God's servant, just as the false prophet will do for Antichrist.

NEBUCHADNEZZAR

Nebuchadnezzar ruled the neo-Babylonian Empire from 605–562 B.C. He was boastful and proud (Daniel 4:29–32) and erected an image that people had to worship or die (Daniel 3:1–7)—just as the Antichrist will do. And in 586 B.C., he destroyed the temple in Jerusalem, just as the Antichrist will do (2 Kings 25:8–10; Revelation 11:1–2).

ALEXANDER THE GREAT

Between 336 and 323 B.C., Alexander led his Greek phalanxes to conquest in Asia Minor, Syria, Egypt, Babylonia, and Persia, becoming a mighty world conqueror and launching the Hellenistic Age. He also declared himself god. He died in Babylonia at the age of thirty-three.

THE ROMAN CAESARS

These men foreshadowed the Antichrist in that they ruled the world and compelled men to worship them as gods.

ANTIOCHUS EPIPHANES

This Seleucid king of Syria is the most pronounced, clearest foreshadowing of Antichrist in the Scripture according to Daniel 8 and 11. Almost all prophecy scholars of every viewpoint agree that Daniel 8:9–14 refers to Antiochus Epiphanes who persecuted the Jewish people and defiled their temple in 167 B.C.

However, it seems that in Daniel 8:15–23 the picture begins to move beyond Antiochus to Antichrist in the end times. In other words, the Antichrist will be a kind of "Antiochus plus." The escalation beyond Antiochus is indicated by several chronological indicators in the text: "the time of the end" (8:17), "the final period of the indignation" (8:19), and "the appointed time of the end" (8:19). Antiochus's oppression provides only a partial fulfillment of the prophetic vision in Daniel 8:23–25. Antichrist will be the complete fulfillment.

This same kind of transition from Antiochus to a future super-Antiochus occurs in Daniel 11. Most prophecy scholars believe that Daniel 11:20–35 refers to the activities of Antiochus Epiphanes. But in verse 35, Daniel refers to "the end time," and in verses 36–45 he goes on to describe "the king" who will do as he pleases. The actions of this king go beyond anything Antiochus ever did. Therefore, it appears that in both Daniel 8 and Daniel 11, Antiochus is purposely set forth as a preview of the final Antichrist.

There are ten ways in which Antiochus Epiphanes parallels Antichrist:

1. Both persecute the Jewish people.
2. Both demand worship.
3. Both establish an image in the temple (abomination of desolation) (Daniel 11:31; 12:11).
4. Both impose an alien belief system on the Jews.
5. Both have a relationship to the Roman empire.
6. Both have a religious leader who aids them—Antiochus had a priest named Menelaus and Antichrist will have the false prophet (Revelation 13:11–18).

7.   Both are opposed by a faithful remnant.
8.   Both are reported dead, but appear alive again (compare the apocryphal book 2 Maccabees 5:5 with Revelation 13:3, 12, 14).
9.   Both are active in the Middle East for about seven years.
10. Both are defeated by the advent of a great deliverer—Antiochus was defeated by Judas Maccabees; Antichrist will be defeated by Jesus Christ (Revelation 19:20–21).

Adolf Hitler

Hitler was the clearest foreshadowing of the Antichrist in modern history.

- He planned to establish a kingdom (reich) that would last one thousand years (a false millennium).
- He came out of Germany, which was part of the old Roman Empire in Europe.
- He was a mesmerizing speaker.
- He rose from insignificance to worldwide power in a short time.
- He had a "false prophet" (Joseph Goebbels) who promoted him.
- He mercilessly slaughtered the Jewish people in the Holocaust.

From the earliest history of man, Satan has tried to promote certain men to world rule so he can achieve his goal of worldwide rule and worship. In the first century the apostle John could say "even now many antichrists have appeared" (1 John 2:18). However, all the antichrists who have come and gone are but dim foreshadowings of the final man of sin. Nevertheless they do give us valuable insight into his attributes and activities.

FIFTY-THREE

IS THE ANTICHRIST ALIVE TODAY?

The clearest, most concise answer to this question is this: No one knows for sure. Many have speculated, but no one really knows.

Pseudoprophet Jeane Dixon has prophesied that a child was born in the Middle East at 7:17 A.M. on February 5, 1962, who will lead the entire world. In her book *My Life and Prophecies,* she relates how this prophecy was received and what she felt it signifies.

> My eyes once again focused on the baby. By now he had grown to manhood, and a small cross which had formed above his head enlarged and expanded until it covered the earth in all directions. Simultaneously, suffering people, of all races, knelt in worshipful adoration, lifting their arms and offering their hearts to the man. For a fleeting moment I felt as though I were one of them, but the channel that emanated from him was not that of the Holy Trinity. I knew within my heart that this revelation was to signify the beginning of wisdom, but whose wisdom and for whom? An overpowering feeling of love surrounded me, but the look I had seen in the man when he was still a babe—a look of serene wisdom and knowledge—made me sense that there was something God allowed me to see without my becoming a part of it.
>
> I also sensed that I was once again safe within the protective arms of my Creator.
>
> I glanced at my bedside clock. It was still early—7:17 A.M.
>
> What does this revelation signify? I am convinced that this revelation indicates a child, born somewhere in the Middle East shortly after 7:00 A.M. on February 5, 1962—possibly a direct descendant of the royal line of Pharaoh Ikhnaton and Queen Nefertiri—will revolutionize the world. There is no doubt that he will fuse multitudes into one all-embracing doctrine. He will form a new "Christianity," based on his "almighty power," but leading man in a different direction far removed from the teaching and life of Christ, the Son.[35]

THE ANTICHRIST OF THE HOUR

While no one—including Jeane Dixon—knows if *the* Antichrist is alive today, I am convinced that *an* Antichrist is alive in the world at this very moment.

Writing late in the first century A.D., the apostle John said that the spirit of Antichrist was already at work undermining and opposing the work of God (1 John 2:18; 4:3). If that's true, then we can be certain that the *spirit* of Antichrist is alive and well today!

You see, the devil doesn't know when the coming of Christ will occur any more than you or I do. So he has prepared an elaborate contingency plan that can be put into effect at a moment's notice (in the blink of an eye, you might say). I believe that Satan has a man ready in every generation—a satanically prepared vessel just waiting to take center stage and rule the world as *the* Antichrist. Satan has always had a Nimrod, a Pharaoh, a Nebuchadnezzar, an Alexander the Great, an Antiochus, a Caesar, a Napoleon, or a Hitler ready. Rest assured that someone alive today is Satan's candidate for the Antichrist should the Rapture happen now.

Movies like *The Omen* that preview what the coming of the Antichrist may be like are make-believe horror films, but often the main premise is biblically sound. There is a gripping scene early in the movie *The Omen*. On the morning after the nightmarish fifth birthday party for Damien (the Antichrist), a Catholic priest named Father Brennan pays an unannounced visit to Ambassador Thorn's office. As soon as Father Brennan is alone with Thorn (Damien's father), he blurts out a warning to the ambassador: "You must accept Christ as your Savior. You must accept him now!"

The same warning is still applicable today. When the Antichrist appears, most people will still refuse to accept Christ and will instead turn to follow the lawless one. Don't put it off any longer. Accept Jesus Christ as your Savior now!

Make no mistake, the Antichrist is coming.

FIFTY-FOUR

WHAT FINALLY HAPPENS TO THE ANTICHRIST?

God's Word is very specific about the doom of the Antichrist. Two main passages in the New Testament spell out how he meets his end.

Second Thessalonians 2:8 says, "Then that lawless one will be revealed whom the Lord will slay with the breath of His mouth and bring to an end by the appearance of His coming." This passage reveals that the Lord Jesus will destroy the power of the Antichrist simply by His spoken word.

The Bible also reveals that the Antichrist's judgment will be quick and severe:

> And I saw the beast and the kings of the earth and their armies assembled to make war against Him who sat on the horse and against His army. And the beast was seized, and with him the false prophet who performed the signs in his presence, by which he deceived those who had received the mark of the beast and those who worshiped his image; these two were thrown alive into the lake of fire which burns with brimstone. And the rest were killed with the sword which came from the mouth of Him who sat on the horse, and all the birds were filled with their flesh. (Revelation 19:19–21)

When the Lord Jesus is revealed in glory, He will destroy all the armies gathered at Armageddon with the sharp sword of His Word that proceeds from His mouth. All He will have to do to destroy all of man's military might is simply say, "Drop dead," and the armies of the world will melt before him like wax.

However, the Antichrist and his henchman, the false prophet, will not be killed like the others. They will be "thrown alive into the lake of fire which burns with brimstone," where they will be joined one thousand years later by the devil, the head of the unholy trinity (Revelation 20:10). Just as two men in the Old Testament went to heaven without dying (Enoch and Elijah), so two men in the New Testament go to hell without dying (the Antichrist and the false prophet).

This is the final doom of the devil's masterpiece: The Antichrist's kingdom will be swept away, and the glorious kingdom of Christ will be established.

> *"But the court will sit for judgment, and his dominion will be taken away, annihilated and destroyed forever."*
> DANIEL 7:26

The Tribulation

"For then there will be a great tribulation,
such as has not occurred since the beginning
of the world until now, nor ever will."
Matthew 24:21

I was born and raised in Oklahoma, and I still live there today. Oklahoma is primarily known for two things: football and tornadoes. A few years ago there was a popular movie titled *Twister.* The climax of the movie focused on a group of Oklahoma "storm chasers" pursuing an F5 tornado (a tornado with winds of 261–316 mph).

A few years after this movie came out, Oklahoma experienced a true terrible "Twister." I'll never forget turning on the television for the evening news on May 3, 1999. What I saw captured my attention for the next four hours. Storm chasers had located a fairly strong and large tornado in southwest Oklahoma.

Unlike most twisters, however, this tornado did not break up, weaken, or recede back into the clouds. Over the next four hours, this "routine" tornado metastasized into a monster without equal. It was a meteorologist's worst nightmare: an F5 tornado one-half mile wide that held together for an extended period of time and hit a major population center (Oklahoma City).

I watched in disbelief as the cyclone effortlessly cut its devastating sixty-mile swath through town after town, neighborhood after neighborhood. When the steamroller finally ran out of energy, it had totally destroyed 1,500 homes, damaged 8,093 homes, and killed 44 people.

After the storm, meteorologists determined that the wind speed generated by the tornado had peaked at 318 mph—the strongest winds ever recorded on earth. The storm was in a category all its own; it may have even created a new F6 tornado rating.

The day after the tornado the local news stations showed aerial views of the damaged areas. The scene was indescribable. Later that week I had the opportunity to view some of the damaged areas in person. I was overwhelmed. It looked like a nuclear weapon had been detonated. The twisted trees with all the bark stripped off defied explanation. When I asked someone why the ground was so bare he told me that the twister had literally sucked away all the grass.

As stunning as this F5 tornado was, the Bible says that someday God is going to unleash His own twister on this earth—an F5 tornado of God's blasting judgment. God's Word declares that a time of unparalleled devastation is coming on all the earth in the future, a time the Bible calls the Tribulation.

This chapter will answer some of the questions you have about this coming period of divine wrath.

FIFTY-FIVE

WHAT IS THE TRIBULATION PERIOD?

God's Word tells us that man will always have trouble in life (Job 14:1; John 16:33). However, the Bible also tells us that there is a concentrated time of tribulation coming on this world unlike anything that has ever come before or will ever come after (Daniel 12:1). The tribulation period is the final 2,520-day (seven-year) period before the second coming of Christ. It is when God will pour out His wrath on this sinful, disobedient world.

The Tribulation begins when Antichrist and Israel sign a covenant with each other (Daniel 9:27) and ends at the Second Coming. The intervening "week of years" (seven years) between these two events is what the Bible calls the seventieth week of Daniel (Daniel 9:25–27).

TIMELINE OF THE SEVENTY WEEKS PROPHECY

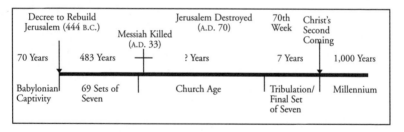

As its name implies, the Tribulation will not be a great time to be alive. Dr. J. Dwight Pentecost provides ten descriptive, biblical words that characterize the coming Tribulation:

- Wrath.
- Judgment.
- Indignation.
- Trial.
- Trouble.
- Destruction.
- Darkness.

- Desolation.
- Overturning.
- Punishment.

Dr. Pentecost concludes his discussion of the Tribulation with this statement, "No passage can be found to alleviate to any degree whatsoever the severity of this time that shall come upon the earth."[36]

The Tribulation will be the darkest hour in human history.

Fifty-six

What are the main events on earth during the Tribulation?

The most complete description of the events of the Tribulation is found in Revelation 6–19. These fourteen action-packed chapters describe the main events, main players, and main places in the seven-year period before the second coming of Christ.

The main thread that runs through this period is God's judgment. This judgment is poured out in three successive waves, each of which contains seven parts: seven seals, seven trumpets, and seven bowls.

The seven seals will be opened during the first half of the Tribulation. The seven trumpets will be blown during the second half of the tribulation. And the seven bowls will be poured out in a very brief period of time just before Christ returns.

Sequence of Judgments

Scripture often compares these judgments to birth pangs (Jeremiah

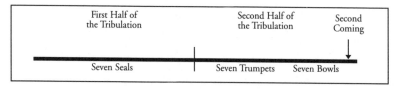

30:4–7; Matthew 24:8; 1 Thessalonians 5:3). As the Tribulation progresses, these pains will intensify in their severity and frequency.

Let's look at these three crashing waves of God's judgment.

The Seven Seals

The initial outpouring of God's wrath on the earth is the seven seal judgments described primarily in Revelation 6. This chart gives an overview of the seven seals.

Seal	Symbol	Meaning	Revelation
First Seal	White Horse	Antichrist	6:1–2
Second Seal	Red Horse	War	6:3–4
Third Seal	Black Horse	Famine	6:5–6
Fourth Seal	Pale Horse	Death and hell	6:7–8
Fifth Seal	—	Martyrs in heaven	6:9–11
Sixth Seal	—	Universal upheaval and devastation	6:12–17
Seventh Seal	The Seven Trumpets	Begins next wave of judgement	8:1–2

THE SEVEN TRUMPETS

The seventh seal contains the seven trumpets. Each trumpet sounds to signal another judgment of God on the earth.

Trumpet	Event	Result	Revelation
First Trumpet	Bloody hail and fire	One-third of vegetation destroyed	8:7
Second Trumpet	Fireball from heaven	One-third of oceans polluted	8:8–9
Third Trumpet	Falling star	One-third of fresh water polluted	8:10–11
Fourth Trumpet	Darkness	One-third of sun, moon and stars darkened	8:12
Fifth Trumpet	Demonic invasion	Torment	9:1–12
Sixth Trumpet	Demonic army	One-third of mankind killed	9:13–21
Seventh Trumpet	The kingdom	The announcement	11:15–19

The Seven Bowls

As bad as the trumpet judgments will be, the seven bowls clearly signal the darkest chapter in the history of mankind. With both the seals and the trumpets there will be an interruption or pause between the sixth and seventh in the sequence. However, there will be no such interruption with the bowls. They will be poured out in quick succession at the very end of the tribulation. Here the birth pangs will have reached a fever pitch, both in frequency and intensity.

As you look at this chart, notice how closely these bowls parallel the plagues on the Egyptians in Exodus 7–11. The difference is that in Revelation these plagues are worldwide in scope.

Bowl	Poured Out	Result	Revelation
First Bowl	Upon the earth	Sores on the worshipers of the Antichrist	16:2
Second Bowl	Upon the seas	Seas turned to blood	16:3
Third Bowl	Upon the fresh water	Fresh water turned to blood	16:4–7
Fourth Bowl	Upon the sun	Intense, scorching heat	16:8–9
Fifth Bowl	Upon the Antichrist's kingdom	Darkness and pain	16:10–11
Sixth Bowl	Upon the Euphrates River	Armageddon	16:12–16
Seventh Bowl	Upon the air	Earthquakes and hail	16:17–21

These twenty-one judgments are staggering. The earth, its environment, and its population will be totally devastated by its Maker.

You would think that all this would bring sinful men and women to their knees before God. Right? Wrong. At the pinnacle of the bowl judgments we see the unbelievable response of sinful man: "They blasphemed the God of heaven because of their pains and their sores; and they did not repent of their deeds" (Revelation 16:11). What a picture of the human heart!

The Tribulation will be the worst time to live in human history. How much better to ask Jesus into your heart now and watch it all from heaven!

FIFTY-SEVEN

IF I'M GOING TO BE RAPTURED TO HEAVEN, WHY SHOULD I CARE ABOUT THE TRIBULATION?

Even though all true believers will be raptured to heaven before the Tribulation, thus escaping the wrath of God, it is still important for us to know about the key players and events of this seven-year period. There are four reasons why we should be concerned about the Tribulation.

First, we should be concerned about the Tribulation because God's Word teaches it. All of Scripture is important and worthy of our careful study and application to our lives (2 Timothy 3:16–17). Since Revelation is part of Scripture, it's profitable for us to study it.

Second, in studying about the Tribulation we learn a great deal about the nature of man, God, and Satan. It teaches us that man is sinful, rebellious, and easily deceived. We learn that God is holy and that He unleashes His wrath against sin, but also that He is gracious and will save millions of people even in earth's darkest hour (Revelation 7:9–14). The Bible also uses the Tribulation passages to teach us about Satan. Authors Timothy Demy and Thomas Ice note:

> The Tribulation is important because, in a sense, Satan is unmasked and we see his ultimate intentions and purposes. Such an understanding of his plan, if properly applied, can aid the believer today in spiritual warfare.
>
> For example, we note that during the Tribulation, Satan uses religion in a false and deceptive way. This stands as a warning for us today.[37]

Third, as we see the signs of the coming Tribulation developing before our eyes, it fills us with hope and expectation that the Lord's coming is near. For instance, I believe that the rise of the European Union, the current trend toward globalism, the available technology for the mark of the beast, and the universal yearning for a Middle East peace plan all point to the imminent fulfillment of the biblical prophecies about the coming Tribulation.

Fourth, though we won't live through the Tribulation if we know the Savior, the Lord loves to take His own people into His confidence and tell them what is going to happen even if it doesn't directly affect their own lives.

In Genesis 18, God came to Abraham and told him that He was going to destroy the wicked cities of Sodom and Gomorrah. This had no immediate impact on Abraham: He didn't live in these cities. But God told Abraham about it anyway. Why? Because Abraham was the friend of God. The Lord said to Abraham, "Shall I hide from Abraham what I am about to do?" (v. 17).

Regarding the Tribulation, God has taken us into His confidence to show us what He will do on earth during those dark days. What a privilege it is to know the mind of God and His prophetic program for the final seven years of this present age!

Fifty-eight

What is the purpose of the Tribulation?

One obvious question at this point is this: Why would God judge with such severity the world He created? Why is such a time of unspeakable trouble necessary?

At least five reasons for the Tribulation are found in Scripture. Each relates to a specific group or person: Israel, the Gentiles, God, Satan, and believers.

A Purpose for Israel

God will use the Tribulation to purge the Jewish people. He will put the nation of Israel into a vice grip from which there is no earthly hope of deliverance. The rebellious nation will be refined by the fires of tribulation.

> "It will come about in all the land,"
> Declares the Lord,
> "That two parts in it will be cut off and perish;
> But the third will be left in it.
> "And I will bring the third part through the fire,
> Refine them as silver is refined,
> And test them as gold is tested.
> They will call on My name,
> And I will answer them;
> I will say, 'They are My people,'
> And they will say, 'The Lord is my God.'" (Zechariah 13:8–9)

As a result of the Tribulation, many of the Jewish people will cry out to God for salvation. They will implore God to split the heavens and come down to save them:

> Oh, that you would burst from the heavens and come down!
> How the mountains would quake in your presence.... But we are
> not godly. We are constant sinners, so your anger is heavy on us.

How can people like us be saved? We are all infected and impure with sin. When we proudly display our righteous deeds, we find they are but filthy rags.... And yet, LORD, you are our Father. We are the clay, and you are the potter. We are all formed by your hand. Oh, don't be so angry with us, LORD. Please don't remember our sins forever. Look at us, we pray, and see that we are all your people. (Isaiah 64:1, 5b–6a, 8–9, NLT)

God will mercifully answer this prayer of confession. As always, He will save a remnant in Israel.

A Purpose for the Gentiles

God will use the tribulation period to punish the Gentile nations and all unbelievers. They will be castigated for their evil in general, for rejecting Jesus Christ, and for persecuting God's people (Isaiah 13:11–13; Joel 3:2; Obadiah 15–16).

A Purpose for God

About thirty-five hundred years ago, Pharaoh mocked the God of heaven: "Who is the LORD, that I should obey him and let Israel go? I do not know the LORD and I will not let Israel go" (Exodus 5:2, NIV). In the next eight chapters of Exodus, God took this brazen challenge and proved to Pharaoh, his magicians, and all the people who He is. When God had finished with the ten plagues, Pharaoh was begging the children of Israel to leave.

In a similar show of bravado the Antichrist will deny the true God and declare himself to be god. God will once again pour out His plagues to prove His power and vindicate His reputation—only this time it will be on a worldwide scale. The tribulation will prove to a rebellious world that He alone is God.

A Purpose for Satan

God will use the Tribulation to unmask Satan. When God removes the restrainer (see question 26), the world will see the devil for who he is—a liar, a thief, and a murderer. Realizing that his time is short, Satan will pour out his venom with force and violence. The people of the world will see him for who he truly is when he unleashes upon them the final firestorm of the dragon.

Therefore rejoice, you heavens
and you who dwell in them!
But woe to the earth and the sea,
because the devil has gone down to you!
He is filled with fury,
because he knows that his time is short. (Revelation 12:12, NIV)

A PURPOSE FOR BELIEVERS

The Lord will graciously use this terrible time of trouble to drive men to Himself in repentance and trust. He will harvest more souls during this time than anyone can count.

> After these things I looked, and behold, a great multitude which no one could count, from every nation and all tribes and peoples and tongues, standing before the throne and before the Lamb, clothed in white robes, and palm branches were in their hands; and they cry out with a loud voice, saying, "Salvation to our God who sits on the throne, and to the Lamb." Then one of the elders...said to me, "These are the ones who come out of the great tribulation, and they have washed their robes and made them white in the blood of the Lamb." (Revelation 7:9–10, 13–14)

When God moves, He always accomplishes many things in many lives. The Tribulation will be no different. Behind every movement of this massive symphony of judgment, there will be God orchestrating it all to His purposes and glory.

FIFTY-NINE

ARE THERE ANY OTHER NAMES OR TITLES IN THE BIBLE FOR THE TRIBULATION?

The following is a list of all the significant terms and expressions in the Bible which I believe refer to the tribulation period.

OLD TESTAMENT TRIBULATION TERMS AND EXPRESSIONS

Tribulation Term	Old Testament Reference
Birth Pangs	Isaiah 21:3; 26:17–18; 66:7; Jeremiah 4:31; Micah 4:10
Day of the Lord	Obadiah 15; Joel 1:15; 2:1, 11,31 ; 3:14; Amos 5:18, 20; Isaiah 2:12; 13:6, 9; Zephaniah 1:7, 14; Ezekiel 13:5; 30:3; Zechariah 14:1
Great and Terrible Day of the Lord	Malachi 4:5
Day of Wrath	Zephaniah 1:15
Day of Distress	Zephaniah 1:15
Day of the Lord's Wrath	Zephaniah 1:18
Day of Desolation	Zephaniah 1:15
Day of Vengeance	Isaiah 34:8; 35:4; 61:2; 63:4
Day of Jacob's Trouble	Jeremiah 30:7
Day of Darkness and Gloom	Zephaniah 1:15; Amos 5:18, 20; Joel 2:2
Day of Trumpet	Zephaniah 1:16
Day of Alarm	Zephaniah 1:16
Day of the Lord's Anger	Zephaniah 2:2–3
[Day of] Destruction, Ruin from the Almighty	Joel 1:15

Tribulation Term	Old Testament Reference
Day of Calamity	Deuteronomy 32:35; Obadiah 12–14
Trouble, Tribulation One Week = (Daniel's Seventieth Week)	Deuteronomy 4:30; Zephaniah 1:16 Daniel 9:27
The [Lord's] Strange Work	Isaiah 28:15, 18
Time/Day of Distress, Anguish	Daniel 12:1; Zephaniah 1:15
The Indignation/The Lord"s Anger	Isaiah 26:20; Daniel 11:36
The Time of the End	Daniel 12:9
The Fire of His Jealousy	Zephaniah 1:18

NEW TESTAMENT TRIBULATION TERMS AND EXPRESSIONS

Tribulation Term	New Testament Reference
The Day	1 Thessalonians 5:4
Those Days	Matthew 24:22; Mark 13:20
The Day of the Lord	1 Thessalonians 5:2
The Wrath	1 Thessalonians 5:9; Revelation 11:18
The Wrath to Come	1 Thessalonians 1:10
The Great Day of Their Wrath	Revelation 6:17
The Wrath of God	Revelation 15
The Wrath of the Lamb	Revelation 6:17
The Hour of Trial	Revelation 3:10
The Tribulation	Matthew 24:29; Mark 13:24
[Time of] Tribulation	Mark 13:19
The Great Tribulation	Matthew 24:21; Revelation 2:22; 7:14
The Hour of Judgment	Revelation 14:7
Birth Pangs	Matthew 24:8

As you can see, the Bible has a great deal to say about this coming seven-year period of divine wrath. Let's continue digging so we can understand more about the key points and key players of this unparalleled period of human history.

Sixty

Who are the 144,000?

In Revelation 7 and 14, we see a mysterious group of people—144,000 strong—who faithfully serve the Lord during the Tribulation. Who are these people?

The Identity of the 144,000

Right away, it is important to make clear who the 144,000 are not. First, they are not the church. I believe the church, depicted as the twenty-four elders, is already in heaven at this point in Revelation.

Second, they are not the Jehovah's Witnesses. Jehovah's Witnesses believe that only 144,000 will go to heaven. Since their number reached 144,000 in 1935, Judge Rutherford, the second president of the Watchtower, shut the door to heaven. According to official doctrine, all Jehovah's Witnesses after 1935 will live forever on earth but will not go to heaven. This is biblical interpretation at its worst.

So, if these 144,000 servants of God are not the church or pre-1935 Jehovah's Witnesses, who are they? If we take the Scriptures at face value, we must conclude that the 144,000 are a group of Jewish men, 12,000 from each of the twelve tribes of Israel, who are raised up by God in the Tribulation to serve Him.

However, when you read Revelation 7 you may notice that one of the twelve tribes is conspicuous by its absence—the tribe of Dan. Why is Dan omitted? I have been asked this question many times. A common answer that goes way back in church history is that the Antichrist will come from the tribe of Dan. However, I believe it is better to explain Dan's omission as due to the fact that Dan was the first of the tribes to go into idolatry (Judges 18:2, 30–31; 1 Kings 11:26; 12:28–30). Deuteronomy 29:18–21 required that the name of anyone who introduced idolatry was to be blotted out.

The Characteristics of the 144,000

Revelation mentions five characteristics that may provide insight into the identity and ministry of these 144,000 servants of God.

They Have Been Purchased

Revelation 14:3 says that the 144,000 "had been purchased from the earth." The purchase price that was paid for these servants of God was the precious blood of Christ. They have been bought with a price. They belong to the Lord as His special possessions.

They Have Been Prepared

Revelation talks about how these 144,000 people are marked as God's own servants:

> "Do not harm the earth or the sea or the trees until we have sealed the bond-servants of our God on their foreheads." And I heard the number of those who were sealed, one hundred and forty-four thousand sealed from every tribe of the sons of Israel. (Revelation 7:3–4)

On earth during the Tribulation, the followers of the beast will bear his mark on their right hand or forehead as evidence that they belong to him (Revelation 13:16). During this same time, the Lord will place His identifying mark—His seal of ownership—on the forehead of the 144,000.

> Then I looked, and behold, the Lamb was standing on Mount Zion, and with Him one hundred and forty-four thousand, having His name and the name of His Father written on their foreheads. (Revelation 14:1)

This seal sets them apart and prepares them for God's service. As New Testament scholar Robert Thomas says,

> It was not uncommon for a soldier or a guild member to receive such a mark as a religious devotee. The mark was a sign of consecration to deity. The forehead was chosen because it was the most conspicuous, the most noble, and the part by which a person is usually identified. It will be obvious to whom these slaves belong and whom they serve.[38]

One question that is often asked is how will these 144,000 Jewish people come to faith in Christ at the beginning of the Tribulation if all believers are raptured to heaven before the Tribulation begins. Who will preach the gospel to them?

While we don't know what means God will use to save the 144,000, one possibility is that they could come to faith in Christ through Bibles and Christian books, videos, tapes, curriculum, software, and music that are left behind.

Or some of the 144,000 may hear the gospel through unsaved pastors and church members who got left behind. When they were not taken, they realized they had never truly known Christ as Lord and Savior, and so they come to Him in sincerity then and take the Good News to the Jewish people.

It is certainly possible, too, that God may give 144,000 Saul of Tarsus "Damascus road experiences." The glorified Christ may reveal Himself personally to these men, calling them to Himself (see Acts 9:1–9).

They Are Protected

God's seal not only prepares the 144,000 for service, but also acts as God's pledge of security. The 144,000 are sealed before the four angels are allowed to bring their judgment on the earth (Revelation 7:1–3). The 144,000 will be exempt from the wrath of God and Satan during the Tribulation (9:4).

In Revelation 14:1–5, John sees the 144,000 at the end of the Tribulation standing triumphantly on Mt. Zion (the city of Jerusalem). Notice that he doesn't see 143,999. All 144,000 have been divinely preserved by the Lord. They have come through the entire Tribulation and are still standing on earth. God will preserve and protect His sealed servants through the seven-year horror of the Tribulation.

They Are Pure

Revelation 14:4 says that the 144,000 are chaste men "who have not been defiled with women." Many interpret this figuratively as saying that they are spiritually undefiled and pure, separated from the corruption and pollution of false religion. However, the fact that the Scripture says that they are not defiled with women seems to point to the conclusion that these servants of God are male, celibate servants of God. In light of the demands of the Tribulation period, they are called by God to abstain from a normal marital life and to devote themselves totally to the Lord's service (see 1 Corinthians 7:29–35).

They Are Persistent

The 144,000 are persistent in their life and service for the Lord even under the most dire circumstances. During the terrible days of the Tribulation they constantly "follow the Lamb wherever He goes" (Revelation 14:4).

Jesus is the Lamb, but He's also the Shepherd. He knows the way, and, like the 144,000, we are to follow Him wherever He leads.

They Are Preachers

The primary ministry of these Jewish servants is to fearlessly proclaim the gospel of Christ during the Tribulation. They will be the greatest evangelists the world has ever seen. There may be a cause and effect relationship in Revelation 7 between the 144,000 in verses 1–8 and the innumerable crowd of believers in verses 9–17.

These sealed servants of God will fulfill Matthew 24:14: "This gospel of the kingdom shall be preached in the whole world as a testimony to all the nations, and then the end will come."

The chief importance of the 144,000 is that they reveal the heart of God to save people even in the midst of the unspeakable judgment of the Tribulation. To the very end, the Savior will graciously continue "to seek and save those who are lost" (Luke 19:10).

Sixty-one

Who are the two witnesses?

As we have seen, during the tribulation period Satan will have two hench-men who will carry out his evil plan for the world: the Antichrist and the false prophet (Revelation 13). What we will look at now is how God will also raise up two special witnesses who will minister on His behalf in the midst of the darkness and devastation (Revelation 11).

Many early Christian leaders, such as Tertullian, Irenaeus, and Hippolytus, believed the two witnesses would be Enoch and Elijah. Others over the years have held that Moses will be one of the two wit-nesses along with either Enoch or Elijah. There are several reasons why these men have been identified as the two witnesses.

Enoch

There are two main arguments given in support of the idea that Enoch will be one of the two witnesses. First, Enoch never died.

> So all the days of Enoch were three hundred and sixty-five years.
> Enoch walked with God; and he was not, for God took him.
> (Genesis 5:23–24)

Second, Enoch was a prophet of judgment in the days before the Flood who announced the coming of the Lord (Jude 14–15). It's possible that Enoch was actually prophesying Jesus' second coming, so it might make sense that he would appear on earth again as a prophet before that time.

Moses

There are three reasons why people have suggested that Moses might be one of the two witnesses. First, the two witnesses will turn rivers to blood and bring plagues on the earth (Revelation 11:6). This is precisely what Moses did in Egypt (Exodus 7:14–25). Second, on the Mount of Transfiguration, which pictured the Second Coming glory of Christ, Moses and Elijah appeared with Christ (Matthew 17:1-11). Third, Moses was a prophet.

Elijah

Five reasons are given for identifying Elijah as one of the two witnesses. First, like Enoch, he never tasted physical death (2 Kings 2:1–11). Second, like Moses, he was present at the Transfiguration. Third, the Scriptures predict that Elijah will come before "the great and terrible day of the Lord" (Malachi 4:5). Fourth, God used him to prevent rain from falling for three and one-half years, just as the two witnesses will do (1 Kings 17:1; James 5:17). And fifth, like the two witnesses, Elijah was a prophet.

Conclusion

Many people favor Enoch and Elijah as the two witnesses because neither of them tasted physical death. Because the Bible says that it is appointed for men to die once (Hebrews 9:27), the argument is that these men have to come back to earth so they can finally die. However, this verse is simply stating the general principle that all people die. It is not stating a requirement. After all, at the Rapture there will be an entire generation of people who will do an end run on the grave!

If I had to select the two men from the past who are the most likely candidates for the two witnesses, I suppose Moses and Elijah would be the best. The ministry of the two witnesses is most like the ministry of these two men, and it was these two who appeared at the transfiguration together with Christ. However, the fact that they are not named in Revelation 11 causes me to reject this theory.

The fact is that, since the Lord doesn't tell us who they are, we really can't know for sure. Therefore, while it is possible that the two witnesses may be two of these great men from the past brought back to the earth, it seems best to view the two witnesses as two men who have never lived before, men whom God will raise up as His special witnesses in the Tribulation.

SIXTY-TWO

IS THE "TRIBULATION" THE SAME AS THE "GREAT TRIBULATION?"

The most commonly used term for the future seven-year period of God's judgment on the world is the "Tribulation." This term is found in Matthew 24:9 in many modern translations. A few verses later (v. 21) the term is intensified: "a great tribulation." The relationship between the phrases *tribulation* and *great tribulation* has confused some people.

God's Word teaches that the future seven-year time of worldwide trouble will be divided into two equal segments of three and a half years. On this point almost all would agree. However, there are several opinions concerning how the terms *tribulation* and *great tribulation* relate to this seven-year period.

Option 1	Initial $3^1/_2$ years = tribulation	Final $3^1/_2$ years = great tribulation
Option 2	Entire 7 years = tribulation	Entire 7 years = great tribulation
Option 3	Entire 7 years = tribulation	Final $3^1/_2$ years = great tribulation

Any of these interpretations is possible. However, I favor option 3.

The term *tribulation* in Matthew 24:9 seems to encompass the entire seven-year period. It is an excellent word to describe the overall nature of the final seven years of this age and is frequently used that way by most students of Bible prophecy. The term *great tribulation,* on the other hand, seems to be used in Matthew 24:21 to describe the more specific time that will follow the setting up of the abomination of desolation (an idolatrous image in the temple) at the midpoint of the seven-year period.

Therefore, it appears that the title "great tribulation" is used to describe the intensification of God's wrath during the final three and a half years of the total seven-year tribulation period.

SIXTY-THREE

ARE WE IN THE TRIBULATION NOW?

On the night before His crucifixion, our Lord reminded His disciples that in this life they would have trouble. "These things I have spoken to you, so that in Me you may have peace. In the world you have tribulation, but take courage; I have overcome the world" (John 16:33). Later Paul echoed this idea: "Through many tribulations we must enter the kingdom of God" (Acts 14:22).

While it is true that we must enter the kingdom through many tribulations, the Bible makes a clear distinction between the general tribulations that all believers in every age will experience and the intense time of worldwide tribulation that will culminate this age.

Nevertheless, because of the difficulty of the Christian journey, some have been led to believe that this present age is the tribulation period. This seems to have been the problem the Thessalonians were having when Paul wrote his second letter to them. Paul addressed this in 2 Thessalonians:

> Now we request you, brethren, with regard to the coming of our Lord Jesus Christ and our gathering together to Him, that you not be quickly shaken from your composure or be disturbed either by a spirit or a message or a letter as if from us, to the effect that the day of the Lord has come. Let no one in any way deceive you, for it will not come unless the apostasy comes first, and the man of lawlessness is revealed, the son of destruction. (2 Thessalonians 2:1–3)

Paul assures the Thessalonian believers and us that the Tribulation—the Day of the Lord—cannot come until two things happen: a great, worldwide rebellion against God, and the unveiling of the Antichrist. Since neither of these things has happened, we cannot currently be in the tribulation period.

Sixty-four

WILL ANYONE SURVIVE THE TRIBULATION?

Even a cursory reading of Revelation can leave you wondering how anyone could survive the last days. As many as two-thirds of the world's Jewish population will be slain during Antichrist's reign of terror (Zechariah 13:8; Matthew 24:9).

In the fourth seal judgment, one-fourth of the earth's population is killed, and in the sixth trumpet judgment, another one-third of the earth is destroyed. That's half of the world's population in just two judgments. Then as the bowls of wrath are poured out in Revelation 16, the total annihilation of the human race looks imminent.

Our Lord knew that people would someday ask this question, so He has already given us His solution to the problem:

> For then there will be a great tribulation, such as has not occurred since the beginning of the world until now, nor ever will. Unless those days had been cut short, no life would have been saved; but for the sake of the elect those days will be cut short. (Matthew 24:21–22)

As an aside, I believe the elect mentioned here are all the Jewish people who will be saved during the Tribulation.

Some have suggested that this passage is saying that the Lord will shorten the tribulation period to make it less than the time He intended. I don't think that's right. Nor do I believe those who say that it means that tribulation days will be shorter than twenty-four hours.

These encouraging words simply mean that there will be a termination of this period of time—that is, the Lord will not allow it to go on indefinitely. He will end it at the divinely appointed time. This is another way of saying that if the Tribulation were allowed to go on indefinitely, no one would survive. The Lord ends the Tribulation when He does for the sake of those who have been saved during this time and are undergoing terrible suffering.

Jesus assures us that there will be many people who will survive the horrors of the Tribulation. All of these people will be gathered together for judgment when Christ returns. The righteous will enter the millennial kingdom and the lost will be cast into eternal fire (Matthew 25:31–46).

SECTION FIVE

ARMAGEDDON

We may be the generation that sees Armageddon.
RONALD REAGAN

Probably the best known word in all of Bible prophecy is the word *Armageddon.* It is the word that everyone uses to refer to the end of the world. In the summer of 1998 a blockbuster movie by that name debuted. It was about an asteroid the size of Texas on a collision course with earth.

As I saw the commercials for this movie and drank my Coke at McDonald's out of a cup with the word Armageddon emblazoned on it, I couldn't help but wonder if the movie producer had any idea what the word Armageddon means. I also wondered how many of the millions of moviegoers had a clue about the true meaning of Armageddon. While this word has become synonymous in our culture with the end of the world, it is used in the Bible to refer to a very specific event in the last days.

Sixty-five

What does the word "Armageddon" mean?

The word *Armageddon* is found only one time in the Bible:

> Then they gathered the kings together to the place that in Hebrew is called Armageddon. (Revelation 16:16, NIV)

The word is made up of two Hebrew words: *Har* (mountain) and *Megiddo* (a city in the northern part of ancient Israel). Megiddo was built on a hill, so the hill was called the mountain (har) of Megiddo—or Armageddon.

The city of Megiddo overlooks a large valley variously known as the valley of Jezreel, the valley of Esdraelon, the plains of Megiddo, and the valley of Taanach. According to Revelation 16:12–16, Armageddon and the nearby valley will be the rendezvous point for the armies gathering to descend upon Israel (Zechariah 12:1–2; 14:1–2).

However, when we use the term Armageddon, we don't usually mean a place. Usually we're referring to the events that follow after this army is gathered. Like Gettysburg, Armageddon is both a place and an event. Let's look at these events in more detail in the next chapter.

SIXTY-SIX

WHAT IS ARMAGEDDON?

On September 2, 1945, aboard the battleship USS *Missouri,* the Japanese government formally surrendered to the Allied forces, thus ending WWII. After the instrument of surrender had been signed by all the representatives, General Douglas MacArthur, the supreme commander of the allied forces in the Pacific, made a powerful announcement:

> Men since the beginning of time have sought peace. We have had our last chance. Military alliances, balances of power, leagues of nations, all in turn failed, leaving the only path to be by the crucible of war. The utter destructiveness of war now blots out this alternative. If we do not devise some greater and more equitable system, Armageddon will be at our door.

MacArthur's words are more true today than ever before. The world is not getting safer or more peaceful. The twentieth century ended with a third of the world's 193 nations embroiled in conflict. The National Defense Council Foundation listed 65 countries in conflict in 1999, up from 60 the year before. This is exactly what the Bible predicts for the last days. As General MacArthur predicted in 1945, Armageddon is at our door.

MISCONCEPTIONS ABOUT ARMAGEDDON

Before we turn to what the Bible says Armageddon is, it is important to discuss what it is not. First, Armageddon is not a battle. Second, it's not the same as the battle of Gog and Magog in Ezekiel. And third, Armageddon is not the final war on earth. Let's look at these one at a time.

Armageddon Is Not a Battle

It is common to hear people refer to the "battle" of Armageddon. But technically speaking, Armageddon will be a war or campaign involving a series of battles in the land of Israel. The word translated "war" in Revelation 16:14 is the Greek word *polemos,* which refers not to an individual battle but to a series of battles—a war.

Armageddon Is Not the Same as the Battle of Gog and Magog

Ezekiel 38–39 records an invasion that many have understood to be synonymous with Armageddon. I do not believe this is so. Here are a few of the significant differences between these two events:

Gog and Magog (Ezekiel 38-39)	Armageddon (Revelation 14:18–20; 16:16; 19:15–21)
Invasion is led by Gog	Invasion is led by Antichrist
Israel is at peace at the time of the invasion	There is no mention of Israel's peace
Armies gather to pluder Israel	Armies gather to fight against Christ
Occurs at the middle of the Tribulation	Occurs at the end of the Tribulation
Russia and her Islamic allies invade Israel	All nations invade Israel
Occurs so that all the nations will know that He is God	Occurs to destroy the nations

Armageddon is Not the Final War on Earth

I often hear people referring to Armageddon as the last great military conflict on earth. However, the last war in history is the one referred to as Gog and Magog in Revelation 20:7–11. It's the final revolt of Satan. I believe it occurs one thousand years after the war of Armageddon is over.

WHAT ARMAGEDDON IS

The following ten Bible passages are the main ones that describe the events of Armageddon.

1. Psalm 2.
2. Isaiah 34:1–16.
3. Isaiah 63:1–6.
4. Joel 3:1–17.
5. Zechariah 12:1–9.

6. Zechariah 14:1–15.
7. Malachi 4:1–5.
8. Revelation 14:14–20.
9. Revelation 16:12–16.
10. Revelation 19:19–21.

The War of Armageddon is the climactic event of the great Tribulation. It will occur when all the armies of the earth gather to come against Israel and attempt once and for all to eradicate the Jewish people (Zechariah 12:1–2; 14:1–2). After Jerusalem is captured, Jesus Christ will return to destroy the invading armies and deliver the faithful Jewish remnant hiding at Petra in modern-day southern Jordan (more about this later).

THE LOCATION OF ARMAGEDDON

The campaign will be spread out over the entire land of Israel from Megiddo in the north to Edom or Bozrah in the south. The theater of battle will span 180–200 miles from north to south and 100 miles from east to west. Within this larger area, the Bible focuses on three specific places where the fighting will be the most intense.

The Valley of Jehoshaphat (Joel 3:2, 12)

This is probably another title for the Kidron valley. This valley is on the east side of Jerusalem and runs between the eastern wall of the city of Jerusalem and the Mount of Olives.

The Valley of Esdraelon (Revelation 16:14–16)

This valley, also known as the valley of Jezreel, the valley of Taanach, and the plains of Megiddo, is a plain 20 miles long and 14 miles wide that lies at the foot of Mt. Megiddo or Armageddon. It is here that the armies of the earth in alliance with the Antichrist will gather and meet their doom. In Mark Twain's book, *The Innocents Abroad,* he called the Plain of Esdraelon "the battlefield of the nations."

Bozrah/Edom (Isaiah 34:1–5; 63:1)

I think it is interesting that the Bible tells us that when Jesus returns one of the very first places He will go will be to Bozrah, royal city of Edom. Bozrah is east of the Jordan river in the modern nation of Jordan. It is near the rock city of Petra.

Why would Jesus go there first? What is His interest in such an insignificant place? The best answer is that Jesus will go there to deliver the Jewish people who are hiding there from the Antichrist.

At the midpoint of the Tribulation, the Antichrist will break his covenant of peace with Israel (Daniel 9:27). He will then invade Israel and desecrate the temple in Jerusalem by sitting in it and declaring himself to be God (Matthew 24:15; 2 Thessalonians 2:4).

The Bible says that when this occurs a great number of Jews (symbolized by a woman in Revelation 12) will flee into the wilderness where God will supernaturally protect them for three and a half years from the ravages of the Antichrist, energized by Satan (Revelation 12:6, 14; see also 13:4). Scripture seems to indicate that this end-times hiding place for the Jews will be the city of Petra in southern Jordan. Petra is close enough for the people to flee and is in the wilderness and mountains (Matthew 24:16; Revelation 12:6, 14). Moreover, Micah 2:12–13 says that the Lord will one day gather His people into a sheepfold and lead them out in victory. The Hebrew word for *fold* is Bozrah.

The location of Bozrah is still disputed today but it seems most logical to identify it with the amazing rock city of Petra. With its narrow passageway and spacious interior surrounded by high cliffs, Petra is like a huge sheepfold.

It appears that after His descent to the Mount of Olives at His Second Coming (see question 72), Christ will lead His army down to Edom to rescue the hiding Jewish remnant there. When He returns from Edom His clothes will be stained with blood and His sword drenched in blood (Isaiah 34:6; 63:1–3). The armies gathered at Petra against the Lord's people will be slaughtered to such an extent that the mountains will flow with blood and the land will be soaked in it (Isaiah 34:2–7).

As you can see, the War of Armageddon will take place in a widely dispersed areas in and around Israel. Fighting will rage from the Valley of Megiddo in the north to Petra in the south, with Jerusalem right in the middle.

Theologian Herman A. Hoyt provides a gripping description of the scope of Armageddon in his book *The End Times:*

> The center of the entire area [of battle] will be the city of Jerusalem (Zechariah 14:1–2). Into this area the multiplied millions of men, doubtless approaching 400 million, will be

crowded for the final holocaust of humanity. The kings with their armies will come from the north and the south, from the east and from the west. There will be an invasion from hell beneath. And entering the scene at the last moment will be an invasion from outer space. In the most dramatic sense this will be the "valley of decision" for humanity (Joel 3:14) and the great winepress into which will be poured the fierceness of the wrath of almighty God (Revelation 19:15).[39]

THE SEVEN KEY PHASES OF ARMAGEDDON

As I have already stated, I believe that Armageddon will be a multibattle war and not a single battle. Scripture outlines several distinct phases of this campaign.

Since the events of Armageddon will transpire over the entire land of Israel, it is a daunting task to put all of the major events together in chronological order. However, I have attempted to do so. The following is a proposed chronology of the key phases of Armageddon.

Phase 1: Euphrates Dries Up

The Euphrates River will be dried up to prepare the way for the kings of the East to move into Israel (Revelation 16:12). All that we know about the kings of the East is that they represent nations east of the Euphrates. A glance at a world map shows that that could include such modern nations as India, Pakistan, Russia, China, and Japan.

Phase 2: Antichrist's Armies Gather

Antichrist's allies (including the kings of the East) will assemble in the Valley of Megiddo or Armageddon (Revelation 16:12–16).

Phase 3: Fall of Jerusalem

Jerusalem will be attacked and will fall to Antichrist's forces (Zechariah 12:1–3; 14:1–2).

Phase 4: Second Coming

Jesus Christ will return personally to the Mount of Olives (Zechariah 14:4). This is the second coming of Jesus Christ.

Phase 5: Jerusalem Rescued

When Antichrist sees the coming Christ and His heavenly army, he will rally his forces to fight against the King of kings (Revelation 19:19). These armies gathered against Jerusalem will be destroyed by Christ and His army in the Valley of Jehoshaphat outside Jerusalem (Joel 3:9–17; Zechariah 12:1–9; 14:3). Jerusalem will be rescued by her Messiah.

Phase 6: Remnant Delivered

Immediately after He comes, Christ will descend upon Edom to deliver the Jewish remnant hiding in and around the city of Petra (Isaiah 34:1–7; 63:1–5; Joel 3:19).

Phase 7: End of the Beasts

The Antichrist and the False Prophet will be seized and cast alive into the lake of fire, where they will be tormented forever (Revelation 19:20). Just as there were two men in the Old Testament who went directly to heaven without dying (Enoch and Elijah), so these two men will go directly to hell without dying.

THE AFTERMATH OF ARMAGEDDON

After the terrible fighting, all that will be left will be the corpses and weapons of the armies of the world. It is impossible for us to envision the scope of the carnage. The final humiliation of the Lord's enemies is what we might call "The Great Vulture Supper" (Matthew 24:28; Luke 17:37; Revelation 19:17–21). A rotting mass of humanity will fill the entire region. The Lord will summon the carrion birds to feed on the putrefying flesh that litters the landscape. Such will be the end of the glory of man in opposition to the King of kings and Lord of lords.

SUMMARY

Vernon Grounds, president emeritus of Denver Seminary, tells the story of some seminary students who often played basketball in a nearby public school. The janitor was an elderly man who always waited patiently for the seminarians to finish playing. As he waited he always sat there reading his Bible.

One day one of the students asked the man what he was reading. The man replied, "The Book of Revelation." Somewhat surprised, the young man asked him if he understood it. "Oh, yes," the man assured him. "I understand it." Doubtfully, the young man said, "Well what does it mean?" Very quietly the janitor answered, "It means that Jesus is gonna win."

What a great summary for our chapter. It's not vital that you know all the details or phases of the War of Armageddon. The point is: Jesus is gonna win.

Sixty-seven

What are some of the other biblical names or titles for the War of Armageddon?

As we have seen in other areas of the end times, the Bible often uses several different titles to describe the same event. It's the same with Armageddon. In the Bible there are seven titles usually interpreted as referring to Armageddon:

1. A day of vengeance (Isaiah 34:8).
2. The great winepress of the wrath of God (Isaiah 63:2; Joel 3:13; Revelation 14:19–20).
3. That great and awesome Day of the Lord (Joel 2:31).
4. The harvest (Joel 3:13; Revelation 14:15–16).
5. The day…burning like a furnace (Malachi 4:1).
6. The great and terrible Day of the Lord (Malachi 4:5).
7. That war of the great day of God, the Almighty (Revelation 16:14).

Sixty-eight

WILL AMERICAN TROOPS PARTICIPATE IN ARMAGEDDON?

As we noted in the first section, there is no specific reference to the United States in the Bible. However, we can confidently say that the United States will participate in Armageddon. This confidence arises from the fact that Scripture indicates that all the nations of the world will be gathered against Israel at Armageddon (Zechariah 12:3; 14:2; Revelation 16:14).

This does not mean that every nation currently in existence will be at Armageddon. The face of the world may change drastically between now and then. However, it does mean that representatives from the nations, including the United States in whatever form it has taken at that time, will invade Israel with the rest of the world at Armageddon.

Today, America is Israel's chief ally and protector. But in the end times even America will follow Antichrist in turning against Israel and the Jewish people.

SIXTY-NINE

DURING THE WAR OF ARMAGEDDON WILL BLOOD LITERALLY FLOW IN THE LAND OF ISRAEL AS HIGH AS A HORSE'S BRIDLE FOR 200 MILES?

The most vivid description of the severity and brutality of Armageddon is found in Revelation 14:

> After that, another angel came from the Temple in heaven, and he also had a sharp sickle. Then another angel, who has power to destroy the world with fire, shouted to the angel with the sickle, "Use your sickle now to gather the clusters of grapes from the vines of the earth, for they are fully ripe for judgment." So the angel swung his sickle on the earth and loaded the grapes in the great winepress of God's wrath. And the grapes were trodden in the winepress outside the city and the blood flowed from the winepress in a stream about 180 miles long and as high as a horse's bridle. (Revelation 14:17–20, NLT)

This passage is often used by prophecy preachers with great effect. They describe in gruesome detail how blood will literally flow four feet deep for 180 miles, which is the entire length of the land of Israel from Megiddo in the north to Bozrah or Petra in the south. Others maintain that this can't be taken literally. They hold that the language is intentionally exaggerated to impress the reader with the extent of the slaughter.

The picture here is drawn from the imagery of the winepress. When grapes were put into a winepress, people inside it would stomp around on the grapes so that the juice would flow down into a collection vat. In Revelation 14, the winepress is "the great winepress of God's wrath." The Lord throws the nations into the winepress and does the stomping (on people, not grapes). And what pours out is not grape juice, but blood (see Isaiah 63:2–3; Joel 3:13; Revelation 19:15).

I don't believe that this passage necessarily means that there will be a four-foot-deep sea of blood, though this is possible. The Lord is saying that His judgment is going to be so fierce that its effect will be felt over the entire land of Israel, from Megiddo to Bozrah.

CONCLUSION

The War of Armageddon will be the climactic event of the great Tribulation. The armies of the world will gather in Israel and be destroyed by the returning King of kings.

This world has an appointment with destiny. It is on the road to Armageddon. When we put our trust in Jesus Christ as our Savior, God graciously transfers us from the road to Armageddon to the road to glory. The good news is that Jesus is coming someday, perhaps today, to take His own out of this world to heaven before the road to Armageddon dead-ends.

If you have never received the pardon that Jesus purchased for you on the Cross, you can receive it right now and get on the road to glory.

THE SECOND COMING

66 percent of Americans,
including a third of those who admit they never attend church,
say they believe Jesus will return to earth someday.
U.S. NEWS AND WORLD REPORT, 1997

As we look around at all the filth, violence, and ungodliness in our world today, it is easy to get discouraged. It often looks like the other side's winning. As the old poem says:

> God's plan made a hopeful beginning,
> But man spoiled his chances by sinning.
> We trust that the story
> Will end in God's glory,
> But, at present, the other side's winning.

What can turn the present situation around? What hope does this world have?

The only hope is the Second Coming of the One who died for the sins of the world and rose triumphantly from the grave. He is the only one who can overcome the enemy.

The Second Coming is not the same thing as the Rapture, though those are often confused. The Rapture is an event that from the human perspective could occur at any moment. It is the moment when Jesus comes *for His saints* before the seven-year tribulation period begins. The Second Coming, on the other hand, is the event at the end of the seven-year Tribulation, when Jesus comes back to earth *with His saints*.

This section will answer the key questions about this, the climactic event of human history.

SEVENTY

CAN WE BE SURE THAT JESUS IS COMING BACK?

There is nothing more clearly stated in the Bible than the fact that Jesus Christ is coming again. The emphasis on the Second Coming and its absolute certainty can be seen in the following Scriptural statistics:

1. Jesus' return is explicitly referred to 1,845 times in the Bible—1,527 times in the OT and 318 times in the NT (for example: Zechariah 14:3–4; 2 Thessalonians 1:7).
2. The Second Coming is mentioned in 23 of 27 New Testament books.
3. Out of the New Testament's 260 chapters, there are 318 references to the Second Coming. On average, then, the Second Coming is referred to more than once a chapter.
4. Jesus' Second Coming is mentioned eight times for every reference to His first coming.
5. For every mention of the atonement in the Bible, there are two references to the Second Coming.
6. Enoch, who lived only seven generations after Adam and is considered the first prophet of the Bible, prophesied about the Second Coming (Jude 14). Therefore, the first prophecy of the Bible concerns the Second Coming.
7. The final prophecy of the Bible deals with the Second Coming (Revelation 22:20).
8. In Revelation we hear Jesus say, "I come quickly" or "I will come like a thief" seven times—three times in the final chapter (2:16; 3:3, 11; 16:15; 22:7, 12, 20).
9. People are exhorted over fifty times to be ready for the return of Jesus (for instance: Luke 12:35–36; Romans 13:11–14).
10. Jesus Christ Himself refers to His return twenty-one times (for example: Matthew 24:2–30; 25:31; John 14:3; 21:2–23).

11. Angels believe and testify that Jesus is coming back. When Jesus ascended to heaven, angels stated that He would return just as He left (Acts 1:9–11).[40]

The Bible is clear that Jesus is coming again. Make no mistake, He is coming back just as He promised!

Seventy-one

How will Jesus return to earth?

In 1999, the Associated Press ranked the top 100 news events of the twentieth century. Some of the century's biggest stories were the stock market crash of October 28, 1929; the bombing of Pearl Harbor on December 7, 1941; the Kennedy assassination on November 22, 1963; and man walking on the moon on July 20, 1969. But the number one story was the Hiroshima bombing on August 6, 1945 that brought about the end of WWII and unleashed the atomic age.

While all of these stories are incredible, the greatest news event of all time is yet to occur: Jesus' return to planet earth. Talk about a front-page story! Just think about it for a moment and it may make the hair on your neck stand on end.

What will it be like when Jesus returns and sets foot on the earth? How will it happen? He will come personally, literally, visibly, suddenly, dramatically, gloriously, and triumphantly.

He Will Come Personally

Jesus will not send someone else on His behalf. He Himself will return.

> And as they were gazing intently into the sky while He was going, behold, two men in white clothing stood beside them. They also said, "Men of Galilee, why do you stand looking into the sky? This Jesus, who has been taken up from you into heaven, will come in just the same way as you have watched Him go into heaven." (Acts 1:10–11)

> Yes, *I* am coming quickly. (Revelation 22:20, emphasis added)

He Will Come Literally

The coming of Jesus is not a spiritual or symbolic coming. He came literally, in the flesh, the first time. He will come literally again.

And I saw heaven opened, and behold, a white horse, and He who sat on it is called Faithful and True, and in righteousness He judges and wages war. His eyes are a flame of fire, and on His head are many diadems; and He has a name written on Him which no one knows except Himself. He is clothed with a robe dipped in blood, and His name is called The Word of God. (Revelation 19:11–13)

HE WILL COME VISIBLY

Jesus will not come back incognito. His coming will be visible to all the world.

Then if anyone says to you, "Behold, here is the Christ," or "There He is," do not believe him. For false Christs and false prophets will arise and will show great signs and wonders, so as to mislead, if possible, even the elect. Behold, I have told you in advance. So if they say to you, "Behold, He is in the wilderness," do not go out, or, "Behold, He is in the inner rooms," do not believe them. For just as the lightning comes from the east and flashes even to the west, so will the coming of the Son of Man be. (Matthew 24:23–27)

BEHOLD, HE IS COMING WITH THE CLOUDS, and every eye will see Him, even those who pierced Him; and all the tribes of the earth will mourn over Him. So it is to be. Amen. (Revelation 1:7)

HE WILL COME SUDDENLY

The Second Coming of Jesus will be sudden. It won't occur over a long period or in stages. It will come suddenly, like lightning (Matthew 24:27) or a thief in the night (Revelation 3:3b).

HE WILL COME DRAMATICALLY

Jesus' coming will be attended by dramatic signs in the heavens.

But immediately after the tribulation of those days THE SUN WILL BE DARKENED, AND THE MOON WILL NOT GIVE ITS LIGHT, AND THE STARS WILL FALL from the sky, and the powers of the heavens will be shaken. (Matthew 24:29)

There will be signs in sun and moon and stars, and on the earth dismay among nations, in perplexity at the roaring of the sea and the waves, men fainting from fear and the expectation of the things which are coming upon the world; for the powers of the heavens will be shaken. (Luke 21:25–26)

HE WILL COME GLORIOUSLY

Jesus will return with great glory, majesty, and dazzling brilliance.

And then the sign of the Son of Man will appear in the sky, and then all the tribes of the earth will mourn, and they will see the SON OF MAN COMING ON THE CLOUDS OF THE SKY with power and great glory. (Matthew 24:30)

The Lord Jesus will be revealed from heaven with His mighty angels in flaming fire. (2 Thessalonians 1:7b)

HE WILL COME TRIUMPHANTLY

Jesus will return as King of kings and Lord of lords riding a milk-white stallion. He is coming back to conquer! Victorious generals in the Roman Empire rode white stallions after great victories to symbolize their conquests. Jesus rides a white stallion as He goes forth to battle. The victory is sure. He will win the battle.

All the armies of the earth will be amassed to meet Him, yet amazingly no struggle is recorded. All Jesus will have to do to completely vanquish His enemies is speak the words, "Drop dead!"

And I saw the beast and the kings of the earth and their armies assembled to make war against Him who sat on the horse and against His army. And the beast was seized, and with him the false prophet who performed the signs in his presence, by which he deceived those who had received the mark of the beast and those who worshiped his image; these two were thrown alive into the lake of fire which burns with brimstone. And the rest were killed with the sword which came from the mouth of Him who sat on the horse, and all the birds were filled with their flesh. (Revelation 19:19–21)

The Second Coming will be so spectacular it's hard for us to imagine. Nothing this world has ever seen can even come close. But we can rest assured that it will happen just the way the Lord has said.

SEVENTY-TWO

WHERE WILL JESUS RETURN TO EARTH?

The Bible says that when Jesus returns to the earth, every eye will see Him (Revelation 1:7; Matthew 24:27). His coming will be witnessed by the entire world. However, while His return will be worldwide in this sense, He has to actually "touch down" somewhere. Where that might be is what many people want to know.

The Bible seems clear that Jesus will return to earth from the same place He left: the Mount of Olives. Three key passages help identify this as the place of His return.

1. Zechariah 14:4 addresses the second coming of Christ. "And in that day His feet will stand on the Mount of Olives, which is in front of Jerusalem on the east; and the Mount of Olives will be split in its middle from east to west by a very large valley, so that half of the mountain will move toward the north and the other half toward the south."

2. Jesus delivered His great prophetic discourse, which gave the signs of His coming, from the Mount of Olives in Matthew 24–25.

3. When Jesus ascended to heaven from the Mount of Olives in Acts 1:9–12, the angels said that He would return just as He had left. While this could simply mean that He will return in the same manner that He left, it might also carry the idea that He will return to the same place from which He left.

As one of my friends likes to say, "When Jesus returns, He will do a perfect two-point landing on the Mount of Olives."

SEVENTY-THREE

WHO ARE THE ARMIES OF HEAVEN THAT RETURN WITH CHRIST?

A Christian woman was once telling a pastor about the assurance of her salvation. She said, "I have taken a one-way ticket to glory and do not intend to come back."

To this the man of God replied: "You are sure going to miss a lot. I have taken a round-trip ticket. I am not only going to meet Christ in glory, but I am coming back with Him in power and great glory to the earth."

Every Christian of the church age has a round-trip ticket. When Jesus Christ returns from heaven to destroy the Antichrist, judge the nations, and establish His glorious kingdom on earth, He will be accompanied by a great multitude. This mighty army following in His train as He splits the clouds will be made up of both angels and redeemed human beings. All who have been raptured to heaven before the Tribulation will return with Jesus back to earth at His second coming at the climax of the Tribulation.

Here are a few of the most familiar verses that describe the armies of heaven that return with the conquering Christ.

Then the LORD, my God, will come, and all the holy ones with Him! (Zechariah 14:5b)

But when the Son of Man comes in His glory, and all the angels with Him, then He will sit on His glorious throne. (Matthew 25:31)

[God will] establish your hearts without blame in holiness before our God and Father at the coming of our Lord Jesus with all His saints. (1 Thessalonians 3:13)

The Lord Jesus will be revealed from heaven with His mighty angels in flaming fire. (2 Thessalonians 1:7b)

Behold, the Lord came with many thousands of His holy ones. (Jude 14b)

And I saw heaven opened, and behold, a white horse, and He who sat on it is called Faithful and True, and in righteousness He judges and wages war. And the armies which are in heaven, clothed in fine linen, white and clean, were following Him on white horses. (Revelation 19:11, 14)

Just imagine what it will be like to follow the King of kings and Lord of lords when He comes again! There we will be at the head of this angelic and saintly army, blazing with fire through the clouds to join in the ultimate battle of the ages!

SEVENTY-FOUR

WHAT WILL JESUS DO WHEN HE COMES BACK?

The Bible identifies six key things Jesus will do when He returns to earth.

CHRIST WILL DEFEAT THE ANTICHRIST AND HIS ARMIES (REVELATION 19:19-21)

The story is told of when the army of Emperor Julian the Apostate (A.D. 332–363) was marching to Persia, some of his soldiers were tormenting a Christian believer. Tiring of their brutal games, they looked down on their poor victim and asked him scornfully, "Where now is your carpenter-God?" The man looked up at them through his bloodied eyes and answered, "He is making a coffin for your emperor."

When the Lord Jesus returns, the Antichrist and all the other Christ-rejecting rulers will be destroyed by the God they had scorned.

CHRIST WILL REGATHER AND RESTORE FAITHFUL ISRAEL (ROMANS 11:26)

Perhaps the most frequently mentioned promise in the Old Testament is God's vow that He would one day regather and restore the nation of Israel (Isaiah 43:5–6; Jeremiah 30:10; 33:6–9; Ezekiel 36:24–38; 37:1–28).

The regathering of Israel began in 1948 when the modern state of Israel was born, and it continues today. This regathering will continue until the second coming of Christ. During the Tribulation, Israel will be scattered for the final time (Zechariah 14:1–2), and then at the Second Coming, Christ will gather the believing Jews together and restore them as His people (Isaiah 11:11–16; Ezekiel 39:25–29).

Matthew 24 describes the scattering of the Jews during the Tribulation (24:15–21) and then the subsequent regathering under Messiah:

> And then the sign of the Son of Man will appear in the sky, and then all the tribes of the earth will mourn, and they will see the SON OF MAN COMING ON THE CLOUDS OF THE SKY with power and great glory. And He will send forth His angels with A GREAT TRUMPET and THEY WILL GATHER TOGETHER His elect from the four winds, from one end of the sky to the other. (Matthew 24:30–31)

CHRIST WILL JUDGE THE LIVING

When Christ returns, all Gentiles alive on the earth who survived the Tribulation will appear before him to determine if they can enter His kingdom (Matthew 25:31–46). This is called the judgment of the "sheep and the goats." Christ will also gather all living Jews in the wilderness to determine who can enter the kingdom (Ezekiel 20:33–38).

CHRIST WILL RESURRECT THE DEAD

After the Second Coming, one of the next events will be the resurrection of Old Testament believers and Tribulation believers. They will be raised and rewarded and will reign with Christ (Revelation 20:4–6; see also Daniel 12:1–4).

New Testament or church age believers will not be included in this resurrection. As you remember from section 2, believers who have died during our current age (the church age) will have already been resurrected at the Rapture, which will have happened seven years before this resurrection.

CHRIST WILL BIND THE DEVIL (REVELATION 20:1-3)

The first thing Jesus will do after His return is bind Satan. A mighty angel will seize him and cast him into the bottomless pit for one thousand years, after which time he will be briefly released.

CHRIST WILL ESTABLISH HIMSELF AS KING (REVELATION 19:16)

Christ returns as King of kings and Lord of lords! He comes to sit on His glorious throne and reign over the earth (Daniel 2:44; Matthew 19:28; Luke 1:32–33).

> Look! He comes with the clouds of heaven. And everyone will see him—even those who pierced him. And all the nations of the earth will weep because of him. Yes! Amen! (Revelation 1:7, NLT)

THE MILLENNIUM

"A larger body of prophetic material is devoted to the subject of the Millennium, developing its character and conditions, than any other one subject."
J. DWIGHT PENTECOST[41]

Man has always dreamed of utopia. We aspire to create a great society, a paradise on earth, a return to the Garden of Eden. But both the Bible and the witness of history are clear that sinful man can never produce such a society on earth. Paradise is lost, and man in his own efforts can never regain it.

However, God's Word tells us that the next great event after the Second Coming is just such a paradise. Jesus will establish on earth a thousand-year reign of glory and peace (Revelation 20:1–6). The millennial age will bring about the complete fulfillment of all that God has promised to the nation of Israel in the Old Testament.

Let's consider some of the most frequently asked questions about this unprecedented, thousand-year period.

SEVENTY-FIVE

WHAT IS THE MILLENNIUM?

A little boy once asked his father, "What is the Millennium?"

His father replied, "Don't you know what a millennium is? It's just like a centennial, only it's got more legs."

The word *millennium* is made up of two Latin words: *mille* (one thousand) and *annum* (years). Thus it means one thousand years.

The main Bible passage that specifically talks about this thousand-year kingdom is Revelation 20:1–7, but the idea of the Millennium is present throughout the Bible. In the Old Testament, there are several key places that describe the millennial reign of Christ on earth (see Isaiah 11:1–10; 35:1–10; Jeremiah 23:5–8; Joel 3:17–21; Zechariah 14:9–21).

Here are some New Testament names and titles for the millennium:

1. The kingdom of heaven (Matthew 3:2; 8:11).
2. The kingdom of God (Mark 1:14).
3. The Kingdom (Matthew 19:28).
4. A kingdom which cannot be shaken (Hebrews 12:28).
5. The world to come (Hebrews 2:5).
6. Times of refreshing (Acts 3:19).
7. The period of restoration of all things (Acts 3:21).

SEVENTY-SIX

HOW CAN THE MILLENNIUM BE ONLY ONE THOUSAND YEARS IF GOD'S KINGDOM IS ETERNAL?

Six times in Revelation 20:1–7, John states that the reign of Christ on earth after His glorious return will be one thousand years. However, in several other places in Scripture it is stated that Christ's kingdom will last forever (Daniel 7:14, 27; Revelation 11:15). This has led many to conclude that the one thousand years in Revelation 20 must not be literal.

The best way to reconcile this apparent conflict is to recognize that both of these statements are true: Christ will rule over His kingdom on this present earth for one thousand years, *and* He will reign forever.

The future kingdom of God has two parts or phases. Phase one is the millennial reign of Christ on this earth (Revelation 20:1–6), and phase two is the eternal state (Revelation 22:5).

As I once heard it described, the Millennium is the front porch of eternity.

Seventy-seven

What will the Millennium be like?

During the millennial reign of Christ, the earth will experience a return to conditions like the Garden of Eden. It will literally be heaven on earth as the Lord of heaven comes to live on earth among His people.

The Bible has a lot more to say about the Millennium than most people realize. Here is a list of the ten most prominent conditions that will prevail on the earth during the reign of Christ.

Peace

P. T. Barnum, the famous circus showman, loved to show visiting preachers his exhibit called "The Happy Family," in which lions, tigers and panthers squatted around a lamb without any aggression. When Barnum was asked by the visiting preachers if the group ever had any trouble, he would say, "Apart from replenishing the lamb now and then, they get along very well together."

This world is not what it is supposed be, but the Bible declares that someday all wars will cease and the world will be unified under the reign of the true King (Isaiah 2:4; 9:4–7; 11:6–9; Zechariah 9:10). Even the animal kingdom will enjoy perfect peace (Isaiah 11:6–9).

Joy

When Isaac Watts wrote the song "Joy to the World," he did not write it to be a Christmas carol. Rather, he penned it to announce the glorious second coming of Christ to rule and reign on this earth.

Think of some of the words: "Joy to the world! The Lord is come; Let earth receive her king…. No more let sins and sorrows grow…. He rules the world with truth and grace."

This is a song of the Millennium—when full joy will finally come to the world (Isaiah 9:3–4; 12:3–6; 14:7–8; 25:8–9; 30:29; 42:1; Jeremiah 30:18–19; Zephaniah 3:14–17; Zechariah 8:18–19; 10:6–7).

HOLINESS

The word *holy* means to be set apart to God for sacred purposes. The kingdom of Christ will be a holy kingdom. The land, the city, the temple, and the subjects will all be holy unto the Lord (Isaiah 4:3–4; 29:19; 35:8; 52:1; Ezekiel 43:7–12; 45:1; Zechariah 8:3; 14:20–21).

GLORY

The luminous glory of God will be fully unleashed in Messiah's kingdom (Isaiah 35:2; 40:5; 60:1–9; Ezekiel 43:1–5).

JUSTICE AND RIGHTEOUSNESS

When the millennial kingdom begins, it will be inhabited only by believers. However, these believers will still have human bodies with a fallen nature capable of sinning.

Man will still sin, but that sin will be judged in perfect justice at the hands of the Messiah (Isaiah 9:7; 11:5; 32:16; 42:1–4; 65:21–23). He will rule with "a rod of iron," restraining and judging sin, so that the prevailing atmosphere in the kingdom will be righteousness (Isaiah 11:1–5; 60:21; Jeremiah 31:23; Ezekiel 37:23–24; Zephaniah 3:1, 13).

DEEPER KNOWLEDGE

The teaching ministry of the Lord and the indwelling Holy Spirit will bring the subjects of the kingdom into a superior knowledge of the Lord's ways (Isaiah 11:1–2, 9; 41:19–20; 54:13; Jeremiah 31:33–34; Habakkuk 2:14).

NO SICKNESS OR DEFORMITY

Our politicians are constantly working on plans to provide better health care for the citizens of our nation. But in the Lord's government, the health plan will be fantastic. The King will be a healer, too. He will heal all the diseases and deformities of His people (Isaiah 29:18; 33:24; 35:5–6; 61:1–2; Ezekiel 34:16).

As a result, people will live extended life spans, just as people did before the Flood. A person who dies at the age of 100 will be considered to have died very prematurely (Isaiah 65:20).

UNIVERSAL WORSHIP OF GOD

All the inhabitants of the earth will join their hearts and voices to worship God and His Christ (Isaiah 45:23; 52:1,7–10; 66:17–23; Zephaniah 3:9; Zechariah 13:2; 14:16; Malachi 1:11; Revelation 5:9–14).

Worship during the Millennium will be centered in the rebuilt temple in Jerusalem. This temple will be the fourth Jewish temple in Jerusalem (see question 12). The millennial temple will be built in Jerusalem after the third temple (the tribulation temple) is destroyed. The Bible never specifically states that the tribulation temple will be destroyed, but the fact that it is replaced with a much larger temple during the Millennium demands that it no longer be in existence.

One important aspect of the worship in the Millennium is that animal sacrifices will be reinstituted in the millennial temple (Isaiah 56:6–7; 60:7; Ezekiel 43:18–27; 45:17–23; Zechariah 14:16–21).

These sacrifices will not be offered to take away sin, since no animal sacrifice can ever take away sin (Hebrews 10:1–2). Rather, these sacrifices will serve as a powerful memorial to the final sacrifice for sin, Jesus Christ. They will serve, like the Lord's Supper today, as a vivid reminder of the holiness of God, the awfulness of sin, and the death the Savior died in our place.

ECONOMIC PROSPERITY

There won't be any need for welfare programs, Social Security, food stamps, or relief agencies in the Millennium. The world will flourish under the hand of the King of heaven. There will be abundance and plenty for all the inhabitants of the world (Isaiah 35:1–2, 7; 30:23–25; 62:8–9; 65:21–23; Jeremiah 31:5, 12; Ezekiel 34:26; 36:29–30; Joel 2:21–27; Amos 9:13–14; Micah 4:1, 4; Zechariah 8:11–12; 9:16–17).

THE PRESENCE OF GOD

The greatest thing about the kingdom is that Christ Himself will be there. God's presence will be fully recognized and the Lord's people will experience a kind of fellowship with the Lord unlike anything they have ever known (Ezekiel 37:27–28; Zechariah 2:10–13). The city of Jerusalem will be called *Jehovah Shammah*—"the Lord is there" (Ezekiel 48:35).

The next time you listen to a politician's list of campaign promises, notice what he mentions. The list will probably look something like the list we have just seen: peace, justice in the courts, safe streets, education, health care, and a prospering economy. No matter what the TV commercials say, no politician can pull it off. These are unsolvable problems for man. However, in the coming kingdom, the Lord will accomplish everything we have longed for all our lives.

One day a professor at Dallas Theological Seminary came into the classroom and abruptly announced to the class that he had become an amillennialist. At DTS, a bastion of premillennialism, this came as quite a shock to the students.

"Let me explain what I mean," he said. "Last night I was thinking about all the problems in our world: the violence, the inequality, the suffering, the wars, the broken homes. As I was thinking about all these things I began to think about what the world will be like when Jesus comes back and takes over. When I thought of how wonderful it will be I leaned back in my chair and said, 'Aaah, millennium.'"

In that sense, I'm an "Aaahmillennialist" too. How wonderful it will be when Jesus comes back to establish His glorious kingdom.

SEVENTY-EIGHT

WHAT WILL EVERYDAY LIFE BE LIKE IN THE MILLENNIUM?

Having looked at the general conditions that will prevail during the Millennium, it's time to get more specific. This chapter will give an overview of what life in the Millennium will be like. Hopefully it will shed some light on this unparalleled epoch in man's history.

To facilitate our understanding, I want to break the information down into seven bite-sized chunks.

THE MILLENNIUM WILL BE UNIQUE BECAUSE OF WHO IS THERE

The Millennium will be inhabited at the outset by two groups of believers. Group 1 will be believers who have survived the tribulation period on earth. These people will enter the kingdom in their natural, physical bodies. They will live in houses, do work, marry, have children, and possibly die (see below), just as people have done since the beginning (Isaiah 65:17–25). They will still possess the sinful nature, therefore they will sin during the Millennium, despite the fact that the devil is not there to tempt them (though sin will be dealt with swiftly—see below).

Group 2 will be made up of believers who either died or were raptured before the Tribulation. They will already have their new, glorified bodies. They will not have the sinful nature and thus will not sin. This group of the redeemed will rule with Christ during the millennial kingdom. It is possible that Group 2 will rule over Group 1 in some way.

Believers in glorified bodies may be able to go back and forth between heaven and earth during the millennial reign. Again we just don't know for sure. However, the fact that both of these groups will exist side by side on the earth is enough to make the Millennium a totally unprecedented experience.

JESUS WILL BE PERSONALLY PRESENT ON EARTH RULING FROM JERUSALEM AS KING

The thing that really makes the Millennium special is that Jesus Christ will be there in person. He will rule the world from Jerusalem. All nations and peoples will flood there to pay homage to the King and His chosen people, the Jews (Isaiah 60:1–14; see also Ezekiel 37:24 and Zephaniah 3:14–17).

ALL MEN WILL BE REQUIRED TO SUBMIT TO THE KING

Read this portion of Psalm 2:

> Now therefore, O kings, show discernment;
> Take warning, O judges of the earth.
> Worship the LORD with reverence
> And rejoice with trembling.
> Do homage to the Son, that He not become angry, and you per-
> ish in the way,
> For His wrath may soon be kindled.
> How blessed are all who take refuge in Him! (Psalm 2:10–12)

PEOPLE WHO ARE IN THEIR NATURAL BODIES WILL LIVE EXTENDED LIFE SPANS

In the Millennium, those in Group 1 will be restored to the extremely long life spans that people enjoyed in the days before the Flood. The Bible says that during this time someone who dies at the age of 100 will be thought to have suffered an untimely death (Isaiah 65:20). I believe that those who submit to God will live the entire thousand years of the Millennium.

We are never told what ultimately happens to those who enter the Millennium in physical bodies and follow the Lord, but it stands to reason that if they live to the end of the thousand years, they will then receive their glorified bodies so they can enter heaven. Flesh and blood cannot enter the spiritual realm of heaven (1 Corinthians 15:50).

NOT ALL PEOPLE BORN DURING THE MILLENNIUM WILL BECOME DISCIPLES

Some of those who are born during the Millennium will not submit to Christ in their hearts. Those who outwardly rebel during the Millennium will be judged quickly by the Lord (Isaiah 9:7; 11:1–4; Zechariah 14:16–18). No war or insurrection will be tolerated by the King (Isaiah 2:4). Those who have disagreements or grievances will bring them to the Lord, who will act as final arbiter and mediator of all disputes, both national and personal (Isaiah 2:3–4).

Others will outwardly conform to avoid judgment, but they will still have a rebellious heart. We know this is true because at the end of the Millennium, when Satan is released for a little while, the Bible indicates that he has no trouble gathering a huge army to rebel against Christ (Revelation 20:7–10).

People Can Get Sick During the Millennium

Since sin and death will still be present during the Millennium, disease will be present, too. But the Lord will heal all who come to Him, much like He did during His first earthly ministry (Matthew 8:16; see also Isaiah 35:5–6). He will be the Great Physician for the world.

Everything Will Revolve around the King

King Jesus will sit on His throne receiving homage, dispensing justice, healing the sick, meting out judgment, and administering all the details of His kingdom. Jesus, who is called "The Last Adam" in 1 Corinthians 15:45, will do perfectly and completely what the first Adam was totally unable to do: He will take dominion over creation and completely fulfill God's original purpose for man.

I'm sure this answer has left you with many more questions. I must admit that I, too, still have a lot of questions about the details of the Millennium. But let's move ahead and consider why there must be a millennium at all.

SEVENTY-NINE

WHY MUST THERE BE A MILLENNIUM?

The Millennium will serve at least four important functions in the eternal plan of God: to reward the faithful, to redeem creation, to fulfill the promises of God, and to reaffirm the total depravity of man.

TO REWARD THE FAITHFUL

During the millennial kingdom, the saints will be awarded positions of authority based on their degree of faithfulness in this life (Luke 19:16–19). We will reign with Christ (Revelation 20:4–6).

TO REDEEM CREATION

When Adam and Eve sinned in the Garden of Eden, God pronounced a series of five curses. These fives curses were pronounced against the serpent, Satan, the woman, the man, and nature (Genesis 3:14–19). From that time until today the earth has been cursed, as evidenced by thorns and thistles and the hard work that is required by man to scratch out a living. The new crop of crabgrass in the lawn each spring is a small, vivid reminder of the curse.

The curse on nature is poignantly described in Romans:

> For all creation is waiting eagerly for that future day when God will reveal who his children really are. Against its will, everything on earth was subjected to God's curse. All creation anticipates the day when it will join God's children in glorious freedom from death and decay. For we know that all creation has been groaning as in the pains of childbirth right up to the present time. (Romans 8:19–22, NLT)

A crucial function of the Millennium is to reverse God's curse on creation. During the kingdom, all animals will revert back to being plant eaters as they were originally (Genesis 1:30). The lion and lamb will lie down together in harmony, and a child will be able to play next to a poisonous snake without fear of harm (Isaiah 11:6–9). The earth will become amazingly productive and beautiful. Deserts will blossom as will the rose (Isaiah 35:1–7). Even the barren area around the Dead Sea will flourish with plants, animals, and fish (Ezekiel 47:8–12).

The whole earth will become like a huge Garden of Eden.

TO RECOGNIZE THE PROMISES OF GOD

God made three great unconditional, unilateral, eternal covenants that will find their fulfillment in the millennial kingdom. These three covenants or promises were made with Abraham, David, and the nation of Israel.

The Abrahamic Covenant

(Genesis 12:1–3; 15:18–21) God promised Abraham three things: descendants, land, and blessing.

1. Descendants—God promised that Abraham's seed or descendants would become a great nation (Genesis 12:1–3; 13:16; 15:5; 17:7; 22:17–18).
2. Land—God promised Abraham that his descendants would be given a piece of land to call their own forever. The land He promised includes the modern-day nation of Israel and parts of modern-day Egypt, Syria, Lebanon, and Iraq (Genesis 15:18–21). This unconditional promise has never been fulfilled in history, but will be fulfilled in the Millennium (Isaiah 60:21; Ezekiel 34:11–16).
3. Blessing—God also promised Abraham that through him and his descendants all the world would be blessed. This prophecy has been partially fulfilled in the blessing that has come to all the world through Abraham's greatest descendant, Jesus Christ. However, the final blessing from Abraham through Christ to all the nations will come during the wonderful conditions that will exist on this earth during the Millennium.

The Davidic Covenant

God made an eternal, unconditional promise to David that someone from his dynasty would sit on his throne and rule over his kingdom forever. This promise will be fulfilled only when Jesus Christ, who is in the line of David, sits on David's throne in Jerusalem ruling over Israel in the coming kingdom and on into eternity (Ezekiel 37:22–25; Amos 9:11–15; Zephaniah 3:14–17; Luke 1:30–33, 69).

God's promise to David has three components (2 Samuel 7:12–16). God promised to give David a house, a throne, and a kingdom.

1. House—this refers to David's dynasty or the royal family.
2. Throne—this refers to David's authority or right to rule.
3. Kingdom—this refers to David's realm or political kingdom, which is the nation of Israel.

These promises in the Davidic covenant concerning the king, the throne, and the kingdom can only be ultimately fulfilled by Jesus during the Millennium.

The New Covenant

At Mount Sinai God gave Moses the old covenant. Eight hundred years later through the prophet Jeremiah, God promised that He would make a new covenant someday with the house of Israel and the house of Judah (Jeremiah 31:31–34). When Jesus died on the Cross, He instituted the New Covenant in His blood. When He returns to set up His kingdom, the spiritual blessings of this covenant will be realized for Israel and Judah.

God's new covenant promise to Israel also contains a threefold promise:

1. The forgiveness of sins—God will forgive Israel for her sins.
2. The indwelling Spirit—God will place His Spirit in the hearts of the people to personally instruct them in His way (Ezekiel 36:24–26).
3. A new heart—God will give His people a new, clean heart with His law inscribed upon it.

While believers today enjoy all of these promises as a result of the new covenant in Christ's blood (Matthew 26:28), the specific promises in Jeremiah 31:31–34 will not find their ultimate fulfillment for Israel until the millennial kingdom when the Jewish people are restored to the land with Christ as their king.

To Reaffirm the Total Depravity of Man

A fourth important reason why there must be a literal millennial kingdom is to once and for all demonstrate the true nature of man. God's Word clearly teaches that man is sinful both by nature and by practice. The millennial kingdom will be the final, conclusive proof of this fact.

Satan will be bound for one thousand years while the Lord Jesus will be personally present to rule and reign on the restored earth. Yet the Bible teaches that in spite of these perfect conditions, a host of people who are born and raised during this time will reject the Lord in their hearts. They will outwardly conform to avoid the Lord's swift judgment, but inwardly they will harbor a rebellious heart against the King of kings.

When Satan is released at the end of the Millennium, he will be able to gather "a mighty host, as numberless as sand along the shore" (Revelation 20:8, NLT) to try to destroy Christ, His city, and His people. The fact that Satan is able to so quickly gather a group of rebels implies that many people during the Millennium will not really submit to the Lord in their hearts.

The millennium will prove beyond any doubt that regardless of man's heredity, circumstances, or environment, he is incorrigibly sinful apart from God's saving grace. As prophecy author J. Dwight Pentecost notes:

> The millennial age is designed by God to be the final test of fallen humanity under the most ideal circumstances, surrounded by every enablement to obey the rule of the king, from whom the outward sources of temptation have been removed, so that man may be found and proved to be a failure in even this last testing of fallen humanity.[42]

Henry Morris, author of *The Revelation Record*, adds this in his commentary on Revelation 20:7–10:

> One of the most amazing commentaries on the fallen human nature to be found in all the Word of God is right here in this passage. After one thousand years of a perfect environment, with an abundance of material possessions and spiritual instruction for everyone, no crime, no war, no external temptation to sin, with the personal presence of all the resurrected saints and even

Christ Himself, and with Satan and all his demons bound in the abyss, there are still a multitude of unsaved men and women on earth who are ready to rebel against the Lord the first time they get a chance.[43]

The Millennium is proof positive that man's heart is black with sin. It proves for all time that Christ's death on the Cross is absolutely necessary for man's salvation. The thousand-year reign of Christ provides overwhelming evidence that we must have a righteousness outside ourselves to come into relationship with a holy God. The righteousness that we need is the very righteousness of Jesus Christ. God credits that righteousness to all who receive His Son by faith (see 2 Corinthians 5:21).

EIGHTY

WHAT WILL BELIEVERS WHO RETURN TO EARTH WITH CHRIST DO DURING THE MILLENNIAL KINGDOM?

When Jesus Christ returns to earth at the Second Coming, He will bring His saints with Him (Jude 14; Revelation 19:14). After He defeats the armies of the Antichrist at Armageddon and judges the nations, He will establish His kingdom on earth. His saints will rule with Him.

While we will certainly worship Jesus and serve Him during the Millennium, the function that Scripture emphasizes is ruling and reigning with Christ. The Bible says that all believers from every age will reign with Christ for these thousand years.

Consider what these passages say about what you will be doing in the kingdom:

> But the saints of the Highest One will receive the kingdom and possess the kingdom forever, for all ages to come. The Ancient of Days came and judgment was passed in favor of the saints of the Highest One, and the time arrived when the saints took possession of the kingdom. Then the sovereignty, the dominion and the greatness of all the kingdoms under the whole heaven will be given to the people of the saints of the Highest One; His kingdom will be an everlasting kingdom, and all the dominions will serve and obey Him. (Daniel 7:18, 22, 27)

> Or do you not know that the saints will judge the world? If the world is judged by you, are you not competent to constitute the smallest law courts? Do you not know that we will judge angels? How much more matters of this life? (1 Corinthians 6:2–3)

> He who overcomes, and he who keeps My deeds until the end, to him I will give authority over the nations; and he shall rule them with a rod of iron, as the vessels of the potter are broken to

pieces, as I also have received authority from My Father; and I will give him the morning star. (Revelation 2:26–28)

Then I saw thrones, and they sat on them, and judgment was given to them. And I saw the souls of those who had been beheaded because of their testimony of Jesus and because of the word of God, and those who had not worshiped the beast or his image, and had not received the mark on their forehead and on their hand; and they came to life and reigned with Christ for a thousand years. Blessed and holy is the one who has a part in the first resurrection; over these the second death has no power, but they will be priests of God and of Christ and will reign with Him for a thousand years. (Revelation 20:4, 6)

What an exciting prospect! We will rule the nations with Christ for a thousand years on earth. We will even judge the angels.

During this present age we are being tested by God to determine our future position of authority and responsibility in the Kingdom. According to Luke 19:11–26, we will be given rulership in the kingdom based on what we did with the treasures and talents God entrusted to us in this life. Some will be governors over ten cities; some will rule over five cities. We will all reign, but the extent and responsibility of that reign is being determined right now in your life and mine. As I once heard a preacher say, "This is training time for reigning time."

I must admit that the Millennium raises many more questions than I have answers for. The Bible simply doesn't tell us everything we want to know about this bizarre era of man's history. As with other aspects of the end times, regarding the Millennium we must be satisfied with what God has chosen to reveal, and we must do the best we can to understand it and live each day in its shadow.

THE AFTERLIFE

To die would be an awfully big adventure.
PETER PAN

Not long ago I was watching a series on the Discovery channel about the ten great mysteries of the world. Some of the mysteries were the lost city of Atlantis, UFOs, Stonehenge, and the Loch Ness monster. But the number one mystery was life after death. It's a subject that everyone wonders about. In every culture throughout the history of man, people have longed to understand the mystery of death and the great beyond.

In this section we want to answer the questions that people like you and me have about the afterlife. I think you'll be amazed at how much the Bible has to say on this intriguing topic.

EIGHTY-ONE

WHAT HAPPENS TO PEOPLE WHEN THEY DIE?

More Americans than ever—81 percent according to one study[44]—now say that they believe in life after death. Since the turn of the century, belief in an afterlife among American Catholics, Jews, and those with no religious affiliation has grown significantly. However, there appears to be an equal decline in the percentage of those who understand what actually happens to people when they die.

In the Bible, death means separation. It does not mean annihilation, destruction, or ceasing to exist. A person who is *spiritually dead* is spiritually separated from God. When a person *dies physically* he does not cease to exist. There is a separation between the material part (body) and the immaterial part (soul/spirit) of the person.

When this separation occurs, the body "falls asleep" and is buried. But the immaterial part of the person immediately goes to one of two places, depending on the person's relationship with Christ. The departed spirit of a believer in Christ goes immediately into the presence of the Lord.

> Now there was a rich man, and he habitually dressed in purple and fine linen, joyously living in splendor every day. And a poor man named Lazarus was laid at his gate, covered with sores, and longing to be fed with the crumbs which were falling from the rich man's table; besides, even the dogs were coming and licking his sores. Now the poor man died and was carried away by the angels to Abraham's bosom; and the rich man also died and was buried. (Luke 16:19–22)

> "And He said to him, 'Truly I say to you, today you shall be with Me in Paradise.'" (Luke 23:43)

> We are of good courage, I say, and prefer rather to be absent from the body and to be at home with the Lord. (2 Corinthians 5:8)

For to me, to live is Christ and to die is gain. But I am hard-pressed from both directions, having the desire to depart and be with Christ, for that is very much better. (Philippians 1:21, 23)

Until the time of the Rapture, the departed believer exists in a spiritual or disembodied state. Scripture likens it to being "naked" or "unclothed" (2 Corinthians 5:1–5). When Christ comes at the Rapture, the perfected spirits of the redeemed will be reunited with their resurrected, glorified bodies (1 Thessalonians 4:14–16). The spirits of Old Testament believers will be reunited with their bodies at the end of the tribulation (Daniel 12:1–3).

The destiny of unbelievers is very different. When an unbeliever dies, his departed spirit goes immediately into Hades to experience conscious, unrelenting torment. In the parable of the rich man and Lazarus in Luke 16:19–31, Jesus tells us what happens to unbelievers at death: "The rich man also died and was buried. In Hades he lifted up his eyes, being in torment, and saw Abraham far away and Lazarus in his bosom" (Luke 16:22b–23).

At the great white throne (Revelation 20:11), the bodies of all the lost will be resurrected and joined with their spirits to appear before the Judge of the universe.

This chart is a simple reference tool to see what happens to those who have already died or will die before the Rapture.

	Old Testament Believers	Deceased New Testament Believers	All Deceased Unbelievers
Body	Asleep now; resurrected at Second Coming	Asleep now; resurrected at the Rapture	Asleep now; resurrected at the end of the Millennium
Spirit	In heaven now; joined with glorified body at Second Coming	In heaven now; joined with glorified body at the Rapture	In hades now; joined with resurrected body at the great white throne

EIGHTY-TWO

WHAT ABOUT NEAR-DEATH EXPERIENCES?

Some of the bestselling books in the last decade are about near-death experiences (NDEs). Books like *Embraced by the Light* and *Saved by the Light* have captured the attention of millions who want to peer behind death's curtain to get a sneak preview of the afterlife.

Two points about NDEs are important to understand. First, they are called "near-death" experiences, not "death" or "afterlife" experiences. The fact that the person came back from whatever state they were in seems to be proof that they didn't really die. Therefore, we shouldn't put any stock in what their stories purport to tell us about the afterlife. After all, these people were only near death, not dead. It's as ridiculous as a woman telling another woman about her "near-pregnancy" experience. You're either pregnant or you're not. Likewise, you're either dead or you're not.

As one writer in *Christianity Today* said, near-death experiences "tell us no more about death than someone who has been near Denver but never within city limits can tell us about that town. Both NDEs (near-Denver and near-death experiences) are bereft of certitude.... In both cases, more reliable maps are available."[45]

The only people who ever really came back from the dead are the few individuals in Scripture that the Lord or one of His servants raised. And none of them wrote a book about their experience or hit the talk show circuit. Even the apostle Paul, who was caught up to heaven on one occasion, did not reveal the things he saw there (2 Corinthians 12:1–5).

Second, the only reliable source of information about the afterlife is the Bible. Much of the idle speculation that is related from NDEs sounds like it has more in common with the occult and the New Age movement than the Bible. We should turn to God's Word to discover what we want to know about the afterlife, and we should be satisfied with what God has chosen to reveal to us about heaven and hell.

For anyone who wants to know more about the afterlife, I would suggest reading the parable of the rich man and Lazarus (Luke 16:19–31) and the description of heaven in Revelation 21–22.

EIGHTY-THREE

WHAT IS HELL LIKE?

USA Today's front page often features statistics that shape the nation. In 1998 the paper presented interesting numbers on how people answered the question: Is there a hell?

- 52 percent of adults are certain there's a hell.
- 27 percent think there might be.

The pollsters then asked people what they think hell will be like.

- 48 percent believe it is a real place where people suffer eternal torment.
- 46 percent say it is an anguished state of existence rather than an actual place.
- 6 percent don't know.

Many have concocted their own theories about hell. Comedian Woody Allen once said, "Hell is Manhattan at rush hour. There is no question there's an unseen world. The question is, how far is it from midtown and how late does it stay open?"

While people might make light of hell, the Bible gives us a terrifying glimpse of it, and it is no joking matter. Here are ten terrible facts about hell.

FACT 1: HELL IS A LITERAL PLACE

In the parable of the rich man and Lazarus in Luke 16:19–31, hades is pictured as a literal place where the unrighteous rich man went immediately upon his death. Eleven of the twelve times the word *gehenna* (hell) occurs in the New Testament, it is found on the lips of the Savior.

Make no mistake, Jesus believed in a literal hell. He talked about it more than did any other person in the Bible. Jesus is our primary source for what hell is like.

FACT 2: HELL IS A LITERAL PLACE DIVIDED INTO AT LEAST FOUR PARTS

There are four different words in the Greek New Testament to describe the underworld. I believe each of these words describes a unique division of the netherworld.

The Abyss or Bottomless Pit

The New Testament refers to this part of hell nine times. This is a place where some demons are presently confined who will be released for a period of five months to afflict the lost during the tribulation (Revelation 9:1–5). It is also the place where Satan will be bound for the duration of the Millennium (Revelation 20:1–3).

Tartarus

Second Peter 2:4 refers to tartarus as a place of confinement where the angels who sinned in Genesis 6:1–4 are being held until they are finally cast in the lake of fire (see also Jude 1:6–7).

Hades

The Greek New Testament refers to hades eleven times. This is the place where the souls of lost people are presently confined while they await the final day of judgment (Luke 16:23; Revelation 1:18; 20:13–14).

Gehenna

This is the most commonly used Greek word for hell in the New Testament: It is used twelve times. Gehenna is the final place of torment for Satan, demons, and all the lost (Revelation 20:10, 14–15). Gehenna is also called "the lake of fire and brimstone" (Revelation 20:10), "the lake of fire" (Revelation 20:14), and "the second death" (Revelation 20:6, 14). It is called the second death because it is a place of final, eternal separation from God.

FACT 3: HELL IS A PLACE OF MEMORY

In hell there will be continued consciousness and immediate awareness of where one is. In Luke 16:19–31, the rich man knew immediately *where* he was. He also remembered *who* he was, implying that personal identity will remain. And there will be memory: The rich man recognized Lazarus and remembered his own brothers.

Fact 4: Hell Is a Place of Torment

The worst part of hell is that there will be torment and agony. The rich man said, "I am in agony in this flame" (Luke 16:24). He described hades as "this place of torment" (Luke 16:28).

Fact 5: Hell Is a Place of Unquenchable Fire

"I am in agony in this flame." Those were the rich man's words as he languished in hades (Luke 16:24b). The New Testament is clear that hell will be a fire.

> "The Son of Man will send forth His angels, and they will gather out of His kingdom all stumbling blocks, and those who commit lawlessness, and will throw them into the furnace of fire; in that place there will be weeping and gnashing of teeth." (Matthew 13:41–42)

> If your eye causes you to stumble, throw it out; it is better for you to enter the kingdom of God with one eye, than, having two eyes, to be cast into hell, where THEIR WORM DOES NOT DIE, AND THE FIRE IS NOT QUENCHED. For everyone will be salted with fire. (Mark 9:47–49)

Fact 6: Hell Is a Place of Separation from God

Those who do not choose Christ as Lord and Savior will spend eternity apart from Him.

> These will pay the penalty of eternal destruction, away from the presence of the Lord and from the glory of His power. (2 Thessalonians 1:9)

Fact 7: Hell Is a Place of Unspeakable Misery, Sorrow, Anger, and Frustration

The Bible indicates that hell is a furnace of fire where "there will be weeping and gnashing of teeth" (Matthew 13:42).

Fact 8: Hell Is a Place of Raging Thirst

Jesus' parable indicates that those in hell will be tortured by unquenchable thirst:

And he cried out and said, "Father Abraham, have mercy on me, and send Lazarus so that he may dip the tip of his finger in water and cool off my tongue, for I am in agony in this flame." (Luke 16:24)

FACT 9: HELL IS THE ONLY OTHER PLACE TO SPEND ETERNITY BESIDES HEAVEN

There are only two places people go after death: paradise or perdition. The rich man went to hades; Lazarus went to heaven. There is no third choice. These are still the only two options today.

FACT 10: HELL IS A PLACE FROM WHICH THERE IS NO ESCAPE

Nothing can change one's fate after death. There is no purgatory, no second chance, no parole for good behavior, and no graduation. As the old saying goes, "As death finds us, eternity keeps us. Hell is truth seen too late."

The lost can never come to heaven. The saved can never end up in hell. Remember Abraham's words to the rich man in hades: "And besides all this, between us and you there is a great chasm fixed, so that those who wish to come over from here to you will not be able, and that none may cross over from there to us" (Luke 16:26).

Hell is a place of eternal destiny!

The only way of escape from this terrible place is through Jesus Christ. On the cross He bore God's full wrath against your sin and mine. He paid the price for our eternal salvation.

Won't you come to Him today?

EIGHTY-FOUR

IS PUNISHMENT IN HELL ETERNAL?

The Thinker, Rodin's famous statue, sits in mute amazement, contemplating the fate of lost souls cast into hell. Thinking about hell should have the same effect on us. The doctrine of hell is undoubtedly the most disturbing subject in the Bible. And the most disturbing truth about hell is its duration.

The idea of people being punished for their misdeeds doesn't bother most people. But the notion that hell will last forever can be totally repugnant to those same people. For this reason, many have tried to soften this truth by adopting a "kinder, gentler" view of hell. They do this in spite of the fact that eternal judgment is one of the elementary teachings of the Bible (Hebrews 6:1–2). That the lost are eternally consigned to hell is part of the spiritual ABCs every believer should understand and believe.

Two erroneous views of the fate of the lost have become popular in recent years. The first of these views is Annihilationism. This is the idea that all souls are created immortal but that the wicked lose their immortality at the final judgment. Their candle is extinguished; their souls are annihilated by God. For annihilationists, the punishment for the lost is permanent extinction.

The second incorrect view is Conditional Immortality. This view teaches that human souls are not inherently immortal. At the judgment the wicked pass into oblivion, which is the natural expectation of all souls, but the righteous are granted immortality.

While both of these views are certainly more appealing to the human mind, the Bible clearly teaches that punishment in hell will last forever.

The Greek word *aionios,* which is translated "eternal" or "everlasting," is used seventy-one times in the New Testament. Fifty-one times it is used of the happiness of the saved in heaven. It is used of both the quality and quantity of the life that believers will experience with God. The word is used another two times of the duration of God in His glory (Romans 16:26; 1 Peter 5:10). One time it is used of the duration of the Holy Spirit (Hebrews 9:14). Ten other times it is used in such a way that no one would question that it means forever (2 Corinthians 4:17–18; 5:1; 2 Peter

2:10). Seven times it is used of the fate of the wicked, and there should be no doubt to an objective mind that in those passages the word signifies time without end (Matthew 18:8; Mark 3:29).

One of the clearest references in the New Testament to the eternality of punishment in hell is in Revelation 14:

> "He also will drink of the wine of the wrath of God, which is mixed in full strength in the cup of His anger; and he will be tormented with fire and brimstone in the presence of the holy angels and in the presence of the Lamb. And the smoke of their torment goes up forever and ever; they have no rest day and night, those who worship the beast and his image, and whoever receives the mark of his name." (Revelation 14:10–11)

In Matthew 25:46, both heaven and hell are described as being eternal: "These [the wicked] will go away into eternal punishment, but the righteous into eternal life." Therefore, if we want to say that eternal punishment is limited for the damned, we must also be willing to say that eternal life is limited for the saved.

I copied these words from a sermon by Charles Spurgeon many years ago. They capture the heart-wrenching despair of hell's eternality:

> In hell there is no hope. They have not even the hope of dying; the hope of being annihilated. They are forever, forever, forever lost. On every chain in hell is written "forever." Up above their heads they read "forever." Their eyes are galled and their hearts are pained with the thought that it is "forever." Oh, if I could tell you tonight that hell would one day be burned out, and that those who were lost might be saved, there would be a jubilee in hell at the very thought of it. But it cannot be. It is forever. They are cast into outer darkness.

Knowing what terrible judgment awaits the lost should cause us to plead earnestly with them to be reconciled to God (2 Corinthians 5:20–21).

EIGHTY-FIVE

WILL EVERYONE BE PUNISHED THE SAME IN HELL?

Since God is a God of justice, His punishment will fit the crime. The Bible seems to teach that there will be degrees of punishment in hell for unbelievers based on the amount and nature of the sin committed and the light that was refused.

Jesus Himself taught that there will be degrees of punishment in the day of judgment: "Truly I say to you, it will be more tolerable for the land of Sodom and Gomorrah in the day of judgment than for that city" (Matthew 10:15).

He made similar statements elsewhere:

Then He began to denounce the cities in which most of His miracles were done, because they did not repent. "Woe to you, Chorazin! Woe to you, Bethsaida! For if the miracles had occurred in Tyre and Sidon which occurred in you, they would have repented long ago in sackcloth and ashes. Nevertheless I say to you, it will be more tolerable for Tyre and Sidon in the day of judgment than for you. And you, Capernaum, will not be exalted to heaven, will you? You will descend to hades; for if the miracles had occurred in Sodom which occurred in you, it would have remained to this day. Nevertheless I say to you that it will be more tolerable for the land of Sodom in the day of judgment, than for you." (Matthew 11:20–24)

The master of that slave will come on a day when he does not expect him and at an hour he does not know, and will cut him in pieces, and assign him a place with the unbelievers. And that slave who knew his master's will and did not get ready or act in accord with his will, will receive many lashes, but the one who did not know it, and committed deeds worthy of a flogging, will receive but few. From everyone who has been given much, much will be required; and to whom they entrusted much, of him they will ask all the more. (Luke 12:46–48)

At the great white throne Judgment, the Lord will open "the books" which contain all the deeds of the lost (Revelation 20:11–12). From these books, the Lord will tailor the exact punishment to meet the crime.

EIGHTY-SIX

IS HEAVEN A REAL PLACE?

In a *Time* magazine article, "Does Heaven Exist?" (3-24-97), people were asked questions about heaven. Here are a few of the responses:

Do you believe in the existence of heaven, where people live forever with God after they die?

- Yes, 81 percent.
- No, 13 percent.

Where do you believe you will go when you die?

- Heaven, 68 percent.
- Hell, 3 percent.

Which of the following do you believe are in heaven?

- Angels, 93 percent.
- St. Peter, 79 percent.
- Harps, 43 percent.
- Halos, 36 percent.

The word *heaven* occurs over five hundred times in the Bible. It is used to describe three different "heavens" that exist. Contrary to popular belief, there is no seventh heaven. The first heaven is the atmospheric heaven (the sky), the second is the stellar or celestial heaven (outer space), and the third is the divine heaven (the abode of God).

When we talk about heaven we are usually referring to the divine heaven or third heaven—the dwelling place of God. The Bible tells us that this heaven is just as real as the first and second heavens that we can see.

There are six reasons why I believe it is a literal place that exists right now:

1. Jesus called heaven "My Father's house" and said He was going there to prepare a "place" for His people (John 14:1–3).

2. Heaven is described in detail as a literal place with walls, gates, foundations, and a street (Revelation 21:9–22:5).
3. Jesus taught that heaven is the present abode or dwelling place of God (Matthew 10:32–33).
4. Paul visited the third heaven where God dwells (2 Corinthians 12:2).
5. Our citizenship is in heaven (Philippians 3:20–21). It wouldn't make sense that our citizenship is in the sky or in outer space. Therefore this must mean the abode of God.
6. Heaven is called a city and our heavenly homeland (Hebrews 11:16).

The story is told of an old missionary named Samuel Morrison who, after twenty-five years in Africa, was returning to the United States to die. As it so happened, he traveled home on the same ocean liner that brought President Teddy Roosevelt back from a hunting expedition.

When the great ship pulled into the New York harbor, the dock where it was to tie up was jammed with what looked like the entire population of New York City. Bands were playing, banners were waving, choirs of children were singing, multicolored balloons were floating in the air, flashbulbs were popping, and newsreel cameras were poised to record the return of the president.

Mr. Roosevelt stepped down the gangplank to thunderous cheers and applause, showered with confetti and ticker tape. If the crowd had not been restrained by ropes and police, he would have been mobbed.

At the same time, Samuel Morrison quietly walked off the boat. No one was there to greet him. He slipped through the crowd alone and unnoticed. Because of the crowd of people there to welcome the president, he couldn't even find a cab. In his heart, he began to complain, "Lord, the president has been in Africa for three weeks, killing animals, and the whole world turns out to welcome him home! I've given twenty-five years of my life in Africa, serving You, and no one has greeted me or even knows I'm here."

In the quietness of his heart, a gentle, loving voice whispered, But My dear child, you are not home yet!

Home!

Heaven is a real place, and it's our true home.[46]

EIGHTY-SEVEN

WHY SHOULD I SPEND TIME THINKING ABOUT HEAVEN?

Many people today spend little or no time thinking about the hereafter. The prevailing attitude today seems to be "heaven can wait." You even find this attitude overtaking the church as well. In churches there is little talk about heaven. No singing about heaven. No excitement about heaven. I even hear Christians sometimes say that you can be so heavenly minded that you're of no earthly good.

Martin Marty, the respected University of Chicago religious historian, says:

> I can recall from my [Lutheran] childhood many sermons on what used to be called the geography of heaven and the temperature of hell. Now the only time you hear of heaven is when somebody has died.[47]

David Wells, a theology professor at Gordon-Conwell Theological Seminary, notes:

> We would expect to hear of it in the Evangelical churches, but I don't hear it at all. I don't think heaven is even a blip on the Christian screen, from one end of the denominational spectrum to the other.[48]

But this is not the picture the Bible paints about what our attitude toward heaven should be. God's Word says heaven will be our eternal home, therefore shouldn't we be deeply interested in what it is like? The greater part of the Bible's last two chapters is devoted to the subject of heaven (Revelation 21:1–22:5).

Think of it in terms of moving to a new city. What do you do when you finally decide you are moving? You visit the new area: You check out the neighborhoods, the schools, the climate, the churches, the restaurants, the athletic fields, the shopping areas, and the entertainment options. You discover everything you can about the new place in advance. Why?

Because it's going to be your new home.

Heaven will be our eternal home. It's only natural that we should want to know all we can about the place where we're going to spend eternity. Besides, God's Word implores us, "Set your mind on the things above, not on the things that are on earth" (Colossians 3:2).

Thinking about heaven has at least five practical effects on our lives here on earth:

1. Focusing on heaven restores our hope in times of suffering (Romans 8:18).
2. Focusing on heaven reassures us that God is on the throne (Revelation 4:1–3).
3. Focusing on heaven reminds us that this world is not all there is (Philippians 3:20).
4. Focusing on heaven refocuses us on the nature of true treasure (Matthew 6:19–21).
5. Focusing on heaven reignites our fervor to serve the Lord (Isaiah 6:1–8).

Being heavenly minded is really the only thing that will make us of any earthly good. C. S. Lewis had it right:

If you read history you will find that the Christians who did the most for the present world were just those who thought most of the next. The Apostles themselves, who set on foot the conversion of the Roman Empire, the great men who built up the Middle Ages, the English evangelicals who abolished the slave trade, all left their mark on earth, precisely because their minds were occupied with Heaven. It is since Christians have largely ceased to think of the other world that they have become so ineffective in this one. Aim at Heaven and you will get earth "thrown in." Aim at earth and you will get neither.[49]

EIGHTY-EIGHT

WHAT WILL HEAVEN BE LIKE?

There's a story about a television producer for the British Broadcasting Corporation who was preparing a documentary about Christianity in England. In the course of his research, he sent a memo to a clergyman who served as an adviser to the BBC on church affairs. The memo read, "How might I ascertain the official church view of heaven and hell?" The clergyman replied with a memo consisting of only one word: "Die."

Happily, we do not have to die to discover God's truth about heaven. We know from God's Word that there is a place where believers will live with God forever. But what else does the Bible tell us about this amazing place?

Revelation 21–22 tell us most of what we know about the eternal state. Though these chapters only give us the briefest of glimpses, they do reveal five key aspects of what heaven will be like.

THE SPLENDOR OF HEAVEN

Heaven will be a glorious, splendid place, both because of what is there and what is not there. There are eleven things that won't be there: sea, sin, death, mourning, crying, pain, night, temple, curse, sun, or moon. The main thing that *will* be there is the glory of God (Revelation 21:11, 23). Heaven will be ablaze with God's radiance. The dazzling brilliance of the Lord will shine and glimmer in the city like a diamond.

THE SIGHTS OF HEAVEN

Heaven is pictured in the Bible as a huge city called the New Jerusalem. It will come down out of heaven to sit on the new earth as the capital city of the new heaven and new earth. Here's a guided tour of the seven key sights in the New Jerusalem (from Revelation 21:9–22:5).

The Wall

The wall is 216 feet thick and 1,500 miles high (seven million feet). The wall tells us that heaven is a place of security.

The Gates

Each of heaven's twelve gates is each made of a single pearl. Every gate is guarded by an angel (there is no mention of Peter at the pearly gates). And each one is inscribed with one of the names of the twelve tribes of Israel. The gates speak of the access of heaven.

The Foundation

Each of the twelve foundation stones is fashioned from a different precious stone. Each is inscribed with one of the names of the twelve apostles. The foundation illustrates heaven's stability and permanence.

The Street

There is only one street in heaven (Main Street). It is made of gold so pure it is like transparent glass. The street reveals that heaven is a place of movement and travel.

The River

A river literally runs through it. The river brings eternal refreshment.

The Throne

God is seated on His throne as the monarch of the universe. The throne reveals God's sovereignty.

The Tree

Man was banned from the tree of life in Genesis 3, but access to the tree is restored in the heavenly paradise in Revelation 2:7 and 22:2.

THE SIZE OF HEAVEN

The size of the heavenly city is 1,500 miles on each side. To give you a sense of scale, the moon is 2,160 miles in diameter. So the city is like an enormous floating continent almost as big as the moon coming down to settle on the new earth.

The shape of the city is a perfect cube. The city contains 2.25 million square miles—or 3,375,000,000 cubic miles—of space. It has enough room to accommodate 100,000 billion people. There will be plenty of room in heaven.

THE SUBSTANCE OF HEAVEN

Heaven won't have any cinder blocks, shag carpet, or particle board doors. Only the best materials in the universe will do for the dwelling place of our glorious God. Here is an overview of the building materials God will use (Revelation 21:11–21).

Object	Material
Wall	Diamond
City	Pure gold
Foundation	Diamond, sapphire (blue), chalcedony (greenish blue), emerald (green), sardonyx (layered stone of red and white), sardius (fiery red), chrysolite (golden yellow), beryl (sea green), topaz (greenish yellow), chrysoprase (gold green), jacinth (violet), and amethyst (purple quartz)
Gates	Twelve pearls
Street	Pure gold

THE SANCTITY OF HEAVEN

There's an old Negro spiritual that says, "Everybody talkin' 'bout heaven ain't goin there." The sanctity of heaven refers to its holiness and separation. Heaven will be a sanctified place where no evil will be present. The list of those who will be excluded is found three times in the final two chapters of Revelation (21:8, 27; 22:15). Not everyone will be there.

The only people who will be there are those whose names are found in the Lamb's Book of Life. This book is heaven's register of all the lost sinners who have given up on saving themselves and have trusted Jesus Christ alone to be their Savior from sin.

The story is told of a Philadelphia law firm that sent flowers to an associate law firm in Baltimore upon hearing of its new offices. Through some mix-up, the ribbon that bedecked the floral piece read, "Deepest Sympathy."

When the florist was informed of his mistake, he let out a cry of alarm. "Good heavens," he exclaimed, "then the flowers that went to the funeral said, 'Congratulations on your new location!'"

Heaven will be a wonderful new location.

EIGHTY-NINE

WILL WE KNOW EACH OTHER IN HEAVEN?

Almost every person has probably asked this question at one time or another. We want to know if we will recognize our friends and loved ones in heaven and if they will know us. Interestingly, in a recent survey, less than 50 percent of the respondents believed they would recognize friends, relatives, or their spouses in heaven.

Well, I've got good news for you: I believe we will not only see our friends and loved ones in heaven, we will know them. In fact, we won't really know each other *until* we get to heaven. Only in heaven, when all the masks and façades are torn away, will we really know one another and enjoy intimate, unhindered fellowship.

The main passage that reveals our ability to recognize each other in heaven is Luke 19:19–31. In that parable the rich man recognizes Lazarus in heaven and remembers all the facts about their relationship on earth. The rich man even remembers his five brothers who are still on earth.

Scripture indicates we will even recognize people we never met here on earth. At the transfiguration of Jesus, Peter knew that the two men with Jesus were Elijah and Moses (Matthew 17:1-4). Obviously, Peter had never met Moses and Elijah. How did he know who they were? It appears that he had an intuitive knowledge that enabled him to know immediately who they were. I believe that it will be the same way in heaven. All of the Lord's people will possess this intuitive knowledge in heaven that will enable us to recognize our friends and loved ones as well as the redeemed of all the ages. We will never meet a stranger in heaven!

NINETY

WHAT WILL WE DO IN HEAVEN?

This really is a most asked question about heaven. I've heard it asked these ways, too: "Will there be football in heaven?" "Will I be able to golf in heaven?" "Will I get bored in heaven?" "Will I sit around all day on a cloud strumming a harp?" Most people seem to view heaven as a place of inactivity and endless boredom. As Rudyard Kipling wrote:

> When earth's last picture is painted
>   and the tubes are twisted and dried;
> When the oldest colors have faded
>   and the youngest critic has died;
> We shall rest, and faith, we shall need it,
>   lay down for an eon or two,
> 'Til the Master of all good workmen
>   shall put us to work anew.

This is a kind of "Rip Van Winkle" view of heaven.

Children have their own perspectives on heaven. Here is how a few children responded to the question, "What do you do in heaven?"

- "You can do anything you want, silly!"
- "You can eat candy, and don't get fat or cavities."
- "You water-skate all day long!" declared one squirmy first grader. When asked, "What's water-skating?" she smiled shyly and replied, "You'll find out."
- "You can stay up all day and all night, and your parents can't make you go to bed because there aren't any—beds. There *are* parents."
- "You help people on earth be smarter."
- "You play the harp all day, whether you like it or not."
- "You have to paint clouds."
- "Most of the time you try to get dry because it seems like it's always raining in heaven."[50]

Before we consider what we will do in heaven, I believe it is important to see at least a little bit of what we won't do in heaven. It's going to be great: We will never sin, make mistakes, need to confess, or have to repair anything (no leaky faucets, no burned-out lightbulbs, no broken-down cars). We will never have to rescue others; defend ourselves; apologize; experience guilt; battle with Satan, demons, or the flesh; defend the gospel of Jesus Christ; be healed or rehabilitated; or experience loneliness, depression, or fatigue.

While the Bible doesn't tell us as much as we would like to know about what we will do in heaven, it does focus on six main things we will do. These provide us with a basic job description. In heaven, we'll be singing, serving, supervising, sharing, studying, and being served.

SINGING (REVELATION 4:10-11; 7:7-12; 11:15-17; 14:3; 15:2-4; 19:4-6)

Robert E. Coleman, a renowned scholar in missions and evangelism, relates this beautiful story:

> In some of the medieval monasteries following the custom in the temple of Israel, it was a rule that hymns of praise to God would never cease. When one of the monks would stop singing, another would pick up the song. Thus, day and night, the joyous sound was heard.
>
> On one occasion a monastery was overrun by a band of Norse raiders. They slaughtered the monks without mercy, including the one who was singing. However, one monk was able to escape and hide in an inaccessible spot, where the attackers were not likely to find him. But when he heard the songs of praise cease, instinctively he took it up, thus betraying his place of refuge.[51]

Heaven is a place of unending worship. Even those who can't carry a tune in a bucket here on earth will be able to sing rapturously in heaven. There will be many songs we won't sing in heaven, such as "When We All Get to Heaven" or "Sweet Hour of Prayer." But I'm sure we will still sing "Great is Thy Faithfulness," "All Hail the Power of Jesus' Name," and "O Worship the King."

Heaven is a place of singing.

Serving (Revelation 1:6; 7:15; 19:5; 22:3)

It's been estimated that there are at least 40,000 different occupations in the United States. Yet very few people are satisfied with their jobs. Personnel problems, inadequate pay, and wearisome hours of routine tasks are just some of the reasons for this dissatisfaction.

However, these problems will be behind us forever in heaven. Every one of us will find full satisfaction as we serve the Lord in the various occupations He has for us in glory. The precise areas of serving the Lord are never clearly spelled out in the Bible, but we can rest assured that every person will have a job specially designed for him by the King.

Supervising (Matthew 25:21; Revelation 22:5)

In the Garden of Eden, Adam and Eve were to rule over the wonderful creation God had made. In the same way, God's people will reign forever over the new heaven and new earth as servant-kings. Creation will come full circle.

Again there are no specifics as to how this will be carried out. We will have to wait until we get to heaven to get our specific job description. But we know we will reign with Christ forever. What a prospect! (See also Luke 19:17–19; 1 Corinthians 6:3; 2 Timothy 2:12; Revelation 3:20–21; 20:4.)

Sharing (1 John 3:2; Revelation 22:4)

In the novel *Pilgrim's Progress*, the hero, Christian, is asked why he has such a strong desire to go to heaven. He responds, "Why, there I hope to see him alive, that did hang dead on the Cross; and there I hope to be rid of all those things that to this day are in me an annoyance to me; there they say there is no death, and there I shall dwell with such company as I like best." Christian desired to go to heaven to be with Christ and enjoy the company of fellow believers.

Have you ever wondered what it would be like to be a member of a perfect church? We will find out in heaven. The fellowship in heaven will be sweet—first with our precious Lord as we share intimate communion with Him, and then with one another.

Nineteenth-century hymn writer Fanny Crosby wrote a beautiful song called "My Savior First of All." Its words are especially poignant because Crosby was born blind.

When my life work is ended, and I cross the swelling tide,
When the bright and glorious morning I shall see,
I shall know my Redeemer when I reach the other side,
And His smile will be the first to welcome me. . . .

Thru the gates of the city in a robe of spotless white,
He will lead me where no tears will ever fall;
In the glad songs of ages I shall mingle with delight
But I long to meet my Savior first of all.

When Fanny Crosby died, I believe the first person she saw—had ever seen—was Jesus Christ. What will our relationship be with the Lord in heaven? We will *see* Him and be with Him. That will be our ultimate satisfaction.

STUDYING (1 CORINTHIANS 13:12)

God's children will spend eternity learning more about God and His ways. God will always be infinite, and we will always be finite. Therefore, we will always be learning more about the wonders and majesty of our great God.

BEING SERVED (LUKE 12:35-37)

It may surprise you to learn that Scripture contains no mention of believers serving each other in heaven—only of us serving God and Him serving us. Luke 12:37 says that when the Lord of Glory comes He "will gird himself to serve, and have them recline at the table, and will come up and wait on them." Ever the servant, the Lord Jesus will wait on us, His beloved bride, and meet our needs forever.

While the jury is still out on golf, chocolate, and "water-skating" in heaven, we do know we will be singing, serving, supervising, sharing, studying, and being served. I don't know about you, but I can't wait.

Ninety-one

ARE THERE REWARDS IN HEAVEN?

Some people have a difficult time accepting the idea that God will give out rewards for faithful service. To them it turns the Christian life into a mercenary activity. Nevertheless, the Bible teaches that God will reward believers according to their works. God is not only a judge but also a rewarder.

Consider these passages on rewards: Psalms 58:11; 62:12; Proverbs 11:18; Isaiah 40:10; 62:11; Matthew 5:12; 6:1–2; 10:4–42; Luke 6:35; 1 Corinthians 3:8, 14; Ephesians 6:8; Hebrews 10:35–36; 11:6, 24–26; 2 John 1:8; Revelation 2:23; 11:18; 22:12.

Just as there will be degrees of punishment in hell for the lost, there will be different degrees of reward in heaven for the Lord's people (Luke 19:11–27; 1 Corinthians 3:10–15).

God will reward church-age believers at what the Bible calls the "judgment seat of Christ" (2 Corinthians 5:10). This judgment will occur immediately after the Rapture (1 Corinthians 4:5).

The purpose of the judgment seat of Christ is not to determine whether people will enter heaven or hell. This issue was already decided when the person believed in Jesus Christ as their Savior from sin. Nor is this judgment for the purpose of meting out punishment for sin. God's Word is clear that His children will never be judged for their sins (John 5:24).

The purpose of the judgment seat of Christ is to review our lives, service, thoughts, words, and motives after we became a Christian—and for Christ to either give or withhold rewards based on His perfect evaluation (Matthew 12:36; 1 Corinthians 4:5; Hebrews 4:13).

CROWNS AS REWARDS

While there are undoubtedly many areas of service, conduct, and ministry that will bring reward, the New Testament focuses on five specific rewards, or crowns, that the faithful will receive at the judgment seat. These crowns are representative of the kinds of conduct and service that will be rewarded by the Lord.

The Incorruptible Crown (1 Corinthians 9:24–27)
This is a reward for those who consistently practice self-discipline and self-control over their physical appetites.

The Crown of Righteousness (2 Timothy 4:8)
A reward for those who eagerly look for the Lord's coming and live a righteous life in view of this expectation.

The Crown of Life (James 1:12; Revelation 2:10)
The sufferer's crown is given to those who faithfully endure and persevere under the trials and tests of life.

The Crown of Rejoicing (1 Thessalonians 2:19)
The soul-winner's crown is given to those who lead people to accept Jesus as their Lord and Savior.

The Crown of Glory (1 Peter 5:1–4)
The crown of glory could be called the shepherd's crown. It is given to those pastors, elders, and church leaders who lovingly oversee God's people.

AN EMBARRASSMENT OF RICHES

What will we do with these crowns? Will we wear them around the streets of gold to show off? Will we compare them to the number of crowns others have received?

Not quite. The Bible is clear that the redeemed, having been rewarded by the Lord, will immediately give all glory and honor for their rewards to the Lord. After receiving these rewards in heaven at the judgment seat, we will fall down and worship the Lord, lay our crowns in front of His throne, and praise Him with all our hearts:

> And they lay their crowns before the throne and say, "You are worthy, O Lord our God, to receive glory and honor and power. For you created everything, and it is for your pleasure that they exist and were created." (Revelation 4:10b–11, NLT)

NINETY-TWO

WHAT KIND OF BODIES WILL WE HAVE IN HEAVEN?

All of us look forward to getting a new body in heaven. This is especially true of those who suffer from one or more of "the five B's of old age": baldness, bifocals, bridges, bulges, and bunions. All of us come to a point in life when we look in the mirror and say, "Mirror, mirror on the wall—you've got to be kidding!"

As our outer man begins to fall apart, we begin to groan for glory. We eagerly anticipate our new, remodeled, perfect body in heaven. As Paul writes in 2 Corinthians:

> For we know that if the earthly tent which is our house is torn down, we have a building from God, a house not made with hands, eternal in the heavens. For indeed in this house we groan, longing to be clothed with our dwelling from heaven. (2 Corinthians 5:1–2)

When we think about our resurrection bodies we often have more questions than answers. Though the Bible doesn't satisfy our curiosity about every detail, it does give us a basic idea of what our new, glorified bodies will be like. We know, for instance, that our new bodies will be similar to the resurrected, glorified body of Jesus.

> For our citizenship is in heaven, from which also we eagerly wait for a Savior, the Lord Jesus Christ; who will transform the body of our humble state into conformity with the body of His glory, by the exertion of the power that He has even to subject all things to Himself. (Philippians 3:20–21)

> Beloved, now we are children of God, and it has not appeared as yet what we will be. We know that when He appears, we will be like Him, because we will see Him just as He is. (1 John 3:2)

What was Christ's resurrection body like? He ate food. He had scars. He must've looked somewhat like He did in life because He was recognized by His disciples. He was not limited by space, walls, or locked doors. On two separate occasions, Jesus came right through the walls of the room where the disciples were meeting (John 21:19, 26).

Our future bodies will be just like Jesus' resurrection body. We will be able to do the same things He did.

First Corinthians 15 is the classic passage on what our glorified bodies will be like:

> But someone may ask, "How will the dead be raised? What kind of bodies will they have?" It is the same way for the resurrection of the dead. Our earthly bodies, which die and decay, will be different when they are resurrected, for they will never die. Our bodies now disappoint us, but when they are raised, they will be full of glory. They are weak now, but when they are raised, they will be full of power. They are natural human bodies now, but when they are raised, they will be spiritual bodies. For just as there are natural bodies, so also there are spiritual bodies.
>
> The Scriptures tell us, "The first man, Adam, became a living person." But the last Adam—that is, Christ—is a life-giving Spirit. What came first was the natural body, then the spiritual body comes later. Adam, the first man, was made from the dust of the earth, while Christ, the second man, came from heaven. Every human being has an earthly body just like Adam's, but our heavenly bodies will be just like Christ's. Just as we are now like Adam, the man of the earth, so we will someday be like Christ, the man from heaven. (1 Corinthians 15:35, 42–49, NLT)

From this passage we can draw seven clues about our resurrected bodies.

SEVEN FABULOUS FACTS ABOUT OUR FUTURE BODIES

1. They will be imperishable—they will never decay or die.
2. They will be heavenly bodies—they will be perfectly suitable to our new environment.
3. Each person's body will be distinct from all others "as star differs from star"—each will be unique (1 Corinthians 15:41–42a).
4. They will be glorious—"full of glory."
5. They will be powerful.

6. They will be spiritual.
7. They will be just like Christ's resurrection body.

The best thing about our new body is number four from the list. First Corinthians 15:43 says that our new bodies will be *full of glory.* To me this indicates that our resurrection bodies will be so wonderful and glorious that it will be exactly what we have always dreamed of in a body. It will never disappoint us.

If you're like me, you probably have one part of your body (or maybe several parts) that you would like to change. Maybe it's your weight, your height, your hair, or something about your face. To make it worse, our culture bombards us daily with images of beautiful, well-built people.

But in heaven, there will be no fad diets, no Weight Watchers, no aerobics, no exercise bikes, no personal trainers, no physical therapists, no StairMasters, no weight rooms, no saunas, no jogging tracks, no low-fat foods, no diet drinks, and no plastic surgeons. God will give every one of His children a glorious, unique, diverse, perfect new body at the Rapture that will never fail or disappoint them.

Our new bodies will be glorious!

NINETY-THREE

HOW OLD WILL WE BE IN HEAVEN?

The Bible never explicitly tells us how old we will be in heaven, so answering this question requires a bit of sanctified speculation. It appears from Genesis that God created Adam and Eve as adults. That is, they were not created as children who went through the normal stages of physical development. Adam and Eve were presumably created at the optimal stage of physical development, because God declared them "very good" (Genesis 1:31).

When Jesus died, He was resurrected at the prime of His physical development. Since scholars now believe that Jesus was born in about 5 B.C. and probably was crucified in A.D. 33, He was at least thirty-five years old when He died and possibly as old as thirty-eight or thirty-nine. When He was resurrected He came back in a body that was recognizable by His followers, so it must have appeared to be about the same age as when they knew Him.

As we have already established, when we receive our resurrection bodies they will be like Jesus' resurrection body (see Philippians 3:20–21). This may mean that we will appear at the same age Jesus appeared in His resurrection body. Whatever it means, we can at least know that our resurrection bodies will be perfect. There will be absolutely no deformities (though scars may remain).

What we can safely say is that the Lord will give us a body that reflects how we looked in the prime of our earthly life. For those who died before they reached the prime of life, the Lord, who knows all things, will give them a body that reflects how they would have appeared at the optimal stage of development in their life.

NINETY-FOUR

WHAT WILL HAPPEN TO PEOPLE WHOSE BODIES WERE CREMATED?

Cremation has become an increasingly popular means for disposing of the physical bodies of the dead. It is estimated that by the year 2010, the percentage of those families choosing cremation for their lost ones will rise to 34 percent.[52]

Hank Hanegraaff, president of the Christian Research Institute, gives three key reasons why believers should choose burial over cremation:

1. Scripture clearly favors burial over cremation in both the Old and New Testaments. Jesus was buried, and our baptism is equated with both burial and resurrection (Romans 6:4).
2. Burial symbolizes the promise of resurrection by anticipating the preservation of the body, while cremation symbolizes the pagan worldview of reincarnation.
3. Burial highlights the sanctity of the human body (Genesis 1:27; 1 Corinthians 6:13, 19–20).[53]

I am against cremation. The reason I oppose it is not because I think God will have some difficulty in resurrecting a cremated body, but rather because I believe burial is the biblical way to honor the sanctity of the body as created by God. However, having said this, I recognize that some believers disagree and have no qualms about choosing cremation as the method for dealing with their body after death. That's okay with me.

Whatever view one takes on the subject of cremation, all believers recognize that God has no problem resurrecting a cremated body. The body of every true believer who has been cremated will be resurrected with the bodies of believers who have been buried, burned, drowned, or devoured. God knows the location of every atom. At the Rapture He will resurrect the body of every one of His children regardless of where their body is or what happened to it after death. "The dead will be raised imperishable" (1 Corinthians 15:52). There are no exceptions!

Ninety-five

How can believers enjoy heaven knowing that people are in hell?

I must confess I have asked myself this question many times. It is a difficult question. After all, we know that heaven is a place of joy, happiness, and delight. There the Lord will wipe away every tear from their eyes. Yet how can we enjoy heaven but experience no sorrow for those in hell—especially those we know and love?

One solution to this apparent dilemma is to conclude that in heaven the Lord will purge our memory of our loved ones and friends and the existence of hell. Several verses have been used to support this position: Deuteronomy 25:19; Psalms 9:5; Psalms 69:28; Psalms 109:13. The main support for this view is drawn from Isaiah 65:

> "For behold, I create new heavens and a new earth;
> And the former things will not be remembered or come to mind.
> But be glad and rejoice forever in what I create;
> For behold, I create Jerusalem for rejoicing
> And her people for gladness.
> I will also rejoice in Jerusalem and be glad in My people;
> And there will no longer be heard in her
> The voice of weeping and the sound of crying."
> (Isaiah 65:17–19)

While these verses could support this idea, the main point of the passage appears to be that in our future state everything will be so wonderful that we will forget the sorrows of this life. But forgetting sorrows because of the joy before us is not the same as forgetting everyone we ever knew. To say that believers in heaven will no longer remember people they knew on earth or even the fact that hell exists is to say that in heaven we will know less than we knew on earth. The Bible seems to teach the opposite.

The best solution to the problem is to recognize that in heaven we will have a perfected spirit with an ability to see things clearly from the divine perspective. In heaven we will know about hell and that people we love are there, but we will also be in the presence of the holy God and we will know that those who rejected Him do not deserve to be in His presence. For the first time in our lives we will fully see sin in the light of His holiness and will understand the extent of what it means for the lost to be Christ-rejecting enemies of God who spurned His gracious offer of salvation.

We will realize that we do not deserve to be in His presence, either. We will understand both His undiminished justice and His undeserved mercy. And in recognizing them we will spend eternity thanking Him for our salvation—and we will understand at least in some measure His righteous, eternal punishment of the lost.

Ninety-six

Will there be animals in heaven?

This question has taken on a special meaning for me. During the week I was writing this chapter my family had to have our dog put to sleep. Roi had been our family pet for six years. He was a loyal, playful Welsh Corgi. He developed lymphatic sarcoma, and we finally decided to bring an end to his suffering. After Roi died my sons asked me: "Dad, will Roi be in heaven?"

It's interesting to me that I have been asked about animals in heaven many times by people of all ages. This issue stirs up a great deal of emotion for those who deeply love their pets.

Questions about whether or not we'll see our pets in heaven should not be our focus. Indeed, when we make it there, it may not even cross our minds. The Lamb of God will be our focus. However, this does not mean that we will not enjoy one another and the beauty of the heavenly paradise. And part of this beauty and enjoyment may include our pets from here on earth.

Although Scripture does not say conclusively whether our pets will be in heaven, three key points lead me to believe that animals in general and pets in particular will be in heaven.

First, animals were part of the original creation of God that was declared "good." The Garden of Eden was filled with animals (Genesis 1:25). Revelation tells us that heaven will contain many of the same things that were in the original creation, such as a river, trees, and fruit. Why not animals too? After all, animals are an integral part of earthly life and testify powerfully of the creative, imaginative genius of God. He created the giraffe, the camel, the platypus, the lion, the pachyderm, and the hummingbird.

As the noted pastor W. A. Criswell says, "God has shown a penchant for varieties of life forms, and it would be difficult to imagine that this would not be perpetuated in the heavenlies."[54]

Concerning the question of animals in heaven, author Peter Kreeft says, "The simplest answer is: Why not? How irrational is the prejudice that would allow plants (green fields and flowers) but not animals in heaven!"[55]

Concerning the more difficult issue of whether the same animals will be in heaven that were here on earth, Kreeft adds:

> Would the same animals be in heaven as on earth? "Is my dead cat in heaven?" Again, why not? God can raise up the very grass; why not cats? Though the blessed have better things to do than play with pets, the better does not exclude the lesser. We were meant from the beginning to have stewardship over the animals; we have not fulfilled that divine plan yet on earth; therefore it seems likely that the right relationship with animals will be part of Heaven; proper "petship." And what better place to begin than with the already petted pets?[56]

Second, the Bible suggests from beginning to end that animals may have souls. In Genesis 1:20, 24, for instance, the Hebrew word *nepesh* is used to refer to animals. While this word can simply mean "creature" or "living thing," in the Old Testament it is often understood to mean "soul." And in Revelation 8:9, the Greek word *psuche*—which can mean heart, mind, or soul—is used about sea creatures.

Of course, the soul of an animal would be very different from the soul of a human being. But the biblical suggestion that animals have souls may indicate that they too will be resurrected in the afterlife.

Third, in the Millennium, animals will be present in abundance. Isaiah paints the well-known picture of animal life in Christ's kingdom:

> And the wolf will dwell with the lamb,
> And the leopard will lie down with the young goat,
> And the calf and the young lion and the fatling together;
> And a little boy will lead them.
> Also the cow and the bear will graze,
> Their young will lie down together,
> And the lion will eat straw like the ox.
> The nursing child will play by the hole of the cobra,
> And the weaned child will put his hand on the viper's den.
> (Isaiah 11:6–8)

While the thousand-year reign of Christ is not heaven, it is the initial phase or "front porch" of the eternal kingdom of God. Therefore, if animals exist in the Millennium, this at least establishes a precedent for suggesting that animals may populate the eternal state, too.

In her book *Holiness in Hidden Places,* Joni Eareckson Tada talks about whether she will see her pet schnauzer, Scrappy, in heaven. Her words are a poignant summary of this issue.

> If God brings our pets back to life, it wouldn't surprise me. It would be just like Him. It would be totally in keeping with His generous character.... Exorbitant. Excessive. Extravagant in grace after grace. Of all the dazzling discoveries and ecstatic pleasures heaven will hold for us, the potential of seeing Scrappy would be pure whimsy—utterly, joyfully, surprisingly superfluous.... Heaven is going to be a place that will refract and reflect in as many ways as possible the goodness and joy of our great God, who delights in lavishing love on His children. So will pets be in heaven? Who knows?[57]

NINETY-SEVEN

IS THERE MARRIAGE IN HEAVEN?

Those who have experienced a long relationship with a spouse they love and cherish often want to know if that relationship will continue after physical death. For many happily married couples it is hard to imagine life without one another—let alone eternity without one another.

However, Jesus clearly stated in Matthew 22:28 that marriage as we know it here on earth will not carry over to the hereafter: "For in the resurrection they neither marry nor are given in marriage, but are like angels in heaven."

Romans 7:1–3 and 1 Corinthians 7:39 also state that marriage *as a physical union* is terminated at the death of either spouse. I've performed dozens of weddings in my ten-plus years as a pastor, and the final line of the declaration of intent for the couple is "till death do you part." Even the wedding vows recognize the fact that marriage terminates at death.

Does this mean that married couples on earth will share no special relationship in heaven? I don't think so. Couples who shared the closest intimacy on earth will continue to know, enjoy, and appreciate each other forever.

I plan to spend all of eternity with Cheryl, but it will be in a relationship that goes far beyond anything we have experienced here on earth. We won't be married to each other in the sense of being joined together to the exclusion of everyone else. Instead, we will both be part of the bride of the Lord Jesus Christ. We will together be married to the heavenly bridegroom.

We'll be part of one body, the Bride's body. We will be more intimately connected with each other—and with all the saints—than we've ever been connected in this life. We will all finally know God's design for full fellowship with others, something that the best of marriages in this life can only begin to taste.

NINETY-EIGHT

IS THERE SEX IN HEAVEN?

No one has ever asked me this in a public Q&A session, but I've been asked it privately many times—always by men.

It shouldn't surprise us that people today are interested in this issue. We are bombarded by sexual messages every day. Sex fills our airwaves, TV sitcoms, magazines, the Internet, movies, novels, plays, and gossip columns.

The answer to this touchy question is yes and no. The reason for this double answer is that sex is both something we are and something we do. We need to consider each of these issues separately.

First, sex is what we are in essence or nature: male and female. How often have you filled out a form or questionnaire that had a blank to fill in asking for your sex? Gender is part of the essence of our being. God created this distinction of the sexes in the Garden of Eden (Genesis 1:27). It is likely that in heaven those who were males on earth will always be males, and females will always be females. God will not *remove* our sexual nature, but will *redeem* and perfect it.

Second, sex is also an act that is performed between husbands and wives for pleasure and procreation. It is doubtful that sex as a physical act will be present in heaven. Sex is an act of intimacy and pleasure reserved for married couples. Since there will be no marriage in heaven or need for procreation, the act of sex will not persist as an expression of love.

In heaven there will undoubtedly be something far greater to enjoy than sexual intercourse. Men and women will enjoy each other in a much deeper way than can be accomplished by physical sex. In heaven they will become one flesh in a way that is far beyond what is possible on earth.

Peter Kreeft, a professor of philosophy at Boston College, provides an excellent illustration of this point:

I think there will probably be millions of more adequate ways to express love than the clumsy ecstasy of fitting two bodies together like pieces of a jigsaw puzzle. Even the most satisfying earthly intercourse between spouses cannot perfectly express *all* their love. If the possibility of intercourse in Heaven is not actualized, it is only for the same reason that lovers do not eat candy during intercourse; there is something much better to do.[58]

So, will there be sex in heaven? Yes and no. Yes in the sense of gender, but no in the sense of the physical act. But don't worry, the intimate fellowship we will enjoy with God and each other in heaven will be, literally, better than sex.

Ninety-nine

Can people who commit suicide go to heaven?

Suicide is a growing problem in our society. In North America, suicide is the third leading cause of death for people fifteen to twenty-five years of age. Amazingly, among children aged five to fourteen, suicide is the sixth most common cause of death. Someone commits suicide in America every seventeen minutes.

Whenever someone commits suicide, people wonder if he can go to heaven. I have been asked this questions many, many times. Most people seem to think that suicide cannot be forgiven because the person cannot repent of the act or ask for forgiveness. However, this is true of all of us: Every believer will die with sins unrepented because he didn't even know about them. Despite this, we continue to expect heaven.

There are seven accounts of suicide in the Bible:

1. Abimelech (Judges 9:50–54).
2. Samson (Judges 16:23–31).
3. Saul (1 Samuel 31:2–4).
4. Saul's servant (1 Samuel 31:5).
5. Ahithophel (2 Samuel 17:23).
6. Zimri (1 Kings 16:15–20).
7. Judas (Matthew 27:3–5).

In none of these cases is it ever stated that the person was condemned to hell for committing suicide. I believe the Bible teaches that the Lord will welcome home any person who has trusted Him, regardless of what he has done. Suicide is not the unpardonable sin.

> For I am convinced that neither death, nor life, nor angels, nor principalities, nor things present, nor things to come, nor powers, nor height, nor depth, nor any other created thing, will be able to separate us from the love of God, which is in Christ Jesus our Lord. (Romans 8:38–39)

Those who have fled to Christ for refuge can never be lost. Praise God for His unending, eternal love that will never let us go!

WILL WE SEE GOD IN HEAVEN?

When I was a young boy, a noted guest speaker came to our church. After one of the services I asked him if he thought we would see God in heaven. He told me that we would see Jesus (who, of course, is God), but that we would not see God the Father because He is spirit. For some reason I was never really sure that he was correct. Something inside told me that I would someday see my heavenly Father, but I didn't have any idea if the Bible supported my impression.

What I didn't realize at that time was that all the Lord's people long to see Him: "As the deer pants for the water brooks, So my soul pants for You, O God. My soul thirsts for God, for the living God; When shall I come and appear before God?" (Psalm 42:1–2). And Phillip, speaking for all the disciples, said to Jesus, "Show us the Father" (John 14:8).

As I grew older I discovered four passages that confirm that we will see the manifestation of God the Father in heaven as well as God the Son: Genesis 3:8; Matthew 5:8; Matthew 18:10; and Revelation 4:2–3. We'll look at all four.

They heard the sound of the LORD God walking in the garden in the cool of the day, and the man and his wife hid themselves from the presence of the LORD God among the trees of the garden. (Genesis 3:8)

If heaven is the restoration of Eden, then it would stand to reason that we will see God in heaven just as Adam and Eve did in the Garden.

In Matthew 5:8, Jesus says, "Blessed are the pure in heart, for they shall see God." I believe this will be more true in heaven than it can ever be here as we endeavor to see Him in our hearts.

"See that you do not despise one of these little ones, for I say to you that their angels in heaven continually see the face of My Father who is in heaven." (Matthew 18:10)

If the angels in heaven see the face of the Father, it seems likely to me that His own children will see His face as well.

> Immediately I was in the Spirit; and behold, a throne was standing in heaven, and One sitting on the throne. And He who was sitting was like a jasper stone and a sardius in appearance; and there was a rainbow around the throne, like an emerald in appearance. (Revelation 4:2–3)

In this passage, the One who sits on the throne is not Jesus, but God the Father. In Revelation 5:13—"And every created thing which is in heaven and on the earth and under the earth and on the sea, and all things in them, I heard saying, 'To Him who sits on the throne, and to the Lamb, be blessing and honor and glory and dominion forever and ever'"—the One who sits on the throne (God the Father) is clearly distinguished from the Lamb (God the Son). We will see the Father in heaven.

Author and Bible expositor John MacArthur supports this view:

> I believe that in heaven we will see God Himself with our physical eyes.... God will reveal the light of His glory, and through perfect eyes we will see the very face of God. God is spirit (John 4:24), and spirit is invisible; therefore, whenever God manifests Himself He does so in the form of light.... Seeing Christ and the Father will eternally awe us.[59]

We will see the manifestation of the Father in heaven as well as the face of our blessed Savior. "They shall see His face, and His name shall be on their foreheads" (Revelation 22:4; see also 1 Corinthians 13:12).

The Top Question for You

Up to this point in the book I have been answering all the questions. But I have saved the final one for you to answer.

DO YOU KNOW FOR SURE THAT YOU WILL GO TO HEAVEN WHEN YOU DIE?

I have saved this question for last because it is by far the most important question a person can ever ask. Knowing for sure whether you will spend eternity in heaven is infinitely more important than knowing all about the end times—or anything else for that matter.

The Bible says that all men are sinners both by nature and by action (Romans 3:23). The Bible also declares that God is infinitely holy, righteous, and just, and therefore cannot accept sinners into His presence (Habakkuk 1:13). So how can anyone go to heaven at all? How can a holy God accept sinful man?

God in His infinite grace formulated a plan to remedy this problem. God the Son agreed to step out of eternity into time, to take on human flesh, to live the sinless life we could never live, and to die in our place. He took all our sins on Himself and took the punishment we deserved. The full wrath of the Father, which should have been poured out on us, was instead heaped upon Jesus when He hung on the Cross.

Just before He died, Jesus cried out, "It is finished!" The debt for your sins and mine was paid in full. Now the holy perfection of Christ is available for you and me to put on, almost like a set of clothes. Wearing His righteousness, we can actually enter the presence of God Himself when we die.

All that remains for you to have a relationship with this holy God forever is for you to accept those "clothes" and put them on. You must recognize your need for salvation, realize that you cannot do anything to earn or merit this salvation, and personally receive as a free gift the full pardon Jesus has already purchased for you. Carefully read these words from Scripture and ask God to make them clear in your heart and mind.

> But to all who believed him and accepted him, he gave the right to become children of God. (John 1:12, NLT)

For the wages of sin is death, but the free gift of God is eternal life through Christ Jesus our Lord. (Romans 6:23, NLT)

God saved you by his special favor when you believed. And you can't take credit for this; it is a gift from God. Salvation is not a reward for the good things we have done, so none of us can boast about it. (Ephesians 2:8–9, NLT)

You can receive Jesus Christ as your personal Savior right now as you read these words. God is offering you the free gift of eternal life through Jesus Christ.

Don't wait.

Receive the Savior now.

Take the free gift of salvation God is offering you. God's Word says that "Whoever will call on the name of the Lord will be saved" (Romans 10:13). Call upon Jesus right now in prayer and He will save you.

It is the greatest decision you will ever make. When you trust Christ you will immediately have a place reserved for you in heaven (1 Peter 1:4). You can be sure from this time on that you will go to heaven either at the Rapture or when the Lord calls you home.

Maranatha (Come, Lord Jesus)!

As you can imagine, there are many ways to fit all the pieces of the end times into a sequence. This outline is my best attempt at this time to put all the pieces together. I certainly wouldn't insist on the correctness of every detail in the outline, but my prayer is that it will help you get a better grasp of the overall picture of the end times.

I. Events in Heaven

A. The Rapture of the Church (1 Corinthians 15:51–58; 1 Thessalonians 4:13–18; Revelation 3:10).

B. The Judgment Seat of Christ (Romans 14:10; 1 Corinthians 3:9–15; 4:1–5; 9:24–27; 2 Corinthians 5:10).

C. The Marriage of the Lamb (2 Corinthians 11:2; Revelation 19:6–8).

D. The Singing of Two Special Songs (Revelation 4–5).

E. The Lamb Receiving the Seven-Sealed Scroll (Revelation 5).

II. Events on Earth

A. Seven-Year Tribulation

   1. Beginning of the Tribulation

      a. Seven-year tribulation begins when the Antichrist signs a covenant with Israel bringing peace to Israel and Jerusalem (Daniel 9:27; Ezekiel 38:8, 11).

      b. The Jewish temple in Jerusalem is rebuilt (Daniel 9:27; Revelation 11:1).

      c. The reunited Roman Empire emerges in a ten-nation confederation (Daniel 2:40–44; 7:7; Revelation 17:12).

   2. First Half (three and a half years) of the Tribulation

      a. The seven seal judgments are opened (Revelation 6).

      b. The 144,000 Jewish believers begin their great evangelistic ministry (Revelation 7).

   3. The Midpoint of the Tribulation

      a. Gog and his allies invade Israel and are decimated by God (Daniel 11:40–45; Ezekiel 38–39).

      b. Antichrist breaks his covenant with Israel and invades the land (Daniel 9:27; 11:40–41).

      c. Antichrist begins to consolidate his empire by plundering

Egypt, Sudan, and Libya, whose armies have just been destroyed by God in Israel (Daniel 11:42–43; Ezekiel 38–39).

d. While in North Africa, Antichrist hears disturbing news of insurrection in Israel and immediately returns there to destroy and annihilate many (Daniel 11:44).

e. Antichrist sets up the abomination of desolation in the rebuilt Temple in Jerusalem (Daniel 9:27; 11:45a; Matthew 24:15; 2 Thessalonians 2:4; Revelation 13:5, 15–18).

f. Sometime during these events, the Antichrist is violently killed, possibly as a result of a war or assassination (Daniel 11:45; Revelation 13:3, 12, 14; 17:8).

g. Satan is cast down from heaven and begins to make war with Israel (Revelation 12:7–13). He uses the two beasts in Revelation to persecute Israel.

h. The faithful Jewish remnant flees to Petra in modern Jordan where they are divinely protected for the remainder of the Tribulation (Matthew 24:16–20; Revelation 12:15–17).

i. The Antichrist is miraculously raised from the dead, to the amazement of the entire world (Revelation 13:3).

j. After his resurrection from the dead, the Antichrist gains political control over the ten kings of the reunited Roman Empire. Three of these kings are killed by the Antichrist, and the other seven will submit (Daniel 7:24; Revelation 17:12–13).

k. The two witnesses begin their three-and-a-half-year ministry (Revelation 11:2–3).

4. Last Half (three and a half years) of the Tribulation

a. Antichrist blasphemes God; the false prophet performs great signs and wonders and promotes false worship of the Antichrist (Revelation 13:5, 11–15).

b. The mark of the beast (666) is introduced and enforced by the false prophet (Revelation 13:16–18).

c. Totally energized by Satan, the Antichrist dominates the world politically, religiously, and economically (Revelation 13:4–5, 15–18).

d. The trumpet judgments are unleashed throughout the

final half of the Tribulation (Revelation 8–9).

    e. Knowing he has only a short time left, Satan intensifies his relentless, merciless persecution of the Jewish people and Gentile believers on earth (Daniel 7:25; Revelation 12:12; 13:15; 20:4).

5. The End of the Tribulation

    a. The bowl judgments are poured out in rapid succession (Revelation 16).

    b. Babylon is destroyed (Revelation 17–18).

    c. The War of Armageddon begins (Revelation 16:16).

    d. The two witnesses are killed by Antichrist and resurrected by God three and one-half days later (Revelation 11:7–12).

    e. Christ returns to the Mount of Olives and slays the armies gathered against Him throughout the land from Megiddo to Petra (Revelation 19:11–16; Isaiah 34:1–6; 63:1–5).

    f. The birds gather to feed on the carnage (Revelation 19:17–18).

6. After the Tribulation: Interval or Transition Period of Seventy-Five Days (Daniel 12:12)

    a. The Antichrist and the false prophet are cast in the lake of fire (Revelation 19:20–21).

    b. The abomination of desolation is removed from the temple (Daniel 12:11).

    c. Israel is regathered (Matthew 24:31).

    d. Israel is judged (Ezekiel 20:30–39; Matthew 25:1–30).

    e. Gentiles are judged (Matthew 25:31–46).

    f. Satan is bound in the abyss (Revelation 20:1–3).

    g. Old Testament and Tribulation saints are resurrected and judged (Daniel 12:1–3; Isaiah 26:19; Revelation 20:4).

B. Thousand-Year Reign of Christ on Earth (Revelation 20:4–6).

C. Satan's Final Revolt and Defeat (Revelation 20:7–10).

D. The Great White Throne Judgment of the Lost (Revelation 20:11–15).

E. The Destruction of the Present Heavens and Earth (Matthew 24:35; 2 Peter 3:3–12; Revelation 21:1).

F. The Creation of the New Heavens and New Earth (Isaiah 65:17; 66:22; 2 Peter 3:13; Revelation 21:1–8).

G. Eternity (Revelation 21:9–22:5).

I hope this book has answered most of your questions about the end times, but I'm sure it's raised some others. Here are some of my favorite resources that will help you if you want to dig deeper into some of the issues we've covered in these pages.

GENERAL OVERVIEW BOOKS

Benware, Paul N. *Understanding End Times Prophecy: A Comprehensive Approach.* Chicago: Moody Press, 1995.

Fruchtenbaum, Arnold G. *The Footsteps of the Messiah: A Study of the Sequence of Prophetic Events.* Tustin, Calif.: Ariel Ministries, 1982.

Hitchcock, Mark. *The Complete Book of Bible Prophecy.* Wheaton: Tyndale House Publishers, 1999.

Hoyt, Herman A. *The End Times.* Chicago: Moody Press, 1969.

Ice, Thomas, and Timothy Demy. *Fast Facts on Bible Prophecy.* Eugene, Ore.: Harvest House Publishers, 1997.

LaHaye, Tim, and Jerry B. Jenkins. *Are We Living in the End Times?* Wheaton: Tyndale House Publishers, 1999.

—————. *Understanding the Last Days: The Keys to Unlocking Bible Prophecy.* Eugene, Ore.: Harvest House Publishers, 1998.

Lightner, Robert P. *The Last Days Handbook: A Comprehensive Guide to Understanding the Different Views of Prophecy.* Nashville: Thomas Nelson Publishers, 1990.

Pentecost, J. Dwight. *Prophecy for Today: God's Purpose and Plan for Our Future,* rev. ed. Grand Rapids: Discovery House Publishers, 1989.

—————. *Things to Come: A Study in Biblical Eschatology.* Grand Rapids: Zondervan Publishing House, 1958.

Walvoord, John F. *End Times: Understanding Today's World Events in Biblical Prophecy.* Swindoll Leadership Library, gen. ed. Charles R. Swindoll. Nashville: Word Publishing, 1998.

—————. *The Prophecy Knowledge Handbook.* Wheaton: Victor Books, 1990.

—————. *Prophecy: 14 Essential Keys to Understanding the Final Drama.* Nashville: Thomas Nelson Publishers, 1993.

Willmington, H. L. *The King is Coming: A Compelling Study of the Last Days.* Wheaton: Tyndale House Publishers, 1973.

Wood, Leon J. *The Bible and Future Events: An Introductory Summary of*

Last-Day Events. Grand Rapids: Zondervan Publishing House, 1973.

THE BOOK OF DANIEL

Campbell, Donald K. *Daniel: God's Man in a Secular Society.* Grand Rapids: Discovery House Publishers, 1988.

Jeremiah, David. *The Handwriting on the Wall: Secrets from the Prophecies of Daniel.* Dallas: Word Publishing, 1992.

Walvoord, John F. *Daniel: The Key to Prophetic Revelation.* Chicago: Moody Press, 1971.

Whitcomb, John C. *Daniel.* Chicago: Moody Press, 1985.

Wood, Leon. *A Commentary on Daniel.* Grand Rapids: Zondervan Publishing House, 1973.

RUSSIA AND THE END TIMES

Hitchcock, Mark. *After the Empire: Bible Prophecy in Light of the Fall of the Soviet Union.* Wheaton: Tyndale House Publishers, 1994.

THE BOOK OF REVELATION

Hindson, Ed. *Approaching Armageddon: The World Prepares for War with God.* Eugene, Ore.: Harvest House Publishers, 1997.

Jeremiah, David. *Escape the Coming Night: An Electrifying Tour of the World As It Races Toward Its Final Days.* Dallas: Word Publishing, 1990.

Stedman, Ray C. *God's Final Word: Understanding Revelation.* Grand Rapids: Discovery House Publishers, 1991.

Thomas, Robert L. *Revelation 1–7: An Exegetical Commentary.* Chicago: Moody Press, 1992.

——————. *Revelation 8–22: An Exegetical Commentary.* Chicago: Moody Press, 1995.

Walvoord, John F. *The Revelation of Jesus Christ.* Chicago: Moody Press, 1966.

THE RAPTURE

LaHaye, Timothy. *No Fear of the Storm: Why Christians Will Escape All the Tribulation.* Portland, Ore.: Multnomah Press, 1992.

Ryrie, Charles C. *Come Quickly, Lord Jesus: What You Need to Know About the Rapture.* Eugene, Ore.: Harvest House Publishers, 1996.

Showers, Renald. *Maranatha: Our Lord, Come!* Bellmawr, N.J.: The Friends of Israel Gospel Ministry, 1995.

Stanton, Gerald B. *Kept from the Hour: Biblical Evidence for the Pretribulational Return of Christ.* Miami Springs, Fla.: Schoettle Publishing Company, Inc., 1991.

Walvoord, John F. *The Blessed Hope and the Tribulation.* Grand Rapids: Zondervan Publising Company, 1976.

—————. *The Rapture Question,* rev. ed. Grand Rapids: Zondervan Publishing House, 1979.

BABYLON

Dyer, Charles H. *The Rise of Babylon: Sign of the End Times.* Wheaton: Tyndale House Publishers, 1991.

THE JEWISH TEMPLE

Ice, Thomas, and Randall Price. *Ready to Rebuild: The Imminent Plan to Rebuild the Last Days Temple.* Eugene, Ore.: Harvest House Publishers, 1992.

Price, Randall. *In Search of Temple Treasures: The Lost Ark and the Last Days.* Eugene, Ore.: Harvest House Publishers, 1994.

—————. *The Coming Last Days Temple.* Eugene, Ore.: Harvest House Publishers, 1999.

SIGNS OF THE TIMES

Dyer, Charles H. *World News and Bible Prophecy.* Wheaton: Tyndale House Publishers, 1993.

Hindson, Ed. *Final Signs: Amazing Prophecies of the End Times.* Eugene, Ore.: Harvest House Publishers, 1996.

Hunt, Dave. *How Close Are We? Compelling Evidence for the Soon Return of Christ.* Eugene, Ore.: Harvest House Publishers, 1993.

THE DANGERS OF DATE SETTING

Hindson, Ed. *Earth's Final Hour.* Eugene, Ore.: Harvest House Publishers, 1999.

JERUSALEM

Hunt, Dave. *A Cup of Trembling: Jerusalem and Bible Prophecy.* Eugene, Ore.: Harvest House Publishers, 1995.

Price, Randall. *Jerusalem in Prophecy: God's Stage for the Final Drama.* Eugene, Ore.: Harvest House Publishers, 1998.

The Judgment Seat of Christ

Lutzer, Erwin W. *Your Eternal Reward: Triumph and Tears at the Judgment Seat of Christ.* Chicago: Moody Press, 1998.

Wall, Joe L. *Going for the Gold: Reward and Loss at the Judgment of Believers.* Chicago: Moody Press, 1991.

The Antichrist

Hindson, Ed. *Is the Antichrist Alive and Well? 10 Keys to His Identity.* Eugene, Ore.: Harvest House Publishers, 1998.

Pink, Arthur W. *The Antichrist.* 1923. Reprint, Grand Rapids: Kregel Publications, 1988.

The Millennium

Ryrie, Charles C. *The Basis of the Premillennial Faith.* Neptune, N.J.: Loizeaux Brothers, 1953.

Walvoord, John F. *The Millennial Kingdom.* Grand Rapids: Zondervan Publishing Company, 1959.

Questions and Answers

Ice, Thomas, and Timothy Demy. *Prophecy Watch: What to Expect in the Days to Come.* Eugene, Ore.: Harvest House Publishers, 1998.

Heaven and Hell

Criswell, W. A., and Paige Patterson. *Heaven.* Wheaton: Tyndale House Publishers, 1991.

Dixon, Larry. *The Other Side of the Good News.* Wheaton: Bridgepoint, 1992.

Eareckson Tada, Joni. *Heaven Your Real Home.* Grand Rapids: Zondervan Publishing House, 1995.

Hanegraaff, Hank. *Resurrection.* Nashville: Word Publishing, 2000.

Ice, Thomas, and Timothy Demy. *The Truth about Heaven and Eternity.* Eugene Ore.: Harvest House Publishers, 1997.

Kreeft, Peter. *Every Thing You Ever Wanted to Know about Heaven But Never Dreamed of Asking!* San Francisco: Ignatius Press, 1990.

Lawson, Steven J. *Heaven Help Us!* Colorado Springs: NavPress, 1995.

MacArthur, John F. *The Glory of Heaven.* Wheaton: Crossway Books, 1996.

Morey, Robert A. *Death and the Afterlife.* Minneapolis: Bethany House Publishers, 1984.

Rhodes, Ron. *The Undiscovered Country.* Eugene, Ore.: Harvest House Publishers, 1996.

Rumford, Douglas J. *What about Heaven and Hell?* Wheaton: Tyndale House Publishers, 2000.

1. John Leland, "Millennium Madness," *Newsweek,* 1 November 1999, 70.

2. J. Barton Payne, *Encyclopedia of Biblical Prophecy* (Grand Rapids: Baker Books, 1980), 674–75.

3. Robert G. Clouse, ed., *The Meaning of the Millennium: Four Views,* (Downers Grove, IL: InterVarsity Press, 1977), 117–118.

4. John Walvoord, *The Nations in Prophecy* (Grand Rapids: Zondervan Publishing House, 1967), 175.

5. Ibid., 173.

6. Ed Dobson, *The End* (Grand Rapids: Zondervan Publishing House, 1997), 167.

7. R. C. Sproul, *Romans* (Scotland, Great Britain: Christian Focus Publications, 1994), 190–91.

8. Walvoord, *Israel in Prophecy* (Grand Rapids: Zondervan Publishing House, 1967), 26.

9. Randall Price, *The Coming Last Days Temple* (Eugene, Ore.: Harvest House Publishers, 1999), 592.

10. Mark Chalemin, *Deciphering the Bible Code* (Richardson, Tex.: Renewal Radio, 1998), 10.

11. Sharon Begley, "Seek and Ye Shall Find," *Newsweek*, 9 June 1997, 67.

12. J. Paul Tanner, "Decoding the Bible Codes," *Bibliotheca Sacra* 157 (April–June 2000): 159.

13. Ray Stedman, *God's Final Word* (Grand Rapids: Discovery House Publishers, 1991), 194–95.

14. Charles Dyer, *Rise of Babylon* (Wheaton: Tyndale House Publishers, 1991), 182.

15. Robert Thomas, *Revelation 8–22* (Chicago: Moody Press, 1995), 307.

16. These points were taken from my Dallas Theological Seminary class notes from Charles Dyer's class *Babylon and the Bible.*

17. C. F. Keil, *Ezekiel, Daniel, Commentary on the Old Testament*, trans. James Martin (Reprint; Grand Rapids: Eerdmans Publishing Company, 1982), 159. Wilhelm Gesenius, *Gesenius' Hebrew-Chaldee Lexicon to the Old Testament* (Grand Rapids: Eerdmans Publishing Comany, 1949), 752.

18. G. A. Cooke, "A Critical and Exegetical Commentary on the Book

of Ezekiel," in *The International Critical Commentary* (Edinburgh: T & T Clark, 1936), 408–9.

19. Gesenius, *Gesenius' Hebrew-Chaldee Lexicon,* 862.

20. H. L. Willmington, *The King is Coming,* (Wheaton: Tyndale House Publishers, 1981), 155.

21. Ibid., 10.

22. Donald Grey Barnhouse, *Thessalonians: An Expositional Commentary* (Grand Rapids: Zondervan Publishing House, 1977), 99–100.

23. Paul J. Alexander, *The Byzantine Apocalyptic Tradition* (Berkeley: University of California Press, 1985), 136.

24. Timothy J. Demy and Thomas D. Ice, "The Rapture and Pseudo-Ephraem: An Early Medieval Citation," *Bibliotheca Sacra* 152 (July–September 1995): 12.

25. Charles H. Dyer, *World News and Bible Prophecy* (Wheaton: Tyndale House Publishers, 1995), 270.

26. H. L. Willmington, *The King is Coming* (Wheaton: Tyndale House Publishers, 1981), 81.

27. Grant R. Jeffrey, *Prince of Darkness* (Toronto: Frontier Research Publications, 1994), 29–30.

28. J. Dwight Pentecost, *Will Man Survive?* (Grand Rapids: Zondervan Publishing House, 1971), 93.

29. Ibid., 81.

30. Willmington, *The King Is Coming,* 95.

31. Walvoord. *The Revelation of Jesus Christ* (Chicago: Moody Press, 1966), 210.

32. Ibid.

33. Ibid., 252.

34. John Phillips, *Exploring Revelation* (Neptune, N.J.: Loizeaux Brothers, 1991), 171.

35. Jeane Dixon, *My Life and Prophecies* (New York: William Morrow and Company, 1969), 179–180.

36. Pentecost, *Things to Come* (Grand Rapids: Zondervan Publishing House, 1958), 235.

37. Thomas Ice and Timothy Demy, *The Truth about the Tribulation* (Eugene, Ore.: Harvest House Publishers, 1996), 46.

38. Robert L. Thomas, *Revelation 1–7: An Exegetical Commentary* (Chicago: Moody Press, 1992), 473.

39. Herman A. Hoyt, *The End Times* (Chicago: Moody Press, 1969), 163.

40. John MacArthur, Jr., *The Second Coming of the Lord Jesus Christ: Study Notes* (Panorama City, Calif.: Word of Grace Communications, 1981), 1.

41. Pentecost, *Things to Come,* 476.

42. Ibid., 538.

43. Henry Morris, *The Revelation Record* (Wheaton: Tyndale House Publishers, 1983), 419–20.

44. Anne Sappington and Mike Paguette, "Life After Death?" *Moody,* January/February 1998, 37.

45. Rodney Clapp, "Rumors of Heaven" *Christianity Today,* 7 October 1988, 20.

46. Anne Graham Lotz, *The Vision of His Glory* (Dallas: Word Publishing, 1996), 225–26.

47. David Van Biema, "Does Heaven Exist?" *Time,* 24 March 1997, 73.

48. Ibid.

49. Cal Thomas, "Not of this World," *Newsweek,* 29 March 1999, 60.

50. Dandi Daley Mackall, *Kids Are Still Saying the Darndest Things* (Rocklin, Calif.: Prima Publishing, 1994), 26–27.

51. Robert E. Coleman, *Singing with the Angels* (Grand Rapids: Fleming H. Revell, 1980), 53.

52. Hank Hanegraaff, *Resurrection* (Nashville: Word Publishing, 2000), 129.

53. Ibid., 130–31.

54. W. A. Criswell and Paige Patterson, *Heaven* (Wheaton: Tyndale House Publishers, 1991), 53.

55. Peter Kreeft, *Every Thing You Ever Wanted to Know about Heaven but Never Dreamed of Asking* (San Francisco: Ignatius Press, 1990), 45.

56. Ibid., 45–46.

57. Joni Eareckson Tada, *Holiness in Hidden Places* (Nashville: J. Countryman, 1999), 133.

58. Kreeft, *Every Thing You Ever Wanted to Know about Heaven but Never Dreamed of Asking,* 131.

59. John MacArthur, Jr., *Heaven* (Chicago: Moody Press, 1988), 90.

Sign of the Times in the 9/11 Aftermath

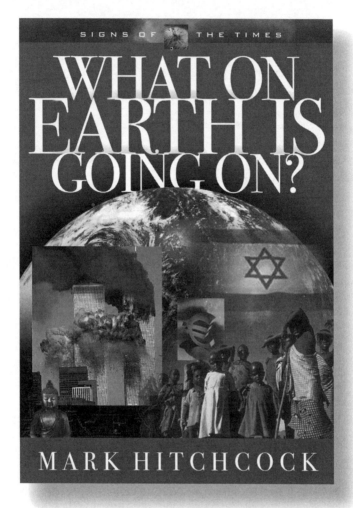

As sensationalists and skeptics wreak havoc with the country's emotions, prophecy expert Mark Hitchcock provides a much-needed definition of what is meant by "signs of the times." In *What on Earth Is Going On?*, Hitchcock discusses the current interest in prophecy caused by the 9/11 attack, presents Jesus' own forecast for the future of the world, and details five major global developments today that discernibly signal Christ's coming. This balanced, concise overview of the real signs of the times will clarify Christ's instructions challenging his followers to be alert in the final days. Readers will easily find and absorb the information they need to prepare for His return.

ISBN 1-57673-853-1

Hitchcock Examines Bible Prophecy's Silence about America

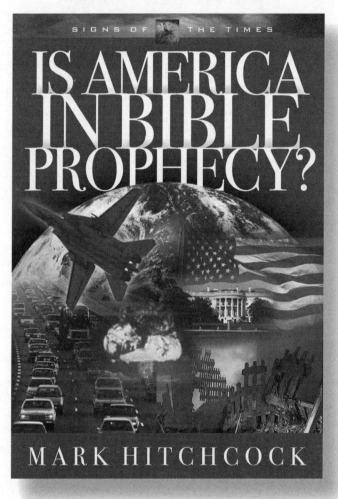

In *Is America in Bible Prophecy?*, expert Mark Hitchcock deals with often-raised questions about America's future. Examining three prophetic passages that are commonly thought to describe America, Hitchcock concludes that the Bible is actually silent about the role of the United States in the End Times. He then discusses the implications of America's absence in prophetic writings. Along with Hitchcock's compelling forecast for the future, he offers specific actions Americans can take to keep their nation strong and blessed by God, as well as an appendix of additional questions and answers.

ISBN 1-57673-496-X